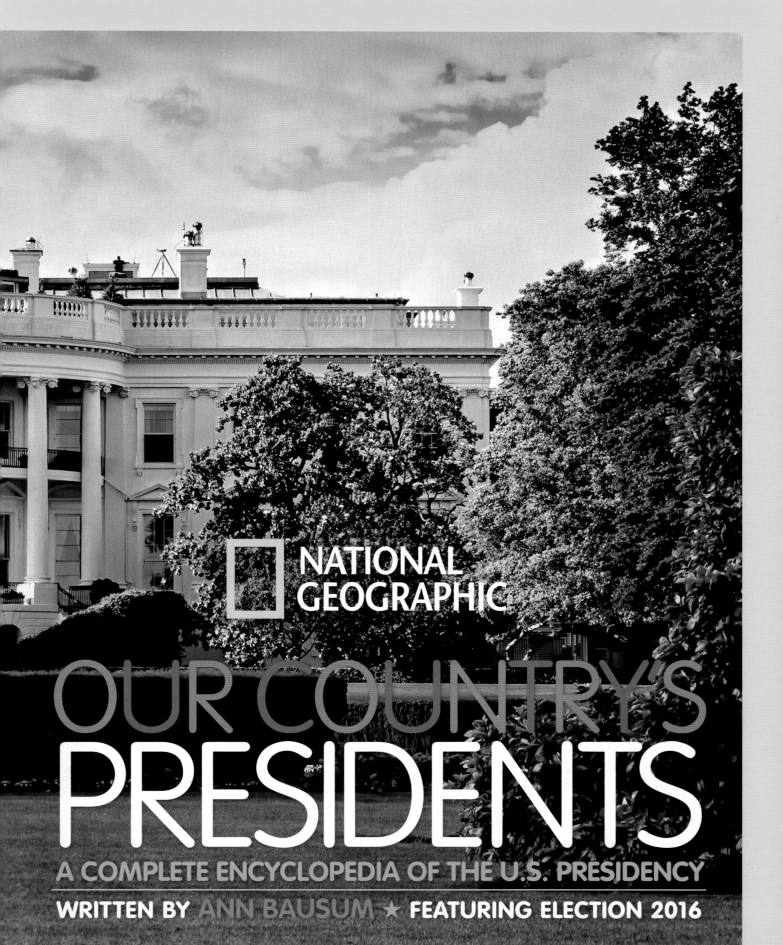

NATIONAL
GEOGRAPHIC

OUR COUNTRY'S
PRESIDENTS

A COMPLETE ENCYCLOPEDIA OF THE U.S. PRESIDENCY

WRITTEN BY ANN BAUSUM ★ FEATURING ELECTION 2016

CONTENTS

VICTORY SPEECH
DONALD TRUMP
45TH PRESIDENT OF THE UNITED STATES

Donald Trump, the winner of the 2016 presidential election, delivered a victory speech during the predawn hours of November 9, 2016, in New York City. Excerpts from his remarks follow; ellipses (...) indicate omitted text. Presidents-elect use such speeches to do more than celebrate their triumphs. These comments can help to heal divisions that have developed during the presidential contest, serve as signposts for how a President will govern, and reassure the world that the peaceful transition of power—a hallmark of democracy—will once again occur.

"Now it's time for America to bind the wounds of division ... To all Republicans and Democrats and independents across this nation, I say it is time for us to come together as one united people ... I pledge to every citizen of our land that I will be President for all Americans ... For those who have chosen not to support me in the past ... I'm reaching out to you for your guidance and your help so that we can work together and unify our great country ...

"As I've said from the beginning, ours was not a campaign, but rather an incredible and great movement made up of millions of hardworking men and women who love their country and want a better, brighter future for themselves and for their family ... Working together, we will begin the urgent task of rebuilding our nation and renewing the American dream.

"I've spent my entire life in business looking at the untapped potential in projects and in people all over the world. That is now what I want to do for our country ... Every single American will have the opportunity to realize his or her fullest potential. The forgotten men and women of our country will be forgotten no longer ... We will embark upon a project of national growth and renewal. I will harness the creative talents of our people and we will call upon the best and brightest to leverage their tremendous talent for the benefit of all ... No dream is too big, no challenge is too great. Nothing we want for our future is beyond our reach ...

"I want to tell the world community that while we will always put America's interests first, we will deal fairly ... with everyone—all people and all other nations. We will seek common ground, not hostility; partnership, not conflict ...

"While the campaign is over, our work on this movement is now really just beginning. We're going to get to work immediately for the American people."

ABOUT THE PRESIDENCY
AN INTRODUCTION

On February 4, 1789, a few dozen men held simultaneous meetings in the various United States. By unanimous vote they selected George Washington to be the nation's first President. These electors hoped Washington would head an unbroken chain of capable national leaders. At that point, though, no one knew for certain whether the American experiment in democracy would last. Only time would tell.

Eleven years later the nation's second President, John Adams, moved into the still unfinished home that is known today as the White House. "May none but Honest and Wise Men ever rule under this Roof," he wrote. Those who followed him to the presidency have tried to honor his hopes, and so will the men and women who become President in the future.

Each President takes a short oath of office: "I do solemnly swear that I will faithfully execute the Office of the President of the United States, and will to the best of my ability, preserve, protect and defend the Constitution of the United States."

Each person must meet a simple list of qualifications in order to seek the presidency: He or she must be born as a U.S. citizen, be at least 35 years old, and have lived in the country for at least 14 years. Each candidate strives to represent the best hopes of fellow citizens for meeting the nation's needs.

Places change over time. The 1790 census counted not even four million people in the United States, including more than half a million slaves. Women, African Americans, Native Americans, and many poor white males had not yet won the right to vote. Over the years, transportation advanced from horse power to steam power to jet power. Inventors, scientists, and explorers changed the landscape with factories, technologies, and discoveries. The United States grew from a tentative experiment in democracy into a world superpower.

U.S. Presidents helped shape this evolving nation. Some, such as Thomas Jefferson, transformed the country's geography and outlook with their visions for change. Others, such as Abraham Lincoln, led the nation through

George Washington (above, far right) was sworn in as the nation's first President on April 30, 1789. The ceremony took place at Federal Hall in New York City, the first seat of national government for the new republic.

Abraham Lincoln, who won the four-way race of 1860 with a plurality of votes (less than 50 percent), spent his presidency trying to unite a divided nation.

"Ask not what your country can do for you—ask what you can do for your country." This challenge in John F. Kennedy's Inaugural Address of 1961 inspired a generation of young people to undertake national service.

Theodore Roosevelt laid the groundwork for the formation of the National Park Service in 1916 through devoted conservation of natural lands during his presidency (above, visiting Yosemite in California, 1903).

critical periods of national and world history. Many left a personal stamp on the outcome of the nation. Most served as good stewards; they tried to do their best work. All marked their place in the history of the nation.

U.S. Presidents are a favorite topic of study for young and old alike. Presidents attract attention for different reasons, whether it's for their bold policies, as with Franklin D. Roosevelt; for their power to inspire, as with John F. Kennedy; or for their adventuresomeness, as with Teddy Roosevelt. Readers are curious about how Presidents coped with the challenges of their eras and how they lived their personal lives.

Presidents come with funny stories (one may have become stuck in a bathtub), unexpected facts (some were slaveholders), and overlooked insights (how they helped establish national traditions). They give us words that inspire ("Government of the people, by the people, for the people shall not perish from this earth"–Abraham Lincoln) and words that reassure ("The only thing we have to fear is fear itself"–Franklin D. Roosevelt).

We give Presidents nicknames—from Uncle Jumbo to Tricky Dick, from Honest Abe to Old Rough-and-Ready. We remember them for their extremes, their milestones, and their originality. Who was the only unmarried President? Who won the closest election? How many Presidents died on the Fourth of July? How many died in office? Who was our youngest President? Who was the oldest? Which Presidents are regarded as our best leaders? Who might be seen as among the worst?

Our Country's Presidents answers these questions and hundreds more. It introduces the Presidents as individuals, with full disclosure of good traits as well as flaws. By viewing the Presidents in full dimension, it is possible to breathe life into the historic portraits that survive them. Readers may measure their own dreams, accomplishments, and challenges against those of their national leaders, perhaps gaining a stronger sense of self as a result.

The Presidents' stories, both personal and professional, are part of the nation's story. When we understand them, they become part of our extended family history. Welcome to the stories of our country's Presidents.

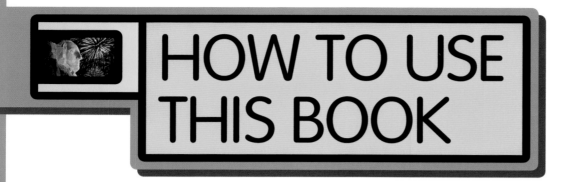

HOW TO USE THIS BOOK

Y ou may choose to read *Our Country's Presidents* from cover to cover, just browse through the photos, or investigate one topic of interest. Knowing a bit more about how the book is organized should help you use it with greater success.

Timelines

This book presents the U.S. Presidents in chronological order grouped by six historical periods. A brief essay explains the common themes shared by the Presidents within these groupings, accompanied by an illustrated timeline that introduces readers to important events of the period, from wars to inventions, from explorations to protests.

Profiles

Individual essays present key elements of the history of each President, including family background, childhood, education, prepresidential careers, election highlights, important events during the presidency, and activities pursued in retirement years. The opening paragraph of each essay summarizes major points about the significance of each leader's administration. Multiple illustrations provide a visual dimension to the story. Profiles range in length from two to six pages depending on the significance of the individual. Longer essays feature notable quotes by the Presidents that have been highlighted in large type.

Presidential Portraits

Each presidential profile is introduced by a full-page reproduction of the leader's official portrait. These paintings are unveiled after the President leaves office and are displayed throughout the White House. The portraits of the most recent Presidents hang in places of honor near the main entrance to the White House.

Fact Boxes

A fact box appears on the opening spread of each profile. It features the President's signature as well as quick reference facts in categories ranging from nicknames to election opponents, from important dates to the number of states in the Union at the start of each presidency. Each box includes a list of selected landmarks to help readers make geographic connections with the lives of the Presidents.

Thematic Spreads

Nearly two dozen two-page spreads are placed strategically throughout the book to explain particular themes that relate to the presidency. By reading these topical essays, you will be able to make connections between Presidents. Your understanding of U.S. history and the operation of the federal government will grow, too. Some essays cover topics of human interest, such as background about the families of the Presidents. Others explain how the government functions, including the workings of the Electoral College and the three branches of government. Additional thematic spreads explore how the Presidents work, play, travel, stay safe, and more—even what they do after they retire from the presidency.

Reference Aids

A summary of U.S. election history introduces the reference material in the final pages of *Our Country's Presidents*. This chart shows the results of every election, including victors and major challengers. It also presents Electoral College tallies and the results of the popular voting that began in 1824. A resource guide follows with ideas for how to find out more about the Presidents. Information on sources used for the book's text and photos as well as a comprehensive index conclude the book.

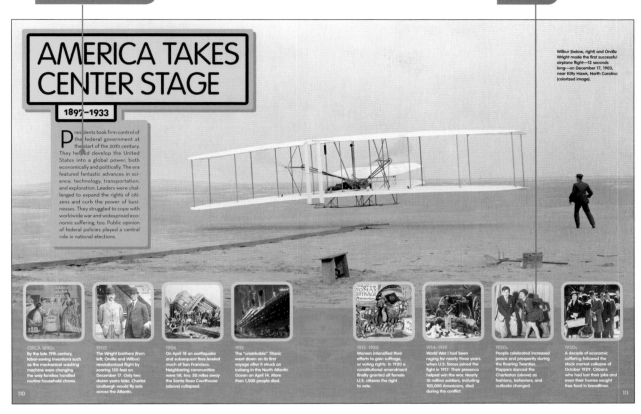

AMERICA TAKES CENTER STAGE

1897–1933

Presidents took firm control of the federal government at the start of the 20th century. They helped develop the United States into a global power, both economically and politically. The era featured fantastic advances in science, technology, transportation, and exploration. Leaders were challenged to expand the rights of citizens and curb the power of businesses. They struggled to cope with worldwide war and widespread economic suffering, too. Public opinion of federal policies played a central role in national elections.

Wilbur (below, right) and Orville Wright made the first successful airplane flight—12 seconds long—on December 17, 1903, near Kitty Hawk, North Carolina (colorized image).

CIRCA 1890s
By the late 19th century, labor-saving inventions such as the mechanical washing machine were changing the way families handled routine household chores.

1903
The Wright brothers (from left, Orville and Wilbur) revolutionized flight by soaring 120 feet on December 17. Only two dozen years later, Charles Lindbergh would fly solo across the Atlantic.

1906
On April 18 an earthquake and subsequent fires leveled much of San Francisco. Neighboring communities were hit, too; 50 miles away the Santa Rosa Courthouse (above) collapsed.

1912
The "unsinkable" *Titanic* went down on its first voyage after it struck an iceberg in the North Atlantic Ocean on April 14. More than 1,500 people died.

1913–1920
Women intensified their efforts to gain suffrage, or voting rights. In 1920 a constitutional amendment finally granted all female U.S. citizens the right to vote.

1914–1919
World War I had been raging for nearly three years when U.S. forces joined the fight in 1917. Their presence helped win the war. Nearly 10 million soldiers, including 100,000 Americans, died during the conflict.

1920s
People celebrated increased peace and prosperity during the Roaring Twenties. Flappers danced the Charleston (above) as fashions, behaviors, and outlooks changed.

1930s
A decade of economic suffering followed the stock market collapse of October 1929. Citizens who had lost their jobs and even their homes sought free food in breadlines.

110

111

ABRAHAM LINCOLN
16TH PRESIDENT OF THE UNITED STATES **1861–1865**

When Abraham Lincoln was inaugurated in 1861, he became President of states that were not united. In fact, after arguing for years about slavery and states' rights, Northerners and Southerners were on the brink of civil, or internal, war. Lincoln, expressing his commitment to the highest ideals of democracy, succeeded in reuniting the country and ending slavery. He was assassinated just after the end of the Civil War in 1865.

Lincoln's humble beginnings are a schoolbook legend. He was born in a log cabin in Kentucky to parents who could neither read nor write. The sum of his schoolhouse education was about one year's time, but he educated himself by reading books he borrowed from others. When Lincoln was nine years old, his mother died. His father, a carpenter and farmer, remarried and moved his family farther west, eventually settling in Illinois. Lincoln was taller (at six feet four inches) than any other President. His high-pitched voice and thick frontier accent (saying "git" for "get" or "thar" for "there") made an odd contrast with his thin but strong and dignified figure.

First Lady Mary Todd Lincoln

Abraham Lincoln's lifelong love of reading whenever and wherever he could began in his youth, when books often took the place of school. Favorite reading included U.S. history, Aesop's Fables, Robinson Crusoe, the Bible, and works by Shakespeare.

Lincoln worked as a flatboat navigator, storekeeper, soldier, surveyor, and postmaster before being elected at age 25 to the Illinois Legislature in Springfield. Once there, he taught himself law, opened a law practice, and earned the nickname "Honest Abe." He served one term in the U.S. House of Representatives during 1847–1849 but lost two U.S. Senate races in the 1850s. However, the debates he had about slavery with his 1858 opponent, Stephen Douglas, helped him earn the presidential nomination two years later. In the four-way presidential race of 1860, Lincoln was the top vote getter. Lincoln gained the presidency on a platform that considered it treason for Southern states to secede, or withdraw, from the nation. It

Abraham Lincoln

NICKNAME
Honest Abe

BORN
Feb. 12, 1809, near Hodgenville, KY

POLITICAL PARTY
Republican (formerly Whig)

CHIEF OPPONENT
1st term: Stephen Arnold Douglas, Northern Democrat (1813–1861); John Cabell Breckinridge, Southern Democrat (1821–1875); John Bell, Constitutional Unionist (1797–1869); 2nd term: George Brinton McClellan, Democrat (1826–1885)

TERM OF OFFICE
March 4, 1861–April 15, 1865

AGE AT INAUGURATION
52 years old

NUMBER OF TERMS
two (cut short by assassination)

VICE PRESIDENT
1st term: Hannibal Hamlin (1809–1891); 2nd term: Andrew Johnson (1808–1875)

FIRST LADY
Mary Todd Lincoln (1818–1882), wife (married Nov. 4, 1842)

CHILDREN
Robert, Edward (died young), William, Thomas (Tad)

GEOGRAPHIC SCENE
23 United States; 11 Confederate States

NEW STATES ADDED
West Virginia (1863); Nevada (1864)

DIED
April 15, 1865, in Washington, DC

AGE AT DEATH
56 years old

SELECTED LANDMARKS
Hodgenville, KY (birthplace); Springfield, IL (home, grave, and library); Lincoln Memorial, President's Cottage, Washington, DC; Mount Rushmore National Memorial, Keystone, SD

80

81

THE PRESIDENCY AND HOW IT GREW

1789–1837

The authors of the U.S. Constitution only sketched a loose outline of the presidency when they defined the federal government in 1787. They expected the first Presidents to work out the details of the job in cooperation with Congress and the Supreme Court. As a result, the first officeholders helped shape the way Presidents make decisions, fight wars, work with Congress, add territory to the country, entertain, and so on. The presidency became a position that could be revised and improved as needed by future Presidents.

1789
Delegates wrote a new set of laws for governing the United States at the Constitutional Convention of 1787. By 1789 the Constitution was ratified, and the nation's first President was in place.

1795
The Constitution put the federal government in charge of issuing money. The $10 "eagle" coin was minted from 1795 to 1933. The capped figure of "Liberty" faced the coin.

1803
Thomas Jefferson offered to buy the Mississippi port of New Orleans. France sold it and the rest of its North American lands to the United States as the Louisiana Purchase.

1804–1806
A handful of men and Sacagawea, a Native American woman, helped Meriwether Lewis and William Clark explore the land between the Mississippi River and the Pacific Ocean.

In 1825 President John Quincy Adams nearly drowned in Tiber Creek (foreground). The water-way now flows through tunnels beneath the nation's capital.

1810
John Marshall served as the nation's Chief Justice longer than anyone else. His 1810 Supreme Court ruling in *Fletcher* v. *Peck* was the first to declare a state law unconstitutional.

1814
Francis Scott Key wrote a poetic description of the British bombardment of Baltimore's Fort McHenry near the end of the War of 1812. It became the U.S. national anthem.

CIRCA 1820
Eli Whitney's cotton gin made it possible for cotton to be grown and processed on a large scale. Slaves labored on sizable plantations to raise more of the crop.

1836
Susanna Dickinson and her baby were among the few survivors of the Battle of the Alamo. Texans battled Mexico for two more months before gaining independence.

GEORGE WASHINGTON
1ST PRESIDENT OF THE UNITED STATES 1789–1797

George Washington helped transform 13 British colonies into a new nation through a lifetime of public service as both a military leader and a statesman. As the first President of the United States, he set precedents, or patterns of behavior, for future Presidents to follow. After his death, he was praised for being "first in war, first in peace, and first in the hearts of his countrymen."

Little is known about the early life of the man who grew up to be called the "Father of His Country." Stories about his virtues—such as his honest confession of chopping down his father's cherry tree—were actually invented by an admiring "biographer" soon after Washington's death. The son of a Virginia landowner and planter, Washington grew up in colonial Virginia. His father died when George was 11, and his older brother, Lawrence, helped raise him. Washington was educated in basic subjects including reading,

George's legendary cherry tree confession

writing, and mathematics, but he did not attend college.

His skill with mathematics led to early work as a surveyor, or measurer and mapper of land. While still a teenager, Washington surveyed the unsettled wilderness of Virginia's Blue Ridge Mountains. He ventured farther west during his 20s—this time as a soldier. Washington fought in the French and Indian War, Great Britain's territorial dispute with France over the lands of the Ohio River Valley. His reputation spread after he published firsthand accounts of his experiences.

Virginians elected Washington to their

George Washington (foreground) survived an icy crossing of the Allegheny River as a British scout in 1753. Later, he made a trustworthy President because citizens knew Washington, being childless, could not place a family heir in power to succeed him. He truly was the "Father of His Country."

NICKNAME
Father of His Country

BORN
Feb. 22, 1732, at Pope's Creek, Westmoreland County, VA

POLITICAL PARTY
Federalist

CHIEF OPPONENTS
none; elected unanimously

TERM OF OFFICE
April 30, 1789–March 3, 1797

AGE AT INAUGURATION
57 years old

NUMBER OF TERMS
two

VICE PRESIDENT
John Adams (1735–1826)

FIRST LADY
Martha Dandridge Custis Washington (1731–1802), wife (married Jan. 6, 1759)

CHILDREN
none; 2 stepchildren from his wife's first marriage

GEOGRAPHIC SCENE
11 states and 2 former colonies still debating ratification of the Constitution

NEW STATES ADDED
North Carolina (1789), Rhode Island (1790), Vermont (1791), Kentucky (1792), Tennessee (1796)

DIED
Dec. 14, 1799, at Mount Vernon, VA

AGE AT DEATH
67 years old

SELECTED LANDMARKS
Pope's Creek Plantation (Wakefield), VA (birthplace); Valley Forge National Historical Park, Valley Forge, PA; Mount Vernon, VA (homestead and grave); Washington Monument, Washington, DC; Mount Rushmore National Memorial, Keystone, SD

General George Washington served as Commander in Chief of the Continental Army throughout the Revolutionary War.

Washington struggled to keep up morale among troops wintering over at Valley Forge, Pennsylvania, in 1777–1778.

colonial legislature, the House of Burgesses, when he was 26. Soon after, Washington married Martha Dandridge Custis, a wealthy widow with two young children. They settled at Mount Vernon, a family home Washington had inherited.

As a colonial legislator, Washington spoke out against unfair aspects of British rule. Later he was one of Virginia's representatives at the First and Second Continental Congresses. These meetings led to the organization of a Continental Army to oppose the British. Washington, who attended the meetings in his military uniform, was chosen by the Continental Congress to head the Army. He was 43 years old. His selection added an influential Southerner to a Revolutionary War movement that was led mostly by Northerners.

Washington held the Continental Army together for six years of fighting against British forces. His troops

suffered significant defeats, but they won important victories in the fight for independence, too. Aided by the French, Washington finally forced the British to surrender most of their troops on October 19, 1781, at Yorktown, Virginia. He retired from the Army after the 1783 peace treaty and returned to private life.

Six years passed between the signing of a peace treaty with Great Britain and the election of Washington as President. During that time the former colonies operated under the Articles of Confederation, a document that reserved most power for the states. Each state printed its own money, for example. There was no national Chief Executive. States sent

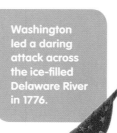

Washington led a daring attack across the ice-filled Delaware River in 1776.

In 1787 Washington presided over the Constitutional Convention in Philadelphia. Delegates drafted a plan for a new national government with hopes that Washington would serve as the country's first President.

New York residents gave George Washington a hero's welcome when he entered the city in 1783 after the end of the Revolutionary War.

representatives to a federal Congress, but this legislature did not even have the authority to collect taxes. Neither the states nor the federal government were able to repay the millions of dollars that had been spent on the Revolutionary War. The states were so poorly linked that their fate as a nation seemed in jeopardy.

In 1787 state representatives gathered in Philadelphia to try to resolve these problems. George Washington, one of Virginia's delegates at this Constitutional Convention, was selected to preside. By the time the convention ended four months later, the delegates had written the Constitution of the United States. This document outlined the basic design for a strong federal government, with two chambers of legislators, a federal court system, and a President. It continues to serve as the foundation for the United States government today.

Nine state governments were required to ratify, or approve, the document before the new federal government could form. By the next summer more than enough states had ratified the Constitution for it to take effect. Following the Constitution's directions, states chose representatives to serve as electors for the President. These members of the first Electoral College cast two votes apiece. All of them gave one vote—for a total of 69—to George

> **"Liberty, when it begins to take root, is a plant of rapid growth."**
>
> George Washington, letter to James Madison, March 2, 1788

Washington, thus making him President. John Adams received the greatest number of remaining votes and became Vice President. Washington was reelected unanimously four years later, with Adams again voted in as Vice President. No other President has ever been unanimously elected.

In 1789 Washington traveled to New York City, then the nation's capital, for his Inauguration. The next year the capital moved temporarily to Philadelphia. Washington brought slaves from his plantation to help staff the President's home. Although Washington helped plan a permanent national capital, his presidency ended before the federal government moved to the city later named in his honor.

President Washington set many precedents for future Chief Executives to follow. A few, like bowing in greeting, quickly went out of fashion. (Thomas Jefferson introduced the custom of shaking hands.) Many other precedents, such as seeking regular advice from department secretaries in Cabinet meetings, remain essential

The small Cabinet of George Washington (above, far right) didn't necessarily make for easy governing. The President had to contend with rival factions of advisers who disagreed about federal versus state powers, foreshadowing the development of political parties.

today. Washington established how the U.S. negotiates treaties, if presidential vetoes could encourage the reworking of legislation (yes), whether the Chief Justice had to be the oldest member of the Supreme Court (no), if the President could decide who would join the Cabinet (yes), and even how many terms he thought a President should serve. He established speechmaking traditions, too, from his Inaugural Addresses to State of the Union messages to a farewell address upon leaving office.

Washington appointed the first federal judges, signed laws that established basic government services like banking and currency, and sought to keep the nation out of wars with Native American and European nations. During his presidency, political parties began to form despite Washington's objections. He became identified with the Federalist Party.

Washington helped lay the cornerstone of the U.S. Capitol during his first year as President.

Martha Washington, who had joined her husband at winter battle camps during the Revolutionary War, left Mount Vernon again to be with him during his presidency. "Lady Washington," as she was called, helped set presidential social customs.

After retiring from the presidency, George Washington returned to his family estate, Mount Vernon, Virginia. An expert horseman, he loved to review his property on horseback. Washington had perfected his skills in the saddle during his youth. As a teenager, Washington had wanted to join the British Navy. His mother, widowed when George was 11, refused to grant his wish.

"Many things which appear of little importance in themselves and at the beginning may have great and durable consequences."

George Washington, letter to John Adams, May 10, 1789

Washington established one more tradition—attending the Inauguration of his successor before he and his wife retired to Mount Vernon in 1797. He was not left at peace for long. In 1798 he agreed to take charge of the Army once more, this time to defend the country in case war developed with France. (It did not, and he was able to complete his service from home.)

In December 1799 Washington became ill after spending hours riding around his property in poor weather. What started as a simple sore throat developed into what was probably a strep infection. Doctors tried the usual cures of the day, including draining nearly a third of the blood from his body, but his condition did not improve. His throat became so swollen that he could not swallow or breathe. He died within two days of falling ill. Washington, one of the largest slaveholders in the country, arranged in his will for his own slaves to be freed by the time of his wife's death.

The former President welcomed a stream of visitors to Mount Vernon, including his Revolutionary War ally the Marquis de Lafayette of France (shown here). His wife, Martha, is seated on the veranda with some family members. Washington's image has been preserved over the years on everything from postage stamps (above) to geographic landmarks. He is the only President to have a state named for him.

JOHN ADAMS
2ND PRESIDENT OF THE UNITED STATES **1797–1801**

John Adams devoted his adult life to the twin causes of creating the United States and securing its long-term survival. Adams—as the President who succeeded, or followed, George Washington—showed that the nation's most important office could survive a change of leadership. He helped his new country avoid war with France during his single term of office.

The man who became known as the "Father of American Independence" was born a British subject in the colony of Massachusetts. The son of an educated farmer and leather craftsman, Adams grew up enjoying toy boats, marbles, kites, hunting, books, and learning. He graduated from Harvard University in 1755 and took up the study of law.

Adams practiced law in Boston for 12 years and served briefly in the state

This pair of farmhouses served as the birthplaces for two U.S. Presidents: John Adams and his son John Quincy Adams.

legislature of Massachusetts before becoming a delegate to the First and Second Continental Congresses. At these meetings in Philadelphia he encouraged the colonists to seek independence from Great Britain. It was Adams who suggested that George Washington

John Adams, the nation's second President, went to school in a setting like the one pictured in this illustration. Adams cherished his status as a U.S. citizen, a right he earned thanks to the American Revolution. "I have not one drop of blood in my veins, but what is American," Adams observed in 1785 while serving as a diplomat in Europe.

Abigail Adams and her husband wrote hundreds of letters to each other during their marriage because John Adams was frequently away on government business. In 1776 when he was a delegate to the Continental Congress in Philadelphia, she reminded him to "remember the ladies. Be more generous and favorable to them than your ancestors." She went on to suggest that women should "not hold ourselves bound by any laws in which we have no voice or representation." It would be the 20th century before women won the right to vote in every state.

John Adams (below, right) at times felt overshadowed by other significant figures of the day. He joked: "The history of our Revolution will be one continued lie from one end to the other. The essence of the whole will be that Dr. Franklin's electrical rod smote the earth and out sprang General Washington. That Franklin electrified him with his rod and thenceforward these two conducted all the policies, negotiations, legislatures, and war."

command the new Continental Army, and Adams coordinated the crafting of the Declaration of Independence.

Adams was overseas during much of the Revolutionary War. He represented his new country to governments in Europe. During his stay in the Netherlands, he arranged for important loans to help fund the Revolutionary War effort. Later he helped negotiate the peace treaty that ended the war with Great Britain.

After the war, Adams served as the first U.S. Ambassador, or representative, to Great Britain. He returned to the United States in 1788 just as a federal government was being organized under the new U.S. Constitution.

He was elected to serve as Vice President to George Washington. Adams held the post for both of Washington's terms, but he found the job dull. He observed: "My country has in its wisdom contrived for me the most insignificant office that ever the invention

John Adams is called the "Father of the American Navy" for establishing a permanent U.S. naval fleet. Among the ships constructed during his presidency was the U.S.S. *Philadelphia*.

The U.S.S. *Constellation* captured *L'Insurgente* of France in 1799 when the two nations were on the brink of war.

of man contrived or his imagination conceived." His efforts while Vice President to establish flattering terms of address for the President (such as "His Highness") only earned him nasty nicknames like "His Rotundity" (Adams was overweight) and "Bonny Johnny Adams."

Whereas Washington had become President by a unanimous vote of the Electoral College, Adams had no such luck. The Constitution originally called for all candidates to be considered for President. It directed that the runner-up, or second-place finisher, become Vice President. This plan failed to anticipate the development of political parties. (A constitutional amendment in 1804 established separate votes for each office.) In 1796 Adams (a Federalist) became President by only a three-vote margin over Thomas Jefferson, a member of the rival Democratic-Republican Party, who became Vice President. Tensions arose between the two men because they represented different political viewpoints. Adams was defeated by Jefferson during his bid for a second presidential term.

Adams devoted much of his presidency to avoiding war with France or Great Britain after fighting broke out in Europe over the increasingly bloody French Revolution. Adams and fellow Federalists tried to stifle their foreign policy critics with the Alien and Sedition Acts. This legislation placed harsh restrictions on immigrants and free speech, among other effects. The President influenced the courts with his judicial appointments, including of Chief Justice

> **"I am but an ordinary man. The times alone have destined me to fame."**
>
> John Adams, diary entry, April 26, 1779

John Marshall, but his so-called midnight judges were named too late to be confirmed.

In 1801 Adams retired to his home in Massachusetts. Throughout his life he had a close, respectful relationship with his wife, Abigail. The pair shared one of the longest marriages of any presidential couple—54 years.

After their presidencies were over, John Adams and Thomas Jefferson restored the friendship of their Revolutionary War days through lively letter writing. The two men were the only signers of the Declaration of Independence to become Presidents. Curiously, they both died on the same day—the 50th anniversary of the approval of the Declaration of Independence. That day, Adams observed: "It is the glorious Fourth of July. God bless it." His final words were: "Thomas Jefferson still survives." He did not know his friend had died only a short while earlier. Adams, who had been ill, stopped breathing later that day.

THE WHITE HOUSE
THE BUILDING AND ITS HISTORY

Since 1800 every U.S. President has lived in the national landmark known today as the White House. George Washington was the only President who never slept there, but he left his mark on the structure by choosing its location and approving its design. The place has been endlessly modified, expanded, and rebuilt ever since John Adams moved into the incomplete house near the end of his term of office.

Thomas Jefferson, the home's second resident, directed many early improvements to the structure and its grounds. Subsequent Presidents have added basic conveniences such as running water, toilets, and electricity; others have modernized it with telephones, elevators, and a movie theater. The West Wing evolved from a temporary office building added by Theodore Roosevelt. Franklin D. Roosevelt added the present Oval Office that has become the President's center of business. Harry S. Truman had the original White House structure shored up and rebuilt after one inspector proclaimed that the building "was

standing up purely from habit." More recently, workers painstakingly removed all of the building's exterior paint, some 40 layers thick, then repainted it its trademark white. Today the President's home includes more than 100 rooms on four floors (plus two basement levels).

Over the years the occupants of the White House have sat for portraits, collected priceless furnishings, and obtained notable works of art. Many of these items remain in use today, making the White House a living museum. Citizens may take a self-guided tour of notable public areas in the White House by obtaining free tickets in advance through their members of Congress. An off-site visitors center provides general information for anyone.

BUILDING THE FIRST WHITE HOUSE

WASHINGTON D.C. 1798

An artist from the 20th century imagined the scene of George Washington and architect James Hoban viewing the construction of what was first called simply the President's House. Slaves and freed slaves provided essential labor during the building's creation.

The modern White House (left, and cutaway and key, opposite) serves as office and residence for the President and family. Its surrounding 18 acres are enjoyed by modern First Families for croquet, tennis, horseshoes, golf, swimming, basketball, and jogging. Interests expressed by White House residents can influence the nation as a whole, from Jacqueline Kennedy's enthusiasm for historic preservation to the Obama family's devotion to organic gardening.

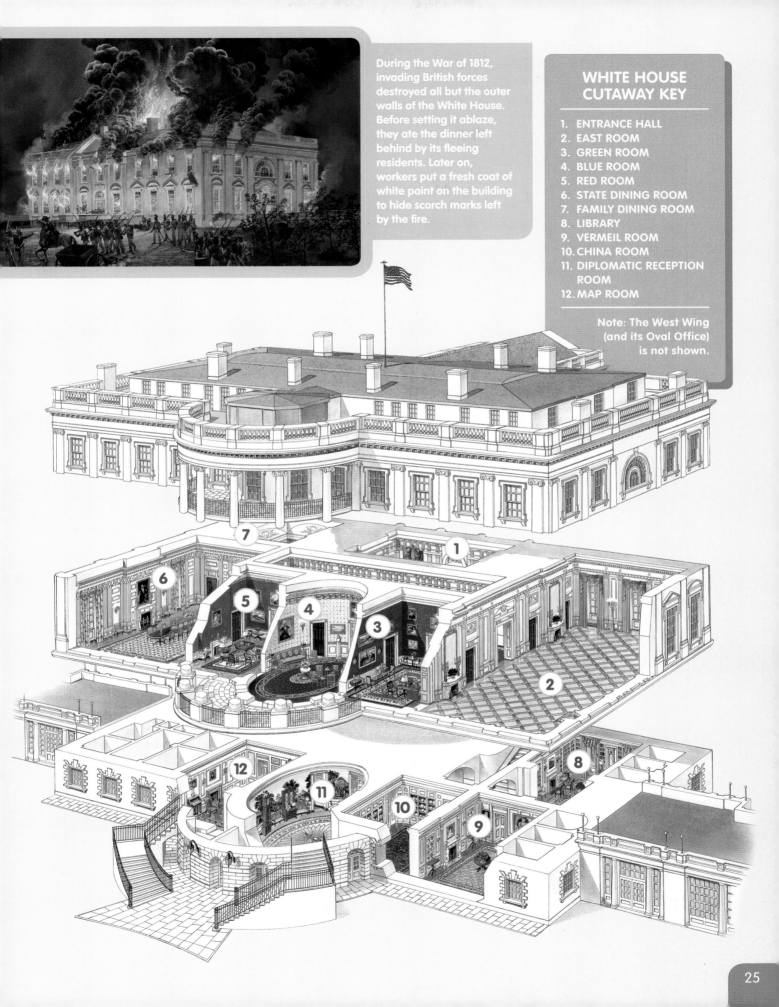

During the War of 1812, invading British forces destroyed all but the outer walls of the White House. Before setting it ablaze, they ate the dinner left behind by its fleeing residents. Later on, workers put a fresh coat of white paint on the building to hide scorch marks left by the fire.

WHITE HOUSE CUTAWAY KEY

1. ENTRANCE HALL
2. EAST ROOM
3. GREEN ROOM
4. BLUE ROOM
5. RED ROOM
6. STATE DINING ROOM
7. FAMILY DINING ROOM
8. LIBRARY
9. VERMEIL ROOM
10. CHINA ROOM
11. DIPLOMATIC RECEPTION ROOM
12. MAP ROOM

Note: The West Wing (and its Oval Office) is not shown.

THOMAS JEFFERSON
3RD PRESIDENT OF THE UNITED STATES 1801–1809

Before his death, Thomas Jefferson listed the accomplishments he wanted carved on his gravestone. Serving as the nation's third President did not make his list. Nonetheless, Jefferson remains one of the most important Presidents in U.S. history. The Louisiana Purchase he made during his first term of office extended the country beyond the Mississippi River toward the Pacific.

Jefferson had the skills for many careers. However, because he came of age during the American Revolution, he devoted himself most notably to service as a statesman. Jefferson was born in 1743 near the Blue Ridge Mountains of colonial Virginia. His father, a landowner, surveyor, and government official, died when his son was 14. From the age of nine, Jefferson studied some

distance from home and boarded with his tutor. Later he enrolled at the College of William and Mary in Williamsburg, Virginia. His education was broad and comprehensive, including science, mathematics, philosophy, law, English language and literature, Latin, Greek, French, and even how to dance at social events.

After college Jefferson became an attorney. By age 26 he was a member of Virginia's House of Burgesses. Jefferson spoke out there against British policies during the final years of colonial government. On June 7, 1776, Jefferson and other delegates at the Second Continental Congress in

Thomas Jefferson (standing) drafted the Declaration of Independence in consultation with, among others, Benjamin Franklin (seated at left) and John Adams. Adams suggested that Jefferson compose the document. "You can write ten times better than I can," said Adams, plus "I am obnoxious, suspected, and unpopular."

NICKNAME
Father of the Declaration of Independence

BORN
April 13, 1743, at Shadwell, Goochland (now Albemarle) County, VA

POLITICAL PARTY
Democratic-Republican

CHIEF OPPONENTS
1st term: President John Adams, Federalist (1735–1826), and Aaron Burr, Democratic-Republican (1756–1836); 2nd term: Charles Cotesworth Pinckney, Federalist (1746–1825)

TERM OF OFFICE
March 4, 1801–March 3, 1809

AGE AT INAUGURATION
57 years old

NUMBER OF TERMS
two

VICE PRESIDENTS
1st term: Aaron Burr (1756–1836); 2nd term: George Clinton (1739–1812)

FIRST LADIES
Dolley Dandridge Payne Todd Madison (1768–1849), friend; Martha (Patsy) Jefferson Randolph (1772–1836), daughter

WIFE
Martha Wayles Skelton Jefferson (1748–1782), married Jan. 1, 1772

CHILDREN
Born to Martha Jefferson (wife): Martha, Mary, plus three daughters and a son who died young; born to Sally Hemings (slave): Beverly, Harriet, Madison, Eston, plus two daughters who died young

GEOGRAPHIC SCENE
16 states

NEW STATES ADDED
Ohio (1803)

DIED
July 4, 1826, at Monticello, Charlottesville, VA

AGE AT DEATH
83 years old

SELECTED LANDMARKS
Monticello, Charlottesville, VA (homestead and grave); Jefferson Memorial, Washington, DC; Mount Rushmore National Memorial, Keystone, SD

During the Tripolitan War of 1801–1805, the U.S. fought with the Barbary pirates and their allies in North Africa to stop lawlessness on the seas.

French troops turned over New Orleans and the territory of Louisiana to U.S. forces on December 20, 1803. During the ceremony (left) the Stars and Stripes of the U.S. replaced the tricolor French flag at the Mississippi River port. Eventually all or parts of 15 states would be carved from Thomas Jefferson's Louisiana Purchase.

Philadelphia were asked to consider whether "these United Colonies are, and of right ought to be, free and independent States."

Soon after, Jefferson, Benjamin Franklin, John Adams, and two others were appointed to draft a declaration, or statement, in favor of independence. Jefferson spent about two weeks putting their ideas on paper. On July 2 the delegates agreed to declare their independence. Two days later, after a few revisions, members approved Jefferson's official declaration. This document is treasured for its persuasive calls for freedom and equality. It is the first achievement Jefferson listed on his gravestone.

During the Revolutionary War, Jefferson tried to put his democratic dreams into action. He wrote the "Statute for Religious Freedom" while serving in the Virginia Legislature. This document called for the separation of church and state, a concept that says it is improper for religious groups and the government to interact. Later this idea was adopted as one of the basic principles of the national government. Jefferson listed this achievement on his gravestone, too.

Over the next 20 years, Jefferson served as governor of Virginia, a representative to the Continental Congress, U.S. minister to France, secretary of state for George Washington, and Vice President for John Adams. These last two posts left Jefferson frustrated. Some government leaders, known as Federalists, favored a strong federal, or national, government ruled by the country's most prosperous and well-educated citizens. Jefferson and his supporters, many of whom were farmers and slaveholders, opposed these ideas. They favored greater freedom for the individual states and called themselves Anti-Federalists or Democratic-Republicans and, eventually, Democrats. Jefferson expressed his dislike of Federalism by resigning from Washington's administration. He also chose not to powder his hair, and he encouraged states to disobey federal laws that they disliked.

When the Electoral College voted in 1800, Jefferson and Aaron Burr tied for the presidency. It took the House of Representatives 36 ballots and two months to decide that Jefferson should be the winner. The Constitution was amended by the time of the next presidential election, so that separate votes were held for President and Vice President. Jefferson was then easily reelected.

As President, Jefferson reversed what he saw as the

> "We hold these truths to be self-evident, that all men are created equal, that they are endowed by their Creator with certain unalienable Rights, that among these are Life, Liberty and the pursuit of Happiness."
>
> Thomas Jefferson,
> Declaration of Independence, July 4, 1776

most offensive Federalist programs. He restored full freedom of speech to the press, reduced restrictions on immigration, increased land sales in the West, ended federal taxation, decreased the national debt, closed the national bank, and canceled the last-minute "midnight judges" appointments that Adams had made as he left office. During his second term, with his approval, Congress ended the practice of importing slaves into the United States from other countries.

Jefferson invented new codes of presidential behavior, too. He dressed casually around guests, even answered the White House door himself sometimes,

Thomas Jefferson is called a "Renaissance man" because of his broad range of talents. He excelled as a farmer, an architect, an inventor, a lawyer, a writer, a musician, and an educator, as well as a statesman. Among his inventions were swivel chairs and the polygraph (right), a machine that duplicated an original document as it was being composed.

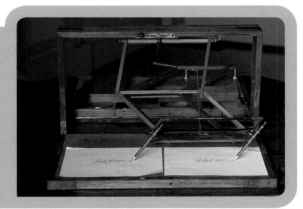

Jefferson designed and founded the University of Virginia in Charlottesville (below) during his retirement years. His personal library of 6,500 books became the foundation for a new Library of Congress after the Library's original collections were destroyed during the War of 1812.

Thomas Jefferson (left) inspects the effectiveness of a plow he invented for use at his estate, Monticello. He depended on slaves to provide the labor there, both in the fields and in his house. Thomas Jefferson is the only person to serve two full terms as President after serving as Vice President. The Jefferson Memorial (below) was constructed in his honor 200 years after his birth.

> **"I shall not die without a hope that light and liberty are on a steady advance."**
>
> Thomas Jefferson, letter to John Adams,
> September 12, 1821

and added an Independence Day open house for ordinary citizens to the White House calendar. His administration, and the two like-minded ones that followed it, led to the end of the Federalist Party.

Jefferson's most noted presidential triumph was the Louisiana Purchase of 1803. When Jefferson tried to buy the port of New Orleans, the French offered to sell all of their western lands, not just the port. They were too busy preparing to fight the British to defend this distant territory. The price was 60 million francs, or about $15 million. The United States nearly doubled in size by gaining more than 800,000 square miles of territory west of the Mississippi River. Many Federalists failed to see the value of buying "a howling wilderness." Jefferson, however, was thrilled.

Even before the Louisiana Purchase, Jefferson had been planning an exploration of the West. He asked Meriwether Lewis, his personal secretary, to lead the trip. News of the Louisiana Purchase reached the U.S. on Independence Day in 1803, just as Lewis was about to set off from the East. Lewis joined forces with William Clark and a small corps of explorers in St. Louis, Missouri. The next spring they set off up the Missouri River in search of a water passageway to the Pacific. Instead they found the Rocky Mountains. They finally reached the Pacific Ocean by way of the Columbia River in December 1805. The Lewis and Clark expedition returned by a similar route to St. Louis the following fall. Their 8,000-mile trip helped open the Louisiana Purchase for settlement.

Jefferson spent five decades perfecting his beloved mountaintop home, Monticello. In Italian, "Monticello" (pronounced mont-ti-CHELL-o) means "little mountain." Jefferson added clever details to his house (above) such as hiding beds, dumbwaiters, octagonal rooms, skylights, revolving storage space, a clock that kept track of the days of the week, and pairs of doors that opened when only one of them was pushed.

Thomas Jefferson married a young widow when he was 28 years old. She died 10 years later; no pictures of her survive. Their daughter Martha (left) served sometimes as her father's First Lady.

As a naturalist, Jefferson enjoyed receiving a live magpie and prairie dog that were collected during the Lewis and Clark expedition.

Jefferson retired to Monticello at the end of his second term. For the remaining 17 years of his life he made improvements to his beloved home, surrounded himself with grandchildren, entertained distinguished guests, and juggled the mounting debts that came with his lavish lifestyle. He accomplished the third and final credit for his gravestone during these years: Jefferson is called the Father of the University of Virginia for designing and organizing this institution. Jefferson, like his old Revolutionary War friend John Adams, died 50 years to the day after the approval of the Declaration of Independence.

Jefferson left a complicated legacy. His estate was so in debt that Monticello and some 200 slaves had to be sold. Historical and scientific evidence, including genetic testing, supports the case that Jefferson had a long-term relationship with his slave Sally Hemings and fathered six children with her. Four of them survived to adulthood; all were eventually freed by Jefferson or released without fear of capture. After his death, Hemings was likewise released, apparently by his daughter Martha.

Today it's hard to reconcile Jefferson's passionate calls for freedom with his lifelong ownership of slaves. He justified his behavior with the long-since discredited view that blacks were intellectually inferior to whites. Yet on some level he seemed to know better, writing: "I tremble for my country when I reflect that God is just." Jefferson knew future generations would have to end slavery and that it could be a devastating process.

JAMES MADISON
4TH PRESIDENT OF THE UNITED STATES 1809–1817

James Madison is remembered most for the hand he had in creating the basic rules for governing the United States—the Constitution and its Bill of Rights. Madison made sure that his new country had a strong and democratic government. Later, as President, he struggled to lead the United States safely through its first war since the American Revolution: the War of 1812.

Madison devoted his adult life to the creation of the United States. Born a British subject in the colony of Virginia, he completed his education at the college that became Princeton University. Madison was the smallest person in the history of the presidency. He stood five feet four inches tall and weighed only 100 pounds.

After serving in the Virginia Legislature and with the Continental Congress, Madison was sent to the Constitutional Convention of 1787. He and other

Dolley Madison

delegates spent 86 days inventing the structure of the U.S. government, including its Congress, presidency, and federal court system. His detailed notes remain a valuable record of the entire event. As one of the authors of *The Federalist Papers*, Madison helped influence states to ratify, or accept, the new Constitution. These 85 essays supported the idea of a

NICKNAME
Father of the Constitution

BORN
March 16, 1751, at Belle Grove, Port Conway, VA

POLITICAL PARTY
Democratic-Republican

CHIEF OPPONENTS
1st term: Charles Cotesworth Pinckney, Federalist (1746–1825); 2nd term: DeWitt Clinton, Federalist (1769–1828)

TERM OF OFFICE
March 4, 1809–March 3, 1817

AGE AT INAUGURATION
57 years old

NUMBER OF TERMS
two

VICE PRESIDENTS
1st term: George Clinton (1739–1812); 2nd term: Elbridge Gerry (1744–1814)

FIRST LADY
Dolley Dandridge Payne Todd Madison (1768–1849), wife (married Sept. 15, 1794)

CHILDREN
none

GEOGRAPHIC SCENE
17 states

NEW STATES ADDED
Louisiana (1812), Indiana (1816)

DIED
June 28, 1836, at Montpelier, Orange County, VA

AGE AT DEATH
85 years old

SELECTED LANDMARKS
Montpelier, Orange County, VA (homestead and grave); The Octagon, Washington, DC (temporary executive home after destruction of the White House)

James Madison had studied hundreds of books on history and government by the time delegates gathered at the Constitutional Convention of 1787 to organize a new government (above). Madison joked that he earned the scar on his nose in "defense of his country." Actually, it resulted from the frostbite he suffered during a long ride home after a 1788 debate with James Monroe during a U.S. congressional campaign.

Forced recruitment of American sailors by the British Navy (right) helped draw the U.S. into the War of 1812 with Great Britain.

strong federal, or national, government. As a representative in the first U.S. Congress, Madison helped secure passage of the Bill of Rights. This companion document to the Constitution sets down the basic civil liberties of the nation's citizens and states. Because Madison played such a central role in these events, he became known as the "Father of the Constitution." Madison preferred to share the credit. The Constitution was not "the offspring of a single brain," he insisted, but "the work of many heads and many hands." Madison and George

Washington are the only signers of the Constitution who later became Presidents.

Madison served four terms in Congress and then worked in Virginia's state government before his friend Thomas Jefferson asked him to join his new presidential administration as secretary of state. At the end of his two terms, Jefferson favored Madison as his successor. Madison easily defeated his opponent, Charles Pinckney, in the Electoral College voting. Pinckney, noting the popularity of Madison's wife, Dolley, observed that he "might have had a better chance had I faced Mr. Madison alone."

When Madison became President, the United States was being drawn into conflict with the British over their war with France. Americans were frustrated because the British were halting U.S. cargo ships bound for France and seizing U.S. sailors and goods. If modern forms of communication had existed in Madison's time, war might have been avoided. Not knowing that the British were ending these seizures, the U.S. declared war against Great Britain. During the War of 1812 (which lasted until 1815) American forces were beaten regularly on land and at sea. The greatest humiliation occurred late in the war when the British entered Washington and set fire to the White House and the U.S. Capitol Building. The final

The War of 1812 featured many battles at sea.

Dolley Madison supervises the packing of White House valuables as the British march on the nation's capital in 1814.

The U.S. gained control of the Great Lakes during the second year of the War of 1812 (Commodore Oliver Hazard Perry, above with sword, on Lake Erie).

"If men were angels, no government would be necessary."

James Madison, *The Federalist Papers*, #51, 1788

contest, the Battle of New Orleans, was fought after a peace treaty had been signed in Europe but before that news could reach North America. Madison was praised after the war for having allowed others to criticize his wartime policies without fear of trial or imprisonment. He insisted it was important for the United States to be able to fight a war without limiting the constitutional rights of its citizens, including the right of free speech.

First Lady Dolley Madison gained lasting fame during the war. She rescued government documents and a famous portrait in the White House of George Washington just hours before the British raided the capital. She was famous, too, for her role as a hostess. She gave lively parties, made pleasant conversation, and dressed lavishly, often topping her head with a turban, jewels, or feathers.

After eight years in the White House, Dolley and her husband, "Jemmey," returned to Montpelier, his family homestead. From there, James Madison helped Jefferson create the University of Virginia, pondered how to end slavery (even as he continued to own slaves), argued against secession (the right of states to withdraw from the Union), and organized his notes from the Constitutional Convention. He outlived all of the other Founding Fathers—the men who had influenced the American Revolution and written the U.S. Constitution. Madison died in 1836, six days shy of the nation's 60th Independence Day celebration.

Francis Scott Key (above, center) captures the drama of a British naval attack at Baltimore in 1814 by writing the poem that became the U.S. national anthem.

THE POWERS OF THE PRESIDENT
THE EXECUTIVE BRANCH IN GOVERNMENT

The structure of the United States government was established by the Constitution in 1787. That document and its 27 amendments explain the basic organization of the nation. The three branches, or divisions, of government are the legislative, executive, and judicial forms of federal power. The legislative branch is represented by the U.S. Congress, which consists of the House of Representatives and the Senate. The judicial branch contains the federal court system, including its Supreme Court. The executive branch includes the President and the departments of the government. Originally there were three departments—State, War, and Treasury. Today (see chart) there are 15 departments.

The Constitution lists the central powers of the President: Serve as Commander in Chief of the armed forces; make treaties with other nations; grant pardons; inform Congress on the state of the Union; and appoint ambassadors, officials, and judges. Over time the government has evolved so the branches operate within a system of checks and balances. For example, most of the President's actions require the approval of Congress. Likewise, the laws passed in Congress must be signed by the President before they can take effect. This system prevents one area of government from becoming so powerful that it overly influences the business of the nation.

Justice Sonia Sotomayor joined the Supreme Court in 2009.

George Washington's first Cabinet had only four members (clockwise from Washington: secretaries of war, treasury, and state plus an attorney general).

The modern Cabinet has grown to reflect the complexity of governing a world superpower. Presidents hold informal meetings, too (gathering in the Oval Office with Barack Obama, far left).

The Government of the United States

THE CONSTITUTION

LEGISLATIVE BRANCH
The Congress:
Senate
House of Representatives

EXECUTIVE BRANCH
The President
The Vice President

JUDICIAL BRANCH
The Supreme Court
of the United States
U.S. Court of Appeals
U.S. District Courts

Department of Agriculture

Department of Commerce

Department of Defense

Department of Education

Department of Energy

Department of State

Department of the Treasury

Department of Justice

Department of Labor

Department of the Interior

Department of Veterans Affairs

Department of Transportation

Department of Housing and Urban Development

Department of Health and Human Services

Department of Homeland Security

The U.S. Constitution divides the nation's government into three branches of responsibility. The President directs the executive branch.

The nation's first two Presidents addressed members of Congress directly (above, John Adams), but the next 24 leaders who followed them did not.

Woodrow Wilson restored the tradition of speaking directly to the nation's legislators (above, asking Congress in 1917 to declare war on Germany).

JAMES MONROE
5TH PRESIDENT OF THE UNITED STATES 1817–1825

James Monroe was the last U.S. President who had been an adult during the Revolutionary War. He presided over a country in the midst of widespread change. New thinking was developing about the role of political parties, the issue of slavery, and the fate of European colonies in the Americas.

Monroe grew up during an earlier period of change. He was born in Virginia as tensions increased between the American colonists and their motherland, Great Britain. Although he entered the College of William and Mary in the colonial capital of Williamsburg, Virginia, he interrupted his education to join in early revolutionary activities. At age 17 he raided the local armory with other students; the next year he dropped out of school to join the Continental Army.

Monroe served under the command of General George Washington, rising in rank to major. He crossed the Delaware River with Washington's troops, was severely wounded during a heroic capture of British cannons in the Battle of Trenton, and wintered at Valley Forge.

Near the end of the war Monroe studied law in Thomas Jefferson's law practice and later opened his own. He also began his lifelong career of public service. Before being elected President, Monroe served in the Virginia Assembly, the Continental Congress, the U.S. Senate, and as governor of Virginia. He held foreign affairs posts under three of the first four Presidents. He was Washington's minister to France, Jefferson's minister to Great Britain, and secretary of state and secretary of war for James Madison.

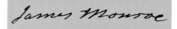

NICKNAME
Era of Good Feelings President

BORN
April 28, 1758, in Westmoreland County, VA

POLITICAL PARTY
Democratic-Republican

CHIEF OPPONENTS
1st term: Rufus King, Federalist (1755–1827); 2nd term: none

TERM OF OFFICE
March 4, 1817–March 3, 1825

AGE AT INAUGURATION
58 years old

NUMBER OF TERMS
two

VICE PRESIDENT
Daniel D. Tompkins (1774–1825)

FIRST LADY
Elizabeth Kortright Monroe (1768–1830), wife (married Feb. 16, 1786)

CHILDREN
Eliza, Maria, plus a son who died young

GEOGRAPHIC SCENE
19 states

NEW STATES ADDED
Mississippi (1817), Illinois (1818), Alabama (1819), Maine (1820), Missouri (1821)

DIED
July 4, 1831, in New York, NY

AGE AT DEATH
73 years old

SELECTED LANDMARKS
Highland (Ash Lawn), Charlottesville, VA (homestead); James Monroe Museum and Memorial Library, Fredericksburg, VA; Hollywood Cemetery, Richmond, VA

James Monroe was a tall President, just over six feet in height. He chose to be inaugurated outdoors in 1817.

In 1803 President Jefferson sent him to France to help negotiate the Louisiana Purchase.

Both Jefferson and his successor, President Madison, favored Monroe's election as President in 1816. Some Democratic-Republicans spoke of their desire to pass over Monroe, a Virginian, and end the "Virginia Dynasty" of Presidents. (Three of the first four Presidents had come from Virginia. Eventually seven of the first 12 would be Virginians.) Monroe's abilities were more important than concerns about his birthplace, though, and he was elected by a wide margin.

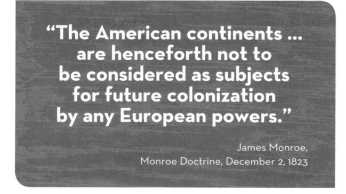

> "The American continents ... are henceforth not to be considered as subjects for future colonization by any European powers."
>
> James Monroe, Monroe Doctrine, December 2, 1823

Monroe added to his popularity as President by taking two extensive "goodwill tours" during his administration. In 1817 he traveled north and west as far as Maine and Michigan. Two years later he headed south to Georgia, went as far west as the Missouri Territory, and traveled back to Washington through Kentucky. He ran for reelection without opposition and earned all but one electoral vote. Legend says he lost this single vote because an elector wanted to preserve George Washington's record of unanimous election. Facts suggest, however, that the elector simply did not support Monroe and put forth another candidate (John Quincy Adams) instead. During his presidency a newspaper credited Monroe with bringing the nation an "era of good feelings." The phrase stuck and came to be associated with him like a nickname.

The United States underwent significant geographic changes during Monroe's leadership. Five new states joined the nation. Only one administration would add

The building of canals and locks expanded the opportunities for travel and commerce during James Monroe's presidency.

The White House (above, center) and adjacent federal office buildings as they appeared in 1820.

As President, James Monroe (standing by globe) framed a new vision for the role of the U.S. government in the Western Hemisphere.

more. (Six states joined the nation during Benjamin Harrison's single term in office.) In addition, Monroe purchased Florida from Spain and resolved key border concerns with Canada. Most important, he stated a vital U.S. position about the Western Hemisphere: The American continents were off-limits for further colonizing by European nations. This policy came to be known as the Monroe Doctrine. It set the stage for the expansion of the United States westward to the Pacific Ocean during the next two decades.

The greatest controversy of Monroe's administration was whether Missouri should enter the Union as a state that permitted slavery. Politicians organized along regional lines—North against South—over this issue. In the end, the Missouri Compromise admitted Missouri as a "slave state" with Maine entering as a "free state." Since each side in the debate gained one state, the balance between opposing viewpoints was maintained. Legislators agreed to prohibit further expansion of slavery north and west of Missouri's southern border. This position would be reconsidered by future administrations during an increasingly tense debate over slavery.

In 1825 Monroe and his wife, Elizabeth, retired to their northern Virginia home, which was designed by Jefferson. When Elizabeth died in 1830, James moved to New York City. He lived there with his younger daughter, Maria, and her family. Within the year Monroe died, too. He was the last U.S. President to die on the Fourth of July. His death followed those of Presidents Jefferson and Adams by exactly five years.

During Monroe's diplomatic service, his wife, Elizabeth, influenced French radicals to free the condemned wife of Revolutionary War ally the Marquis de Lafayette.

JOHN QUINCY ADAMS
6TH PRESIDENT OF THE UNITED STATES 1825–1829

John Quincy Adams, like his father, earned more lasting fame for his accomplishments beyond the White House than for his presidency. His single term of office took place following important overseas service and preceded a celebrated career in Congress. Adams was the only son of a Chief Executive to seek and gain the presidency until George W. Bush did so in the 2000 election.

Adams grew up in Massachusetts during the American Revolution. He witnessed the Battle of Bunker (Breed's) Hill at age eight. He traveled abroad while his father was a diplomat and later earned a degree from Harvard University. After studying law, he served his country with each of the nation's first Presidents. He was a U.S. ambassador for both George Washington and his father, a senator under Thomas Jefferson, an ambassador for James Madison, and secretary of state for James Monroe.

The 1824 electoral votes failed to give majority support to one candidate. After an ugly debate, the House of Representatives named Adams the victor. As Chief Executive, Adams ignored political strategy, stuck to his principles, and found himself generally miserable. It seemed that no one supported him. Jealous political rivals accused him of corruption. Congress refused to fund his plan for a national transportation system of roads and canals. Newspapers slandered him. In 1828 Adams felt it was undignified to personally campaign for reelection and lost the first presidential election influenced by popular vote.

John Quincy Adams enlivened his

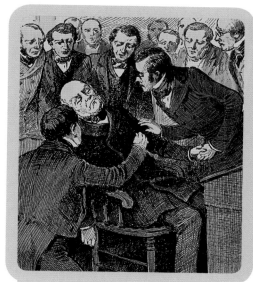
John Quincy Adams, who was elected to Congress after his presidency, becomes ill at his desk.

gloomy White House years by playing billiards, writing in his diaries, and exercising. Often he swam nude in the Potomac River. Once someone stole his clothes, and he had to ask a passing boy to fetch new ones for him from the White House.

Adams is the only President to later serve in the House of Representatives. He won election to the chamber in 1830 at age 63. Adams earned the nickname "Old Man Eloquent" for his passionate arguments. He fought for eight years to overturn the 1836 "gag rule" that prohibited discussion of slavery. His speeches were fiery, both about the restrictions and, after they were lifted, about slavery itself. On February 21, 1848, Adams had a stroke at his desk on the House floor. Realizing he was deathly ill, Adams asked to be tended to in a nearby office so he could die in his beloved Capitol Building. He did so two days later.

John Quincy Adams

NICKNAME
Old Man Eloquent

BORN
July 11, 1767, in Braintree (now Quincy), MA

POLITICAL PARTY
Democratic-Republican

CHIEF OPPONENTS
Andrew Jackson, Democratic-Republican (1767–1845)

TERM OF OFFICE
March 4, 1825–March 3, 1829

AGE AT INAUGURATION
57 years old

NUMBER OF TERMS
one

VICE PRESIDENT
John Caldwell Calhoun (1782–1850)

FIRST LADY
Louisa Catherine Johnson Adams (1775–1852), wife (married July 26, 1797)

CHILDREN
George, John, Charles, plus a daughter who died young

GEOGRAPHIC SCENE
24 states

NEW STATES ADDED
none

DIED
Feb. 23, 1848, at the U.S. Capitol, Washington, DC

AGE AT DEATH
80 years old

SELECTED LANDMARKS
Adams National Historical Park, Quincy, MA (birthplace and family home); United First Parish Church, Quincy, MA (grave)

WHITE HOUSE TRADITIONS
FROM EASTER EGGS TO PRESIDENTIAL PORTRAITS

John and Abigail Adams established one of the oldest and longest-lasting White House traditions soon after their arrival at the incomplete mansion in the fall of 1800. The following New Year's Day they invited members of the public to visit their home at an open house. All were welcomed. Those first guests would have exchanged bows with the presidential couple, but from Thomas Jefferson's presidency on, handshakes came into fashion.

As the popularity of the New Year's Day open house grew, so did the length of the lines of waiting visitors. Abraham Lincoln found himself shaking hands for three hours on New Year's Day in 1863. Herbert Hoover ended the tradition of greeting the public on New Year's Day in 1932.

A newer tradition that continues to this day is the annual Easter Egg Roll on the South Lawn of the White House. This activity migrated to the President's yard in 1878 after it was banned from the lawn of the U.S. Capitol as too damaging to the turf. The custom has continued with some interruptions (such as during wartime) ever since and has gained in popularity in recent decades. The tradition of decorating a Christmas tree at the White House dates back almost as far as the Easter Egg Roll; it began in 1889 during Benjamin Harrison's administration.

The Easter Egg Roll gets under way as children race to the finish line on the South Lawn of the White House. In 1933 Eleanor Roosevelt greeted visitors and listeners to the Egg Roll for the first time over the radio. She introduced games at the event, but the most famous activity during the modern Easter Egg Roll, the egg-rolling race, began in 1974. More than 20,000 children participate annually.

When the Presidents, Premiers, and rulers of other countries visit the U.S., they are guests of honor with the nation's First Family at what is called a state dinner. Tradition calls for the presidential cou-

At state dinners, world leaders exchange toasts of praise and thanks (above, Barack Obama during a visit by Canada's Prime Minister in 2016).

ple to escort the visiting dignitaries to dinner by way of what is known as the grand staircase of the White House. The U.S. Marine Band performs, and the presidential party pauses for news photographers when they reach the adjoining entrance hall. If dancing is planned, custom dictates that the presidential couple exchange dances with their guests of honor. They usually offer gifts to one another, too, and deliver ceremonial toasts to the health of the leaders and their nations.

Guests lucky enough to be invited to stay at the White House often sleep in what is known as the Lincoln Bedroom. Lincoln never actually slept there, but furnishings from his administration help decorate the room.

First Lady Caroline Harrison helped establish the tradition of preserving and displaying china and other dishes used at official events. Periodically a presidential couple will order new dishes for the White House. Considerable thought is given to the design and manufacturing of the china. In early administrations, such tableware had to be imported from Europe; now preference is given to goods made in the United States.

Over the years, it has become a tradition for portraits to be painted of the President and spouse as their stay in the White House comes to a close. The portraits remain behind, taking their places alongside those of past Presidents and First Ladies.

First Lady Mamie Eisenhower (above, right) admired her official portrait prior to its hanging in the White House.

Tradition calls for the portraits of the most recent Presidents to be hung in a place of honor on the main floor of the White House. The portrait of the departing President takes the place on the wall held by the painting of his predecessor, and that portrait moves to a spot of honor nearby—a reminder that Presidents are an integral part of the traditions and history of the White House.

ANDREW JACKSON
7TH PRESIDENT OF THE UNITED STATES 1829–1837

The election of Andrew Jackson put in the White House for the first time a man who seemed to represent the background and ambitions of "ordinary" Americans. His leadership style differed from that of his predecessors, too. Jackson set new patterns for presidential power that continue to be used today.

Jackson grew up earning his "man of the people" reputation. He was the son of Scotch-Irish immigrants, born to a family on the move following the sudden death of his father just a few days earlier. His exact birthplace remains uncertain. He is considered the first of the log cabin Presidents. In 1776 he was able, at age nine, to read aloud the text of the new Declaration of Independence to non-reading neighbors. Although he never

The Inauguration of Andrew Jackson, 1829

learned proper written grammar and spelling, he was well-spoken.

Jackson's education was interrupted by the American Revolution. At age 13 he served as a messenger for American troops and was captured by the British. Jackson is the only President who was a prisoner of war, and the last one who served in the Revolutionary War.

A British officer attacked Andrew Jackson (above) after he refused to polish his captor's boots during the Revolutionary War. Jackson's face bore a lifelong scar from his wound.

Andrew Jackson

NICKNAME
Old Hickory

BORN
March 15, 1767, in the Waxhaw border region of North and South Carolina

POLITICAL PARTY
Democrat (formerly Democratic-Republican)

CHIEF OPPONENTS
1st term: President John Quincy Adams, National Republican (1767–1848);
2nd term: Henry Clay, National Republican (1777–1852)

TERM OF OFFICE
March 4, 1829–March 3, 1837

AGE AT INAUGURATION
61 years old

NUMBER OF TERMS
two

VICE PRESIDENTS
1st term: John Caldwell Calhoun (1782–1850);
2nd term: Martin Van Buren (1782–1862)

FIRST LADY
Emily Donelson (1807–1836), niece

WIFE
Rachel Donelson Robards Jackson (1767–1828), married Aug. 1791 and Jan. 17, 1794

CHILDREN
Andrew (adopted)

GEOGRAPHIC SCENE
24 states

NEW STATES ADDED
Arkansas (1836), Michigan (1837)

DIED
June 8, 1845, in Nashville, TN

AGE AT DEATH
78 years old

SELECTED LANDMARKS
The Hermitage, Nashville, TN (homestead and grave)

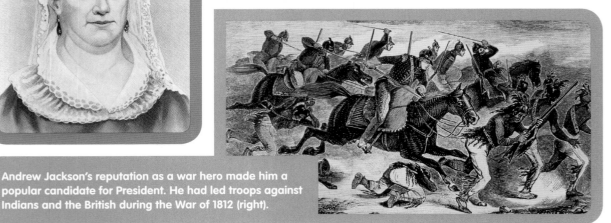

Rachel Jackson was alive when her husband won the presidential election of 1828, but she died before he could take office. Female relatives served as First Lady in her place.

Andrew Jackson's reputation as a war hero made him a popular candidate for President. He had led troops against Indians and the British during the War of 1812 (right).

Jackson tried several professions after the war before he took up the study of law and became an attorney. He settled in Tennessee. Jackson practiced law there and established a cotton plantation, worked by slaves, named the Hermitage. Later he served briefly in both the House and Senate of the U.S. Congress.

More than a decade later—during the War of 1812—Jackson earned the national reputation that carried him to the White House. He served as an officer for volunteers from Tennessee and became a U.S. general. General Jackson became famous for his leadership during the Battle of New Orleans, the last conflict in the War of 1812. Jackson's soldiers thought their leader was as tough as an old hickory tree. The nickname "Old Hickory" stuck with Jackson for life.

During the 1828 presidential election, the opposition party sought to discredit Jackson. It issued a thick booklet about his "youthful indiscretions," or mistakes, including accounts of his numerous fights and duels. (Jackson lived the last four decades of his life with a bullet lodged near his heart from one of his duels.) Jackson's supporters dished out their own round of slander, and Jackson defeated his rival, President John Quincy Adams. Jackson's wife, Rachel, became ill when she learned that their marital history was a campaign issue. The couple had been married twice; the second ceremony occurred after they learned that their first wedding had taken place before she was properly divorced from an earlier husband. Rachel died of a heart attack before her husband became President.

Citizens stormed the White House during Jackson's Inaugural Reception. They were eager to see the "People's President." Guests with muddy boots climbed on silk chairs, fists flew, china crashed, and ladies fainted in the crush of visitors. Jackson escaped out a back door to the safety of a hotel. Finally, staff members placed tubs of punch on the White House lawn to lure the crowd outside, and then they locked the doors.

Jackson marked his two terms of office by assuming greater powers of leadership than any prior President.

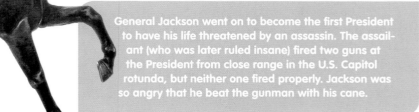

General Jackson went on to become the first President to have his life threatened by an assassin. The assailant (who was later ruled insane) fired two guns at the President from close range in the U.S. Capitol rotunda, but neither one fired properly. Jackson was so angry that he beat the gunman with his cane.

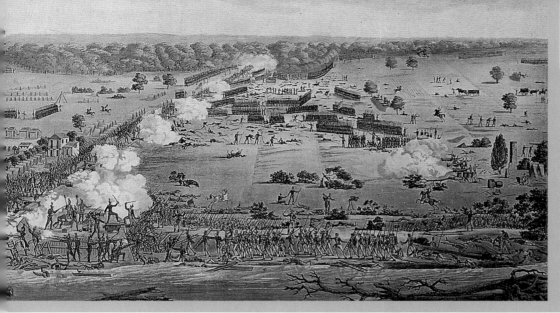

General Andrew Jackson became the "hero of New Orleans" after his forces killed or wounded 2,000 British soldiers who were attacking the city at the end of the War of 1812. U.S. casualties were only 71. Jackson's fame helped earn him the presidency 14 years later.

Andrew Jackson, who grew up in a simple log cabin, was called "a barbarian who ... hardly could spell his own name" by political rival John Quincy Adams.

Jackson's final home, the Hermitage, reflected the advances he had made during his lifetime. In 1833 Jackson responded playfully to his introduction, delivered in Latin, at a Harvard University ceremony in his honor. He joked: "All the Latin I know is *E pluribus unum.*" (This motto, which appears on the U.S. seal, means "out of many, one.") The crowd applauded with delight.

Critics nicknamed him "King Andrew the First." Future Presidents would thank him for setting standards that fortified their own administrations. Jackson insisted that Presidents could hire and fire their Cabinet members, and he replaced one who refused to follow his orders. He upheld the authority of the U.S. government over state governments by insisting it was treasonous for South Carolina to ignore federal import tax law. He encouraged the practice of awarding federal jobs to political supporters. He defied the Supreme Court by ignoring its support of Cherokee Indians. Jackson forced Native Americans living east of the Mississippi to move against their will to new land in the West.

Though his bold actions shocked many politicians, they were generally popular with citizens. Jackson was the last two-term President until Abraham Lincoln. After his second term he retired to the Hermitage, where he continued to influence politics. He took particular pleasure in the election to the presidency of two of his protégés—his own Vice President, Martin Van Buren, and, later on, James K. Polk, a fellow Tennessean. "Old Hickory" died shortly after Polk became President.

> "The great can protect themselves, but the poor and humble require the arm and shield of the law."
>
> Andrew Jackson, 1821

FROM SEA TO SHINING SEA

1837–1861

Presidents faced a delicate balancing act before the Civil War. Efforts to expand U.S. landholdings always seemed to spark renewed debate over whether to expand slavery as well. Presidents had greater success at adding land than at resolving what to do about slavery. Native Americans suffered when they were pushed from their homelands by new waves of settlers. None of the Presidents from this era served more than one term in office. Rather, they left by choice, lost reelection bids, or died in office.

1845
Frederick Douglass increased public concern over the treatment of slaves when he published his autobiography. He worked with abolitionists to end slavery.

CIRCA 1846
By 1846 large parties of settlers were traveling the Oregon Trail from Missouri to the western United States. They rested at Independence Rock (above) before crossing the Rocky Mountains.

1846–1848
The Mexican War began with battles at disputed Texas border spots such as Palo Alto. By the end of the war, U.S. boundaries stretched to California.

1849
The 1848 discovery of gold in California triggered a massive gold rush the next year. Prospectors flocked to the region in search of the valuable metal.

Travelers head west on the Oregon Trail with livestock and belongings (an artist's rendering of the scene circa 1869).

1850s
The number of miles of railroad track in use throughout the United States tripled during the 1850s. A spreading web of routes moved people and freight across vast distances.

1854
Commodore Matthew C. Perry, backed up by a strong show of military might, established trading rights between the United States and Japan during his visit there.

1860
By 1860 more than one-third of all Southerners—nearly four million people—were slaves. Disagreement over the expansion of slavery erupted into the Civil War a year later.

1860–1861
Pony Express riders could deliver mail between Missouri and California in 10 days or less. Rides ceased after telegraph wires spanned the continent in October 1861.

MARTIN VAN BUREN
8TH PRESIDENT OF THE UNITED STATES 1837–1841

Martin Van Buren earned the respect and support of the Democratic Party by developing new ways to conduct politics. The financial panic that began soon after he entered the White House in 1837 clouded his bright prospects as President. This popular Vice President of Andrew Jackson failed to win election to a second term.

Van Buren was an unlikely President to lose a reelection bid. He had spent his adult life creating the political system that earned him his first term in office. A native of New York, he was the first President born as a citizen of the United States. (Earlier Presidents, although born as British subjects, were considered U.S. citizens by their association with the new nation.) Van Buren, the descendant of Dutch immigrants, completed his formal schooling before his 14th birthday. He then took up the study of law. By age 21 he was a practicing attorney.

A successful political career followed. Between 1812 and 1829 Van Buren—originally a Democratic-Republican—served

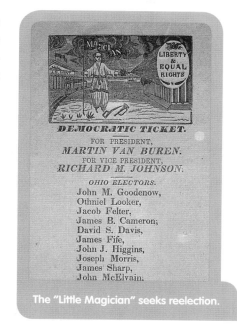

DEMOCRATIC TICKET.
FOR PRESIDENT,
MARTIN VAN BUREN.
FOR VICE PRESIDENT,
RICHARD M. JOHNSON.
OHIO ELECTORS.
John M. Goodenow,
Othniel Looker,
Jacob Felter,
James B. Cameron;
David S. Davis,
James Fife,
John J. Higgins,
Joseph Morris,
James Sharp,
John McElvain.

The "Little Magician" seeks reelection.

as a member of the New York State Senate, then as a U.S. senator, and briefly as governor of his home state. Along the way he revolutionized party politics. Van Buren wanted to defeat those who held office as a result of their personal wealth and influence. He worked with others who shared this view to stir up popular support over issues such as the costly

NICKNAME
Little Magician

BORN
Dec. 5, 1782, in Kinderhook, NY

POLITICAL PARTY
Democrat

CHIEF OPPONENT
William Henry Harrison, Whig (1773–1841)

TERM OF OFFICE
March 4, 1837–March 3, 1841

AGE AT INAUGURATION
54 years old

NUMBER OF TERMS
one

VICE PRESIDENT
Richard M. Johnson (1780–1850)

FIRST LADY
Angelica Singleton Van Buren (1816–1878), daughter-in-law

WIFE
Hannah Hoes Van Buren (1783–1819), married Feb. 21, 1807

CHILDREN
Abraham, John, Martin, Smith

GEOGRAPHIC SCENE
26 states

NEW STATES ADDED
none

DIED
July 24, 1862, in Kinderhook, NY

AGE AT DEATH
79 years old

SELECTED LANDMARKS
Lindenwald, Kinderhook, NY (homestead); Kinderhook Cemetery, Kinderhook, NY

Martin Van Buren's birthplace (left) was in Kinderhook, New York. Van Buren earned many nicknames because of his political cleverness and success. He was called the "Little Magician," "Enchanter," "Wizard," and "Red Fox of Kinderhook." In 1840 Democrats in New York City formed the "O.K. Club," after "Old Kinderhook," another Van Buren nickname. Soon "OK" came to mean "all right."

A HARD ROAD TO HOE!

Martin Van Buren's presidency was troubled by obstacles, such as how to manage the federal money supply and how to overcome the popular frontier-style image—complete with hard cider—of his 1840 political opponent, William Henry Harrison. By the time Van Buren became President, the nation's population had almost quadrupled to more than 15 million people since the start of George Washington's administration nearly 50 years earlier.

Early financial crises were named panics after the hysteria that accompanied them. A shortage of funding in banks led to the Panic of 1837. Hardships followed for the rest of Van Buren's presidency (right, a cartoon depicts homelessness, unemployment, and despair).

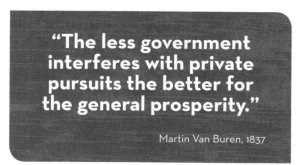

construction of canals. He and his supporters identified themselves by displaying the tail of a buck deer on their hats. The "Bucktail" Democrats gained broad influence by unseating their aristocratic rivals.

Once in power, the Bucktails rewarded their supporters with thousands of state jobs, thus ensuring continued loyalty to the party. This practice came to be known as the "spoils system" because it distributed the riches, or spoils, of office among party members. It was these supporters who helped Van Buren get elected to the U.S. Senate. Later, Andrew Jackson gained his place in the White House thanks, in part, to the practice of Van Buren–style politics. Jackson rewarded Van Buren for his support by naming him secretary of state. When Jackson ran for reelection, he chose Van Buren as his Vice President. He supported Van Buren's own bid for the presidency four years later.

Van Buren gained Jackson's post in the election of 1836, but he did not enjoy the same popularity as his

> **"The less government interferes with private pursuits the better for the general prosperity."**
>
> Martin Van Buren, 1837

predecessor. Nor did his administration enjoy the same prosperity. Soon after his Inauguration, the national economy collapsed in what became known as the Panic of 1837. Banks failed, businesses closed, and tens of thousands of workers lost their jobs. In some cities, angry residents rioted and stole food. It was the worst financial crisis the nation had ever experienced, and it lasted for five years. Van Buren handled the problem poorly. He continued Jackson's financial policies without realizing they were making matters worse, not better.

Van Buren had better luck managing other threats to the nation. Using diplomacy, he quieted tensions with Mexico over the newly independent Republic of Texas. His anti-statehood position on Texas helped reduce North-South concerns over the possible expansion of slavery there. He avoided war with Great Britain in two disputes, one over the Maine-Canada

During Martin Van Buren's presidency, federal troops drove some 15,000 Cherokee out of their homes in or near Georgia to the Indian Territory in present-day Oklahoma. Close to a third of these Native Americans died because of the harsh conditions along what became known as the Trail of Tears.

Hannah Hoes Van Buren died when she was 35 years old, 18 years before her husband became President. In 1837 their four grown sons moved into the White House with their widowed father.

border and the other regarding American support of rebels from Ontario, Canada.

Van Buren continued the Indian Removal Act policies of the Jackson Administration. As a result, the United States waged a vicious war against Seminole Indians in Florida, forcing survivors to move West. These battles and other Indian removal efforts cost the federal government some $50 million. This flow of money unexpectedly helped improve the economy, although not early enough before the election to earn Van Buren a second term in office. The "Little Magician" found himself out of tricks when faced for the second time with a challenge by William Henry Harrison. Van Buren was defeated by someone whose own party had grown stronger using the same tactics Van Buren had promoted earlier with the Democrats.

Van Buren returned to his hometown in upstate New York. He lived at Lindenwald, an estate he had purchased there some years earlier. Van Buren made two more unsuccessful runs for the White House, most notably in 1848 with the short-lived Free Soil Party. He supported President Abraham Lincoln's pro-Union policies during the Civil War but died before the end of the conflict.

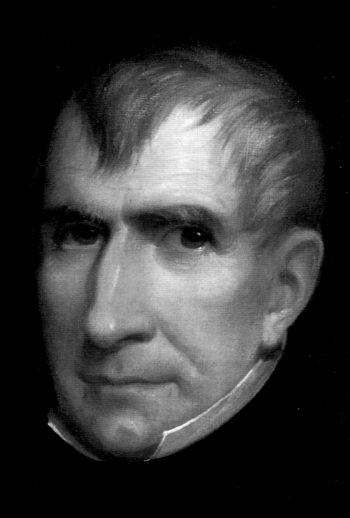

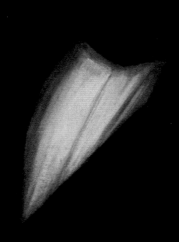

56

WILLIAM HENRY HARRISON
9TH PRESIDENT OF THE UNITED STATES 1841

William Henry Harrison had a presidency of extremes. At age 68 he was the oldest person at that point in time to become President. He gave the longest Inaugural Address ever—one hour and 40 minutes, and he was the first President to die in office. But Harrison is remembered most for having the shortest term of office: one month.

Harrison was also the last President born before the start of the American Revolution. Harrison's father signed the Declaration of Independence when William Henry was three years old. Harrison attended Hampden-Sydney College in Virginia before studying medicine and becoming a soldier. He battled Indians at the Tippecanoe River (hence his nickname) and fought in the War of 1812. He was the governor of Indiana Territory, an Ohio state senator, the ambassador to Colombia, and a U.S. representative and senator before seeking the presidency. Harrison represented the Whigs, a new party that evolved from the Federalists. He and his 1840 presidential running mate were billed as the ticket of "Tippecanoe and Tyler Too." They won.

Harrison delivered his lengthy Inaugural

William Henry Harrison's efforts to take over Native American lands made tribal leader Tecumseh furious during their 1810 meeting.

Address outdoors in brisk weather, yet he refused to wear a hat or coat. He became ill soon after, a fact that many attributed to his disregard of the weather. Renewed study of the historical record, however, suggests a different cause: contaminated drinking water due to an open sewer located near the White House. Harrison died five days later, exactly one month after taking office. His death triggered the first promotion of a Vice President to the presidency without benefit of an election. Years later, Harrison's grandson Benjamin Harrison became the nation's 23rd President.

NICKNAME
Tippecanoe

BORN
Feb. 9, 1773, in Charles City County, VA

POLITICAL PARTY
Whig

CHIEF OPPONENT
President Martin Van Buren, Democrat (1782–1862)

TERM OF OFFICE
March 4, 1841–April 4, 1841

AGE AT INAUGURATION
68 years old

NUMBER OF TERMS
one (cut short by death)

VICE PRESIDENT
John Tyler (1790–1862)

FIRST LADY
Jane Irwin Harrison (1804–1845), daughter-in-law

WIFE
Anna Tuthill Symmes Harrison (1775–1864), married Nov. 25, 1795

CHILDREN
Elizabeth, John, Lucy, William, John, Benjamin, Mary, Carter, Anna, plus a son who died young

GEOGRAPHIC SCENE
26 states

NEW STATES ADDED
none

DIED
April 4, 1841, in the White House, Washington, DC

AGE AT DEATH
68 years old

SELECTED LANDMARKS
Berkeley Plantation, Charles City County, VA (birthplace); Grouseland, Vincennes, IN (family home); Harrison Tomb State Memorial, North Bend, OH

The Whig Party urged voters to "keep the ball rolling on to Washington" by supporting its candidate.

JOHN TYLER
10TH PRESIDENT OF THE UNITED STATES 1841–1845

John Tyler was the first Vice President to complete a different Chief Executive's term. He took firm command of the office immediately after the death of William Henry Harrison. This confident action set the standard for future midterm successions.

A Virginian like his predecessor, Tyler was a graduate of the College of William and Mary in Williamsburg. Before being named to the 1840 presidential ticket, he had served Virginia in the state legislature, as governor, and in the U.S. House and Senate.

Tyler was dubbed "His Accidency" after Harrison's unexpected death. The Constitution was vague about how a Vice President should take over as President. Tyler insisted that he was a true President, not an acting one. He took the oath of office, moved into the White House, and prepared to serve out Harrison's term. He even delivered a brief Inaugural Address (and did not catch cold).

As President, Tyler favored greater power for state governments and less for the federal government. His policies added to North-South tensions and helped lead the country to civil war later

During John Tyler's administration the Morse telegraph machine revolutionized long-distance communication by sending coded messages with electric current.

on. Tyler supported settlement of the West, helped resolve a dispute with Great Britain over Canada's boundaries with Maine, and led efforts to bring the Republic of Texas (then an independent country) into the Union.

Tyler was kicked out of the Whig Party after he vetoed its pro-banking legislation. Without the backing of a party, he had no easy way to seek reelection. Tyler, who was married twice, had 15 children—more than any other President. He and his family retired to Virginia. When civil war seemed likely, Tyler, who was a slaveholder, encouraged his state to leave the Union. He was elected to serve in the Confederate Congress, but he died before he could take office.

John Tyler and his future wife, Julia, escaped harm in 1844 when a cannon misfired during their visit to the warship *Princeton*. After Julia hosted a popular White House ball at the end of her husband's presidency, Tyler, who had been kicked out of his political party, joked: "They cannot say now that I am a President without a party."

John Tyler

NICKNAME
His Accidency

BORN
March 29, 1790, in Charles City County, VA

POLITICAL PARTY
Whig

CHIEF OPPONENT
none; succeeded William Henry Harrison

TERM OF OFFICE
April 6, 1841–March 3, 1845

AGE AT INAUGURATION
51 years old

NUMBER OF TERMS
one (partial)

VICE PRESIDENT
none

FIRST LADY
Letitia Christian Tyler (1790–1842), first wife (married March 29, 1813); Priscilla Cooper Tyler (1816–1889), daughter-in-law; Letitia Tyler Semple (1821–1907), daughter; Julia Gardiner Tyler (1820–1889), second wife (married June 26, 1844)

CHILDREN
Born to Letitia Tyler (first wife): Mary, Robert, John, Letitia, Elizabeth, Alice, Tazwell, plus a daughter who died young; born to Julia Tyler (second wife): David, John, Julia, Lachlan, Lyon, Robert, Pearl

GEOGRAPHIC SCENE
26 states

NEW STATES ADDED
Florida (1845)

DIED
Jan. 18, 1862, in Richmond, VA

AGE AT DEATH
71 years old

SELECTED LANDMARKS
Sherwood Forest Plantation, Charles City County, VA (homestead); Hollywood Cemetery, Richmond, VA

THE VICE PRESIDENTS
LEADERS JUST A HEARTBEAT AWAY

Forty-eight individuals have served as Vice President of the United States since 1789. Fourteen have eventually become President, starting with John Adams, the first Vice President. The others, although important political figures in their day, have tended to fade from popular memory.

The vice presidency was created at the same time as the presidency with the writing of the U.S. Constitution in 1787. The office received only brief definition. It took two constitutional amendments to clarify how Vice Presidents should be chosen and what role they should play when a President becomes ill or dies in office.

The earliest Vice Presidents earned their posts by being the runners-up in the voting for President by the Electoral College. By the late 1820s, as citizens began voting for President, political parties began identifying their own candidates for the two offices. Today such selection is directed by each presidential nominee. Then and now, vice presidential nominees often balance and broaden the appeal of an election ticket by representing, for example, a different age and geographic region.

Early Vice Presidents were not seen as Presidents-in-waiting the way they are today. In fact, lawmakers disagreed over whether the Vice President even had this responsibility. It was not until the death of President William Henry Harrison in 1841 that this uncertainty was resolved. John Tyler, Harrison's Vice President, insisted that he deserved all the rights and responsibilities of President. His decisive example set the pattern for future presidential successions.

The Constitution spells out one main responsibility for the Vice President: to preside over the U.S. Senate. In that role, the Vice President is expected to cast deciding votes whenever the tally of senators' ballots results in a tie. Vice President John Adams was called upon to fulfill this duty on 29 occasions, more than any other Vice President.

With such a limited job description, early Vice Presidents often spent little time in the nation's capital, especially

The Vice President's official residence lies a short drive from the White House.

Aaron Burr was among the most notorious Vice Presidents, particularly after he shot Alexander Hamilton in an 1804 duel (above). Hamilton later died, leaving Burr open to murder charges as Thomas Jefferson's Vice President.

when the Senate was out of session. Many returned to their home states and took up old responsibilities. It was not until the 1970s that the Vice President even earned an official residence. The home is a 33-room house on the grounds of the U.S. Naval Observatory, a short drive from the White House. Walter Mondale, second in command to Jimmy Carter, became the first Vice President to inhabit this space.

Over the years Vice Presidents have shared similar

Modern Vice Presidents serve many functions in support of the nation's Chief Executives, such as speaking on behalf of the President (Vice President Joe Biden talks about rising college costs during a 2012 visit to Florida).

Vice Presidents represent the administration at events (Hubert Humphrey greets Martin Luther King, Jr., at a dinner in New York, 1965).

Only two Vice Presidents, John C. Calhoun and Spiro T. Agnew, have resigned from office. Calhoun left Andrew Jackson's administration to become a U.S. senator. Agnew (right), Richard Nixon's Vice President, resigned after admitting he had cheated on his income taxes. Ten months later, scandal forced Nixon to resign, too.

The complexity of national affairs makes Vice Presidents valuable advisers and consultants for their bosses (Al Gore at work with President Bill Clinton).

backgrounds with Presidents, starting with a common average age of about 55 years. New York State, a popular home for Presidents, gave more Vice Presidents to the country than any other state. Eight were born there, and four others settled there before taking office. Like Presidents, many Vice Presidents served first as governors (16) or members of Congress (35) before assuming national office. Many had presidential ambitions of their own but settled for the post of Vice President, perhaps with the hope that the job would serve as a stepping-stone to the presidency later on.

More than half of the Vice Presidents have served at least one four-year term in office; only nine have completed two terms as Vice President. Others either succeeded to the presidency by death (on eight occasions), or because of resignation (once), died in office themselves (in seven instances), resigned from their duties (twice), or filled unexpired terms of other Vice Presidents (once). Former Vice Presidents have variously retired from political life; won seats in Congress; or, in the case of five men, gone on to be elected President. Charles Dawes (Coolidge's Vice President) and Al Gore (Bill Clinton's) even earned Nobel Peace Prizes.

Until the U.S. Constitution was amended in 1967, vacancies in the office of Vice President remained unfilled until the next presidential election. Now the 25th Amendment asks the President to nominate someone to serve as Vice President, subject to approval by a majority of the members of Congress. Richard Nixon was the first President to use this provision. Before then there had been 19 occasions totaling nearly 38 years when the nation had no one serving as Vice President.

The role a Vice President plays in an administration is set by each individual President. During the 20th century, Vice Presidents gained greater influence and were given increasingly important duties. Today's Vice Presidents juggle a growing range of responsibilities. At the same time, they live each day knowing they are but a heartbeat away from becoming President of the United States.

JAMES K. POLK
11TH PRESIDENT OF THE UNITED STATES 1845–1849

Using a combination of war and rough diplomacy, James Knox Polk significantly increased the nation's size. By the end of his single term, he had taken control of the land that would form almost all of the 48 contiguous United States. However, disagreements over the expansion of slavery into the new territories left the nation more divided than ever.

Polk came to Washington with the nickname "Young Hickory" because of his ties to Andrew Jackson, the famed "Old Hickory" President. Like Jackson, Polk was born in the Carolinas and settled in Tennessee. He was the son of a prosperous landowner, planter, and slaveholder. Polk's formal education began at age 17. He earned a degree with honors from the University of North Carolina, studied law, became an attorney, and sought a career in politics.

Polk camps with his father on a surveying trip.

After a few years in the Tennessee Legislature, Polk gained election to the U.S. House of Representatives. He served there for 14 years and was eventually elected speaker, or leader, of the House. He earned Andrew Jackson's friendship

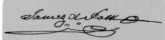

NICKNAME
Young Hickory

BORN
Nov. 2, 1795, near Pineville, Mecklenburg County, NC

POLITICAL PARTY
Democrat

CHIEF OPPONENT
Henry Clay, Whig (1777–1852)

TERM OF OFFICE
March 4, 1845–March 3, 1849

AGE AT INAUGURATION
49 years old

NUMBER OF TERMS
one

VICE PRESIDENT
George Mifflin Dallas (1792–1864)

FIRST LADY
Sarah Childress Polk (1803–1891), wife (married Jan. 1, 1824)

CHILDREN
none

GEOGRAPHIC SCENE
27 states

NEW STATES ADDED
Texas (1845), Iowa (1846), Wisconsin (1848)

DIED
June 15, 1849, at Nashville, TN

AGE AT DEATH
53 years old

SELECTED LANDMARKS
Pineville, NC (reconstructed birthplace); State Capitol Grounds, Nashville, TN (grave)

James K. Polk grew up in the backwoods of North Carolina and Tennessee. As President, he pushed the U.S. boundaries to the Pacific Ocean. The first U.S. postage stamps, the U.S. Naval Academy, and the Smithsonian Institution all began during his administration.

Posters compare the candidates for President in 1844. James K. Polk was a "dark horse," or unexpected choice, for his political party. When word of his nomination reached Washington, D.C., by the new Morse telegraph, some doubted that the machine was working correctly.

> "The people of this continent alone have the right to decide their own destiny."
>
> James K. Polk,
> Message to Congress, December 2, 1845

in those years by supporting the President's policies. Later Polk served as governor of Tennessee.

Despite this record of public service, the nomination of Polk for President in 1844 came as a surprise. Most Democrats had expected the party to renominate former President Martin Van Buren, with Polk as a possible vice presidential candidate. Van Buren, however, had lost favor because of his antislavery stand against Texas statehood. Polk, a slaveholder, supported bringing Texas into the Union as a slave state and became the compromise nominee. He narrowly defeated the noted statesman Henry Clay at the polls.

Polk came into office determined, as were many citizens then, to expand his country's borders to the Pacific Ocean. This belief—that the U.S. had the right to take over lands in the West—was called Manifest Destiny. This unquestionable confidence was used to justify the nation's expansion regardless of how it forced Native Americans from their homelands.

Polk started with the Oregon Territory. Previously, this northwestern region, which included parts of present-day Oregon, Idaho, Washington State, and Canada's British Columbia, had been settled by British and Americans alike. U.S. pioneers traveled to it by way of the Oregon Trail. Polk bluffed that he expected the British to give up all land south of latitude 54° 40' N, the southern border of Russia's Alaskan Territory.

An artist illustrated Polk's policy of Manifest Destiny by showing the symbolic figure of Columbia leading settlers westward.

Otherwise he would fight to take it. Hence the popular slogan "fifty-four forty, or fight." In the end, Polk was delighted to settle on the 49th parallel, which still forms most of the U.S.-Canada border.

Next Polk concentrated on the southern U.S. border. Texans had won their independence from Mexico in 1836. Polk angered Mexico by granting Texas statehood soon after he became President. Then a boundary dispute erupted over the new state's southern border. Mexico insisted the Nueces River, the boundary of Texas as a Mexican state, was still its southern border. The U.S. claimed territory all the way to the Rio Grande—about half of the country of Mexico.

On Polk's instructions, U.S. soldiers provoked the Mexicans to attack by crossing into the disputed region in early 1846. From then on, U.S. forces never lost a battle in a war that ultimately took them all the way to Mexico City. When the Mexican War ended in the fall of 1847, the United States had gained not only the border it wanted for Texas but considerable other new land as well. Eventually, some or all of the states of Arizona,

This political cartoon questions whether trouble caused by President Polk's policies will collapse on him like a house of cards.

California, Colorado, Nevada, New Mexico, Utah, and Wyoming would take shape in the extra territory. The U.S. government paid Mexico $15 million for its loss of land. Ulysses S. Grant, the future Civil War general and U.S. President, was among those who fought in the war. He described it as "one of the most unjust ever waged by a stronger against a weaker nation."

In all, Polk added 1.2 million square miles of territory to the United States. It came with a heavy price. Northerners opposed to the expansion of slavery and Southerners who supported it debated furiously over whether slavery had a place in the vast new lands. The two sides seemed ready to come to blows over the issue, and they finally did when the Civil War erupted some dozen years later.

Polk left the White House after one term, fulfilling an election promise not to run again. He enjoyed the shortest retirement of any President—three months—in part because he had literally exhausted himself on the job. Polk became ill, possibly with cholera, and died. His wife, Sarah, lived in their Tennessee home 42 years longer, remaining neutral during the Civil War.

James K. Polk and his wife, Sarah (left), had no children. They retired to "Polk Place" (above) after his presidency. Sarah was well educated, and she devoted her energies to her husband's career. She traveled with him, helped with his speeches, reviewed newspapers for him, and served as the White House hostess. Because of her religious beliefs, she disapproved of alcohol, gambling, and dancing. When she entered the room for her husband's Inaugural Ball, the dancing ended. The Polks started the White House traditions of an annual Thanksgiving dinner and the playing of "Hail to the Chief" for the President's arrival.

WE WANT TO VOTE
BATTLES FOR THE BALLOT

The range of people denied the right to vote over the course of history in the United States has included women, slaves, African Americans, Native Americans, Asian Americans, immigrants, the impoverished, people convicted of a felony, and adults unable to read and write.

Changes in voting rights have come gradually and in steps. The granting of rights at one time hasn't necessarily guaranteed their continuation at other times, and the adoption of laws expanding the franchise hasn't always been accompanied by enforcement of the laws. Yet, by degrees, Americans have gained the right to voice their preferences in the country's elections.

In an effort to restrict the ability of others to vote, authorities have imposed taxes on the voting process (known as poll taxes), redrawn the boundaries of voting districts to suit a political advantage (a process called gerrymandering), required long periods of residency, constructed illogical tests and other obstacles to registration, refused to comply with laws, and harassed and even murdered people attempting to register, or prove their qualifications, for voting.

Although the federal government has the last word on voting rights, states administer the casting and counting of votes, and state laws vary over who can vote, how people register to vote, and the ways people vote. A series of amendments to the U.S. Constitution has helped

It took almost two centuries for a nation born out of a desire for equality to achieve something close to universal suffrage—that is, the right of all citizens to have a voice in their governance. Early efforts to extend voting rights to African-American males occurred after the Civil War, but it took another 100 years for people of color to achieve equal suffrage.

The dramatic 1965 voting rights march in Alabama (led by Martin Luther King, Jr., center, and other activists) influenced Congress to pass the year's landmark Voting Rights Act. Five decades later, states began challenging the ongoing federal review of their voting laws.

In 1971 18-year-olds became eligible to vote. Until then, voters had to be 21 years of age.

Women (shown marching for voting rights in 1912) gained access to the ballot box during the 20th century.

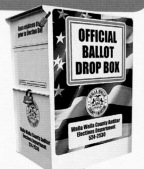

In 1993 passage of the so-called Motor Voter Act made it easier for everyone to register—even at state motor vehicle offices. Political parties may work to expand voting rights because they hope to attract the votes of the newly enfranchised. Or they may back laws that make it easier for their traditional supporters (or harder for their opponents' supporters) to vote. Sometimes leaders even set politics aside and embrace the arguments of those who want to vote.

In 1971 Americans expanded the suffrage again when the 26th Amendment lowered the voting age from 21 to 18. A period of war contributed to this constitutional change. At the height of the Vietnam War, young people objected to forced military service for 18-year-olds who could not yet vote on government policies. Such objections led Congress and the states to reduce the voting age to match the age for military service.

Wars had influenced passage of the previous suffrage amendments as well. The Union victory in the Civil War directly contributed to the granting of voting rights to former male slaves, and the national commitment to supporting democracy abroad during World War I led to the granting of voting rights to women at home.

ensure that more and more people can vote and that authorities enforce laws designed to protect voting rights.

The 15th Amendment to the Constitution was ratified in 1870; it granted African-American males the right to vote. Although the amendment initially enabled thousands of former slaves to vote, its effectiveness faded after whites used intimidation and legal maneuvers to prevent blacks from voting. Not until the federal government passed the Voting Rights Act of 1965 were local authorities forced to uphold the 15th Amendment.

Starting in 1848, women mounted a 72-year-long struggle to gain their voting rights. Only after ratification of the 19th Amendment in 1920 did they secure those rights. The majority of African-American women waited another 45 years to have their voting rights enforced along with those of black men.

Counting ballots deposited in collection boxes is time-consuming. Machines now speed up the work.

OFFICIAL BALLOT DROP BOX

Walla Walla County Auditor Elections Department
524-2530

Debates continue over who should vote and how. Should voters have to obtain photo IDs to prove their identities? Should there be a paper record of every vote cast? Should convicted felons who have served their sentences nonetheless be banned from ever voting? Should immigrants be allowed to vote, even if they are not yet citizens? Should the voting age be lowered to 16? How will such debates be settled? Maybe they will be put to a vote!

ZACHARY TAYLOR
12TH PRESIDENT OF THE UNITED STATES 1849–1850

Zachary Taylor was a soldier by training, not a politician, but he discovered unexpected similarities between those two professions after becoming President. Politicians in the nation's capital could become as combative as soldiers, he learned, particularly when the matter of slavery was discussed. He threatened to use military force to settle the debate over slavery; then he died in office before he could.

Taylor was the first President who had never held another elected office. In fact, he had never even voted in a presidential election because he felt his loyalty as a soldier for the U.S. government required him to stay neutral politically. Born in Virginia, Taylor was raised on a plantation in Kentucky and was one of the last slave owners to become President. He never attended college. Instead, he entered into a 40-year career as an officer in the U.S. Army. His relaxed style of military dress, reputation for bravery, and consistent victories earned him the nickname "Old Rough-and-Ready."

Being a military hero helped Taylor win the election, but his Army career was poor training for the national debate on slavery. An uproar developed after he suggested that new states

Taylor's 1848 running mate succeeded him as President after Taylor's death.

should decide for themselves whether to be slave or free. Northerners wanted Taylor to restrict slavery, not expand it. Southerners feared new antislavery states would diminish their own pro-slavery influence in Congress. When Southerners threatened to secede from, or leave, the Union, Taylor offered to lead the U.S. Army against them. We must "preserve the Union at all hazards," he said.

Then Taylor died. Evidence now suggests that he, as with William Henry Harrison, may have become ill because of contaminated drinking water. He died within days of contracting an intestinal infection.

NICKNAME
Old Rough-and-Ready

BORN
Nov. 24, 1784, in Orange County, VA

POLITICAL PARTY
Whig

CHIEF OPPONENT
Lewis Cass, Democrat (1782–1866)

TERM OF OFFICE
March 4, 1849–July 9, 1850

AGE AT INAUGURATION
64 years old

NUMBER OF TERMS
one (cut short by death)

VICE PRESIDENT
Millard Fillmore (1800–1874)

FIRST LADIES
Margaret Mackall Smith Taylor (1788–1852), wife (married June 21, 1810); Mary Elizabeth Taylor Bliss (1824–1909), daughter

CHILDREN
Ann, Sarah, Mary, Richard, plus two daughters who died young

GEOGRAPHIC SCENE
30 states

NEW STATES ADDED
none

DIED
July 9, 1850, in the White House, Washington, DC

AGE AT DEATH
65 years old

SELECTED LANDMARKS
Zachary Taylor National Cemetery, Louisville, KY

General Zachary Taylor often wore old farm clothes into battle. He made a straw hat part of his standard battle dress. Zachary Taylor's legs were so short that he needed help mounting a horse. He liked to ride sidesaddle.

MILLARD FILLMORE
13TH PRESIDENT OF THE UNITED STATES 1850–1853

Millard Fillmore offered compromise, in contrast to the threatening style of his predecessor, as a way to end the ongoing tense debate over slavery. Despite being born a Northerner, Fillmore seemed to sympathize with Southern concerns. In the end, the compromises he signed only delayed civil war between North and South.

Born in a log cabin in upstate New York, Fillmore fulfilled the American dream of rising from simple beginnings to national importance. He was poorly educated. He is said to have seen his first map of the United States upon entering school at age 19. (Later he married his schoolteacher.) He never attended college, but he trained himself to be a lawyer. He won election to government posts in New York State and the U.S. House of Representatives before agreeing to run for Vice President on Zachary Taylor's ticket in 1848.

When Fillmore became President after Taylor died in office, he chose to compromise with lawmakers over quarrelsome debates about slavery. Their five agreements became known as the Compromise of 1850. These deals admitted California as a free state, settled

Millard Fillmore failed to regain the presidency in 1856.

border disputes between Texas and New Mexico, gave territory status to New Mexico, closed the slave markets in the nation's capital, and allowed federal law officers to return runaway slaves to their owners. Each side gained something, and war seemed less likely.

Fillmore showed little interest in the next election, so the Whigs selected a different candidate and lost in 1852, making him the "Last of the Whigs" when the party disintegrated. Some former Whigs supported the new Know-Nothing Party and nominated Fillmore for President in 1856. Fillmore disapproved of the group's anti-immigrant views but ran and finished third. He died in Buffalo, New York, in 1874.

NICKNAME
Last of the Whigs

BORN
Jan. 7, 1800, in Cayuga County, NY

POLITICAL PARTY
Whig

CHIEF OPPONENT
none; succeeded Taylor

TERM OF OFFICE
July 10, 1850–March 3, 1853

AGE AT INAUGURATION
50 years old

NUMBER OF TERMS
one (partial)

VICE PRESIDENT
none

FIRST LADIES
Abigail Powers Fillmore (1798–1853), wife (married Feb. 5, 1826); Mary Abigail Fillmore (1832–1854), daughter

SECOND WIFE
Caroline Carmichael McIntosh Fillmore (1813–1881), married Feb. 10, 1858

CHILDREN
Born to Abigail Fillmore (first wife): Millard, Mary

GEOGRAPHIC SCENE
30 states

NEW STATES ADDED
California (1850)

DIED
March 8, 1874, in Buffalo, NY

AGE AT DEATH
74 years old

SELECTED LANDMARKS
Fillmore Glen State Park, Moravia, NY (reconstructed birthplace); The Millard Fillmore House, East Aurora, NY; Forest Lawn Cemetery, Buffalo, NY

Millard Fillmore was tall, handsome, and well mannered, in striking contrast with the rough-and-ready image of his predecessor. He and his wife Abigail established the first permanent library at the White House. Abigail traveled in an elegant carriage (right). Sadly she caught cold and died after attending the inauguration of Franklin Pierce, her husband's successor.

THE TIMETABLE FOR ELECTIONS
CAMPAIGN STRATEGIES AND PARTY POLITICS

The presidential campaigns of modern times are vastly different from those waged by earlier candidates for President. In fact, the concept of campaigning for the presidency did not even gain favor until well into the 19th century. Prior to that time, supporters spoke on behalf of candidates. Sitting Presidents, in particular, preferred not to mix the politics of campaigning with their work as Chief Executive.

Today's candidates begin their official presidential campaigns more than a year before Election Day and raise hundreds of millions of dollars in order to support their bids for votes. During the opening months of an election year, members of the various political parties compete against one another in a series of statewide contests called primaries and caucuses. Votes earned at the state level determine how many delegates will support each candidate during the parties' summer nominating conventions.

The party conventions bring thousands of delegates and leaders together to make official their nomination for President based on the statewide spring elections. Each presidential candidate has the responsibility of selecting a vice presidential running mate, and that person's nomination is made official at the conventions, too. Other convention business includes determining the party's platform, a statement that summarizes what the party and candidates will stand for if elected.

The fall campaign season pits candidates from the major parties against one another in a series of debates and political activities. Political campaigns compete for support for their candidates through advertising blitzes and weeks of cross-country appearances where the candidates deliver stump speeches, similar material repeated over and over for new audiences. Campaigns employ each innovation in communications technology—from radio to television to the Internet to cell phones and Twitter—in an effort to influence voters.

Election Day occurs in November on the first Tuesday after the first Monday in the month. U.S. citizens age 18 or older, regardless of race, gender, or beliefs, may register to vote. Voter turnout, the number of people who actually

When rail travel served as the best link between cities, politicians often embarked on so-called whistle-stop campaigns (above, Warren G. Harding in 1920).

The first televised presidential debate took place in 1960 when Richard Nixon faced off against John F. Kennedy. Kennedy's youthful, tanned physique led viewers to judge him more favorably, while radio listeners thought Nixon had performed the best.

In 2008 a record-breaking crowd of more than 80,000 people gathered in Denver at its Mile High Stadium to celebrate the nomination of Barack Obama as the Democratic Party's nominee for President. The occasion featured political speeches, performances by pop stars, and celebration.

vote on Election Day, can be a critical factor in a candidate's success or defeat. Although a surprising number of people choose not to vote even when they are eligible to do so, many others value this action as one of their most cherished responsibilities as citizens. The final outcome of the election is determined by tallies within each state that identify the Electoral College support of each candidate.

Usually the results of elections are known within hours after the closing of all polls. Winning candidates celebrate with victory speeches, while the losers concede, or admit defeat, in concession speeches. Occasionally election results are unclear or become controversial, and some time may be required in order to determine who will emerge victorious.

A President's level of support during an election is seen as a measure of national confidence in that person. Someone who wins by a wide margin is said to hold a mandate, or the sign of widespread national support. Presidents elected with a mandate bring considerable political influence to their new position.

Opportunities to vote increased during the 1960s when reforms ended an era that sought to exclude African Americans from participating in Southern elections (above, marking ballots in Alabama, 1966).

Controversies can occur when ballots are counted (left, in Florida during the 2000 election).

FRANKLIN PIERCE
14TH PRESIDENT OF THE UNITED STATES 1853–1857

When Franklin Pierce became President, the national debate about slavery had quieted. Pierce, a man with an undistinguished record in public office, renewed the controversy by supporting the option of slavery in Kansas Territory. This stand reopened the slavery issue and helped push the country closer to civil war.

In large part, Pierce was nominated for President because he had not made many political enemies or taken a firm stand on slavery. His party decided it would be easier to elect "Handsome Frank" than other, more controversial Democrats. Pierce had been born in a log cabin in New Hampshire. A graduate of Maine's Bowdoin College, he took up law and served in the New Hampshire Legislature. Later he spent 10 years in Washington, D.C., as a representative and a senator. While there Pierce earned more notice for his heavy drinking than for his lawmaking. Democrats campaigned for his presidency with the slogan: "We Polked you in 1844; we shall Pierce you in 1852."

Benjamin Pierce (above, with his mother) died in a train crash shortly before his father's Inauguration.

As President, Pierce infuriated Northerners by supporting the Kansas-Nebraska Act of 1854. This measure ended the Missouri Compromise of 1820 by permitting slavery to spread north of Missouri's southern border. Using a policy called popular sovereignty, the act suggested that residents of new states should determine for themselves whether to permit slavery within their borders. Casualties climbed to about 200 in "Bleeding Kansas" after both proslavery and antislavery settlers rushed to the territory and began fighting.

The Democratic Party was so embarrassed by the scene that it did not renominate Pierce for a second term. Pierce retired to New Hampshire in disgrace. His death in 1869 went largely unrecognized.

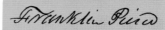

NICKNAME
Handsome Frank

BORN
Nov. 23, 1804, in Hillsborough (now Hillsboro), NH

POLITICAL PARTY
Democrat

CHIEF OPPONENT
Winfield Scott, Whig (1786–1866)

TERM OF OFFICE
March 4, 1853–March 3, 1857

AGE AT INAUGURATION
48 years old

NUMBER OF TERMS
one

VICE PRESIDENT
William Rufus De Vane King (1786–1853)

FIRST LADY
Jane Means Appleton Pierce (1806–1863), wife (married Nov. 10, 1834)

CHILDREN
Frank, Benjamin, plus a son who died young

GEOGRAPHIC SCENE
31 states

NEW STATES ADDED
none

DIED
Oct. 8, 1869, in Concord, NH

AGE AT DEATH
64 years old

SELECTED LANDMARKS
Hillsboro, NH (boyhood home); Concord, NH (adult home); Old North Cemetery, Concord, NH

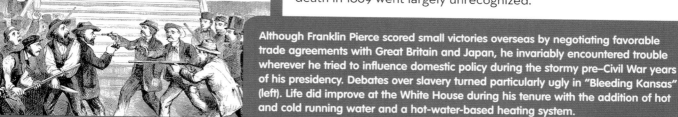

Although Franklin Pierce scored small victories overseas by negotiating favorable trade agreements with Great Britain and Japan, he invariably encountered trouble wherever he tried to influence domestic policy during the stormy pre–Civil War years of his presidency. Debates over slavery turned particularly ugly in "Bleeding Kansas" (left). Life did improve at the White House during his tenure with the addition of hot and cold running water and a hot-water-based heating system.

JAMES BUCHANAN
15TH PRESIDENT OF THE UNITED STATES 1857–1861

James Buchanan, in an effort to hold the Union together, offered concession after concession to the South, regardless of the anger his actions provoked in the North. When Southern states began to secede anyway, he protested but claimed to have no constitutional authority to force them to come back.

Buchanan's dissatisfying single term in the White House followed a distinguished, 40-year career of public service in the United States and abroad. Buchanan was born in a log cabin in Pennsylvania. Buchanan had one good eye for each type of vision—close up and distant. In order to see well, he cocked his head to one side or the other, depending on which eye he needed to use. The son of an Irish immigrant, he graduated from Dickinson College, studied law, and ran for public office. He served briefly in the state legislature and then spent a decade each in the U.S. House and Senate. In addition, he was minister to Russia under Andrew Jackson, James K. Polk's secretary of state, and minister to Great Britain for Franklin Pierce. This final post helped earn him the presidential nomination. By being abroad he had avoided the latest slavery debates.

The slave Dred Scott lost his bid for freedom in 1857.

Shortly after Buchanan's Inauguration, the Supreme Court issued its *Dred Scott* ruling. The slave Dred Scott had argued he should be free if his master moved with him to a free state. The Court disagreed, saying slaves were property, not citizens, and remained slaves anywhere. Although Buchanan disliked slavery (he even bought slaves in order to free them), he hated breaking laws even more. (His nickname recalled his insistence on precise bookkeeping, for example.) Buchanan stood by the ruling, infuriating Northerners. He could not resolve the financial Panic of 1857 or the secession of Southern states from the Union. Having stated he would serve only one term, Buchanan was delighted to leave office. The only President who never married, he retired to Pennsylvania to write his memoirs. He died in 1868.

NICKNAME
Ten-Cent Jimmy

BORN
April 23, 1791, in Cove Gap, PA

POLITICAL PARTY
Democrat

CHIEF OPPONENT
John C. Frémont, Republican (1813–1890)

TERM OF OFFICE
March 4, 1857–March 3, 1861

AGE AT INAUGURATION
65 years old

NUMBER OF TERMS
one

VICE PRESIDENT
John Cabell Breckinridge (1821–1875)

FIRST LADY
Harriet Lane (1830–1903), niece

WIFE
never married

CHILDREN
none

GEOGRAPHIC SCENE
31 states

NEW STATES ADDED
Minnesota (1858), Oregon (1859), Kansas (1861)

DIED
June 1, 1868, in Lancaster, PA

AGE AT DEATH
77 years old

SELECTED LANDMARKS
Mercersburg Academy, Mercersburg, PA (relocated boyhood home); Wheatland, Lancaster, PA (homestead); Woodward Hill Cemetery, Lancaster, PA

"Don't fire 'til I get out of office," exclaims James Buchanan (at right in this political cartoon). The departing President told his successor, Abraham Lincoln: "If you are as happy, my dear sir, on entering this house as I am on leaving it and returning home, you are the happiest man on earth."

A NEW BIRTH OF FREEDOM

1861–1897

Years of disagreement between Northerners and Southerners over slavery and related issues finally led to civil war between the two regions. After the four-year war ended in 1865, a series of Presidents struggled with Reconstruction, the process of reuniting and rebuilding the splintered nation. Post–Civil War Presidents more often found themselves watching history unfold than shaping it. The growth of industry in the East and the expansion of western settlement drove the United States toward its modern form.

1863
Union forces defeated Confederate troops at the Battle of Gettysburg after the Southern army crossed over onto Northern soil. The four-year-long Civil War ended in 1865.

1869
A continuous railway line spanned the country coast to coast for the first time on May 10 when a ceremonial gold spike was pounded into place at Promontory, Utah.

1871
Fires burned across Chicago for more than 24 hours beginning on October 8. The city rebuilt itself into a vibrant midwestern business center, complete with early skyscrapers.

1879
Thomas Edison invented the electric lightbulb. Other inventions by Edison included the phonograph, microphone, and motion pictures. He developed the scientific research laboratory, too.

Union admiral David G. Farragut's three-masted ship fights its way up river to New Orleans in April, 1862. The city fell from Confederate control soon after.

1886
The Statue of Liberty became a beacon of welcome to immigrants after its dedication. Within a decade, more than 350,000 newcomers were arriving annually. That figure had more than doubled by 1906.

1889
When the federal government opened up central Oklahoma for settlement in April, some 50,000 "sodbusters" rushed to stake their claims in the new territory on a single day.

1890
Susan B. Anthony worked most of her life on the fight to earn women the right to vote. In 1890 she became president of the National American Woman Suffrage Association. The cause succeeded 30 years later.

1893
The Duryea brothers built the first successful gasoline-powered car in the United States. Within a dozen years, more than 1.5 million cars were being produced in the country.

ABRAHAM LINCOLN
16TH PRESIDENT OF THE UNITED STATES 1861–1865

When Abraham Lincoln was inaugurated in 1861, he became President of states that were not united. In fact, after arguing for years about slavery and states' rights, Northerners and Southerners were on the brink of civil, or internal, war. Lincoln, expressing his commitment to the highest ideals of democracy, succeeded in reuniting the country and ending slavery. He was assassinated just after the end of the Civil War in 1865.

Lincoln's humble beginnings are a schoolbook legend. He was born in a log cabin in Kentucky to parents who could neither read nor write. The sum of his schoolhouse education was about one year's time, but he educated himself by reading books he borrowed from others. When Lincoln was nine years old, his mother died. His father, a carpenter and farmer, remarried and moved his family farther west, eventually settling in Illinois. Lincoln was taller (at six feet four inches) than any other President. His high-pitched voice and thick frontier accent (saying "git" for "get" or "thar" for "there") made an odd contrast with his thin but strong and dignified figure.

First Lady Mary Todd Lincoln

Lincoln worked as a flatboat navigator, storekeeper, soldier, surveyor, and postmaster before being elected at age 25 to the Illinois Legislature in Springfield. Once there, he taught himself law, opened a law practice, and earned the nickname "Honest Abe." He served one term in the U.S. House of Representatives during 1847–1849 but lost two U.S. Senate races in the 1850s. However, the debates he had about slavery with his 1858 opponent, Stephen Douglas, helped him earn the presidential nomination two years later. In the four-way presidential race of 1860, Lincoln was the top vote getter. Lincoln gained the presidency on a platform that considered it treason for Southern states to secede, or withdraw, from the nation. It

Abraham Lincoln's lifelong love of reading whenever and wherever he could began in his youth, when books often took the place of school. Favorite reading included U.S. history, *Aesop's Fables*, *Robinson Crusoe*, the Bible, and works by Shakespeare.

Abraham Lincoln

NICKNAME
Honest Abe

BORN
Feb. 12, 1809, near Hodgenville, KY

POLITICAL PARTY
Republican (formerly Whig)

CHIEF OPPONENT
1st term: Stephen Arnold Douglas, Northern Democrat (1813–1861); John Cabell Breckinridge, Southern Democrat (1821–1875); John Bell, Constitutional Unionist (1797–1869); 2nd term: George Brinton McClellan, Democrat (1826–1885)

TERM OF OFFICE
March 4, 1861–April 15, 1865

AGE AT INAUGURATION
52 years old

NUMBER OF TERMS
two (cut short by assassination)

VICE PRESIDENT
1st term: Hannibal Hamlin (1809–1891); 2nd term: Andrew Johnson (1808–1875)

FIRST LADY
Mary Todd Lincoln (1818–1882), wife (married Nov. 4, 1842)

CHILDREN
Robert, Edward (died young), William, Thomas (Tad)

GEOGRAPHIC SCENE
23 United States; 11 Confederate States

NEW STATES ADDED
West Virginia (1863), Nevada (1864)

DIED
April 15, 1865, in Washington, DC

AGE AT DEATH
56 years old

SELECTED LANDMARKS
Hodgenville, KY (birthplace); Springfield, IL (home, grave, and library); Lincoln Memorial, President's Cottage, Washington, DC; Mount Rushmore National Memorial, Keystone, SD

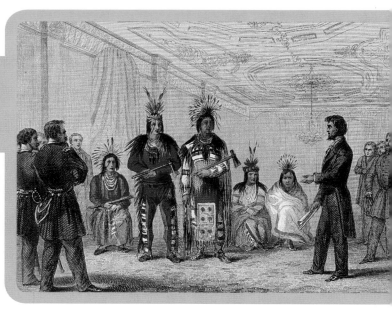

Lincoln grew strong by splitting logs into thousands of rails for fences. At age 21 he "paid" 400 rails per yard for pants fabric.

agreed to continue slavery in the South but outlawed its spread elsewhere. Southern leaders threatened to secede rather than accept this Republican plan. After Lincoln's victory, but before his Inauguration, these states began to act on their threat to leave the Union. The Civil War officially began on April 12, 1861, at Fort Sumter, South Carolina, when forces from the new Confederate States of America attacked this U.S. fort.

Lincoln had promised in his Inaugural oath to "preserve, protect, and defend" the Union. Now he began to act, competing with Confederate leaders for the allegiance of states not yet committed to either side. With Congress out of session until July, Lincoln broke laws when they stood in his way of protecting the Constitution. "Often a limb must be amputated to save a life," he reasoned. Lincoln expanded the size of the Army and Navy, jailed people who might encourage secession of Border States, stopped trade with the Confederacy, and spent government funds without the approval of lawmakers. His efforts strengthened the Northern cause; later they were approved by Congress and the courts. In the end, 11 states joined the Confederacy and 23 remained in the Union, including the Border States of Missouri, Kentucky, Maryland, West Virginia, and Delaware.

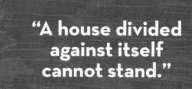

"A house divided against itself cannot stand."

Abraham Lincoln, June 1858

The outcome of the Civil War remained unclear during the early years of fighting. While the North held the upper hand on the seas, the South generally beat Union forces on land. It was not until the Battle of Gettysburg, in July 1863, that Southern dominance of the battlefield ended. Through speeches such as his Gettysburg Address, Lincoln encouraged Northerners to keep fighting, whatever the costs. In this famous dedication of the battlefield cemetery, he urged citizens to ensure "that these dead shall not have died in vain—that this nation, under God, shall have a new birth of freedom—and that government of the people, by the people, for the people, shall not perish from the earth." Earlier that same year Lincoln called for the end of slavery in his Emancipation Proclamation.

Consistent military victories, including the capture of Atlanta, Georgia, in September 1864, helped Lincoln win reelection. He selected as his running mate Andrew Johnson, who was Southern-born but Union-loyal, in an effort to represent the complexity of the divided nation. Only Union states participated in the election. By the following March, Northern victory in the war was certain; the only question was when. Lincoln's second Inaugural Address made it clear that the Union states would keep fighting "until every drop of blood drawn with the lash, shall be paid by another drawn with the sword." Yet Lincoln urged citizens to end the war free from bitterness, "with malice toward none; with charity for all." Victory came on April 9, 1865, at Appomattox Court House, Virginia, when Confederate general Robert E. Lee surrendered to Union general Ulysses S. Grant. Some 750,000 soldiers had died during the four-year conflict.

Seeing the Union successfully through the Civil War was Lincoln's greatest presidential responsibility, but it was not his only accomplishment. Together with Congress, he inaugurated a national banking system; established the Department of Agriculture; standardized paper currency; supported the development of a transcontinental railroad; enacted the Homestead Act, which opened up vast holdings of federal land to settlers; and crafted the 13th Amendment, which ended slavery.

Lincoln's personal life in the White House revolved around his wife, Mary, and two young sons, William and Thomas, better known as Willie and Tad. (Their oldest son, Robert, was studying at Harvard.) Lincoln often romped with his sons and their friends. A teenage guest recalled how she once entered a room to find the President flattened on the floor with four boys holding down his limbs. "Come quick and sit on his stomach," invited Tad. Lincoln forgave the boys their wildness. "It's a diversion," he told a visitor, "and we need diversion at the White House." Lincoln told jokes, tall tales, anecdotes, and stories to relieve wartime tensions.

FREE SPEECH
FREE HOMES
FREE TERRITORY

PROTECTION TO AMERICAN INDUSTRY

FOR PRESIDENT
ABRAHAM LINCOLN

FOR VICE PRESIDENT
HANNIBAL HAMLIN
OF MAINE

Northerners and Southerners differed for years over whether the federal government had the right to control the practice of slavery. Disagreement about matters such as returning runaway slaves to their owners caused Southern states to secede from the Union and led to the Civil War.

Lincoln and his running mate, Hannibal Hamlin, won the 1860 election even though their names were omitted from the ballots of 10 slave-owning states.

Photographic portraits of Abraham Lincoln document the toll the four-year-long Civil War took on the President (photo taken November 15, 1863).

In 1862 humor lost its place for a while when Willie became the only child to die in the White House. He was a victim of typhoid fever. Mary, already saddened by criticism of her performance as First Lady, grieved deeply and long. First falsely accused of being sympathetic to the Confederacy (because some Southern relatives fought for the Confederacy), then scolded for her lavish spending, she was now chided by the public for neglecting her official duties. The subsequent deaths of her husband and Tad left her so grief-stricken that some people considered her insane.

Left to right: Mary, Willie, Robert, Tad, and Abraham Lincoln. By 1871 only Mary and Robert remained alive.

Lincoln spent much of the final weeks of his life away from the White House. He met with military commanders, such as Ulysses S. Grant (who would become the 18th President), and discussed surrender terms. Lincoln's plans for Reconstruction, or the reorganizing of the United States, were flexible and generous. However, he would barely live to enjoy the end of the war, much less shape its peace. He became the first President to be assassinated when he was shot on April 14, 1865.

Lincoln had received thousands of death threats since 1860. The day he was shot, he confided to his daytime bodyguard that he had recently dreamed of being assassinated. His nightmare became a reality that evening when he went out to see a play. Lincoln and his wife watched the performance from box seats that could be accessed by a private door. This entrance was poorly guarded, allowing the actor John Wilkes Booth to enter the seating area uninvited. Booth hoped to revive the Confederate cause by killing the President. He shot

From the Lincoln-Douglas Debates of 1858 to the Emancipation Proclamation (above, left) and Gettysburg Address of 1863 (above, right), Lincoln promoted freedom and unity.

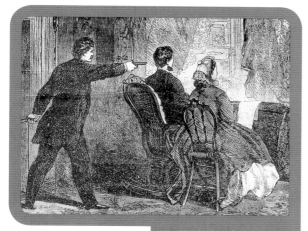

In 1865 Lincoln became the first President to be assassinated.

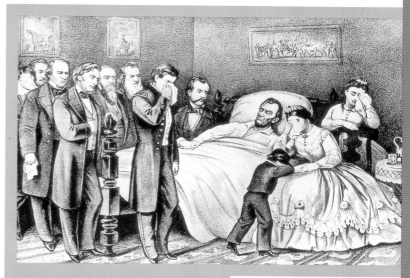

The President's death at the end of the Civil War unsettled the fragile nation.

Lincoln in the back of the head, then jumped to the stage floor, breaking his leg in the process. He escaped the theater nonetheless and remained on the loose for nearly two weeks. He was shot during his eventual capture and died from his wounds.

The wounded and unconscious President was carried to a boardinghouse across the street. His long body had to be placed diagonally across the standard-size bed in order to recline properly. He died the following morning, said to be wearing an expression of happiness and repose on his face. His body lay in state at the U.S. Capitol and at other sites in the North before traveling home for burial in Illinois.

"All persons held as slaves within any State ... in rebellion against the United States, shall be then, thenceforward, and forever free."

Abraham Lincoln,
Emancipation Proclamation,
January 1, 1863

ANDREW JOHNSON
17TH PRESIDENT OF THE UNITED STATES 1865–1869

The crisis of war between the states was followed by a crisis within the U.S. presidency. It began with the assassination of Abraham Lincoln and continued through the presidency of his successor, Andrew Johnson. The climax came with Johnson's impeachment and near removal from office by Congress.

Johnson grew up with more poverty and hardship than any other President. His parents were illiterate laborers; his father died when Andrew was three. He never attended a day of school. Nonetheless, by age 20 Johnson had been elected to be an alderman, or city legislator. Later he became a mayor, then a Tennessee state senator, U.S. representative, Tennessee governor, and U.S. senator. Johnson was the only Southern legislator who stayed on to work in the U.S. Senate during the Civil War. Southerners branded him a traitor, but Lincoln rewarded him by making him the military governor of Tennessee and, later on, his vice presidential running mate in the election of 1864.

Although Johnson was a Democrat, Republicans put him on Lincoln's 1864 presidential ticket as a representative from the South. Thus, the party of the presidency changed from Republican to Democrat with Lincoln's death. Johnson was the last slave owner to become President. He argued with politicians about how to "reconstruct" the United States after the Civil War. He routinely vetoed, or rejected, Congress's ideas and became known as the "Veto President."

His leadership style angered

Andrew Johnson opened a tailor's shop when he was 17. He continued to make his own clothes even after becoming a legislator.

legislators so much that, in 1868, the House of Representatives impeached him, or charged that he should be removed from office. House members identified 11 articles, or reasons, for removal. Nine of them dealt with the President's controversial firing of his secretary of war, an ally of the Republican-led Congress. The Senate considered the House charges but fell one vote short of convicting Johnson, so he completed his term of office.

During his presidency the U.S. purchased the territory Alaska from Russia. In 1875 the retired President returned to the U.S. Senate. No other President has gone on to become a senator. At his request he was buried wrapped in a U.S. flag with his head resting on his copy of the Constitution.

NICKNAME
Veto President

BORN
Dec. 29, 1808, in Raleigh, NC

POLITICAL PARTY
Democrat

CHIEF OPPONENT
none; succeeded Lincoln

TERM OF OFFICE
April 15, 1865–March 3, 1869

AGE AT INAUGURATION
56 years old

NUMBER OF TERMS
one (partial)

VICE PRESIDENT
none

FIRST LADIES
Eliza McCardle Johnson (1810–1876), wife (married May 17, 1827); Martha Johnson Patterson (1828–1891), daughter

CHILDREN
Martha, Charles, Mary, Robert, Andrew, Jr.

GEOGRAPHIC SCENE
36 states

NEW STATES ADDED
Nebraska (1867)

DIED
July 31, 1875, in Carter's Station, TN

AGE AT DEATH
66 years old

SELECTED LANDMARKS
Mordecai Historic Park, Raleigh, NC (relocated birthplace); Andrew Johnson National Historic Site, Greenville, TN (includes two residences and grave)

Andrew Johnson—the first President ever impeached—receives a summons for his Senate trial.

U.S. POLITICAL PARTIES
THE TWO-PARTY SYSTEM

The Founding Fathers hoped that representatives of the new United States government would work together in harmony without dividing into opposing groups called parties. Yet, soon after George Washington became President, political parties began to form. Leaders partnered with others who shared their geographic background, foreign policy beliefs, or other ideas for governing the country.

Today, as then, the party with the largest number of elected members in the U.S. House of Representatives and the U.S. Senate holds a majority of influence over those chambers. Its members outnumber those of the minority, or opposing, parties. Occasionally the same party will control both chambers of Congress and the presidency. With that much political power, it can significantly influence the nature of government. Usually each party will control only one or two of these three areas. In that case, political parties will have to compromise and cooperate with one another in order to enact new laws and policies.

During George Washington's presidency, lawmakers divided into two groups, depending on whether or not they believed that a strong federal government should oversee weaker state governments. Ever since, although names and opinions may change, two political parties have dominated the U.S. government. Today's leaders are primarily members of the Democratic and Republican Parties. Each group can trace its origins well back into the 19th century.

A 19th-century political cartoonist popularized the use of animals to symbolize the Republican and Democratic Parties. He drew an elephant to represent the colossal size of Republican Party support in 1874. He chose a donkey for the Democrats, knowing that Andrew Jackson had adopted that symbol after being called a jackass during the feisty campaign of 1828.

The Democratic Party evolved from the early groups who opposed a strong federal government. Leaders such as Thomas Jefferson shaped these lawmakers into a collection of politicians who referred to themselves by such terms as Anti-Federalists and Democratic-Republicans. By 1828 they were known simply as Democrats.

The modern Republican Party was formed during the 1850s to combat the spread of slavery. Its first successful presidential candidate was Abraham Lincoln. Sometimes it is referred to as the Grand Old Party (GOP).

The Democratic and Republican Parties have shared fairly equally in the control of the White House. There have been several occasions, however, when one party has had a long period of domination. From Lincoln's election in 1860 through the election of 1908, for example, all but two Presidents were Republicans. The Democratic Party earned its longest streak of control—20 years—from 1933 to 1953. Its predecessor, the Democratic-Republican Party, had an even longer streak—28 years, from 1801 to 1829.

Two other political parties had members become Chief Executives, too. Washington and his successor, John Adams, were associated with the Federalist Party. The Whig Party evolved from these early Federalists. Four of its members became President. Two Whigs won outright election: William Henry Harrison and Zachary Taylor. Both of them died in office. Their Whig Vice Presidents, John Tyler and Millard Fillmore, replaced them.

A campaign banner promotes the 1920 ticket of the Democratic Party. (It lost.)

The Republican Party was founded in Ripon, Wisconsin, in 1854. It is still going strong more than 150 years later.

The Democratic Party became fully formed with the presidency of Andrew Jackson. Franklin D. Roosevelt led the Democrats for 12 years following the election of 1932 (above). There have been many attempts to start new parties over the years. These range from the Free Soil and Know-Nothing Parties of the 19th century to the Libertarian and Green Parties of modern times. These third parties may try to offer an alternative to the established parties on all fronts or may form around a single issue.

Often the presidential ballot will include candidates from third parties, those groups that exist beyond the two major parties. Occasionally a candidate will run for office as an "independent"—that is, without the support of a political party. No independent or third-party candidate has ever made it to the White House. Even so, these candidates may influence an election by dividing the support of voters or by directing attention to a particular issue or cause. In recent decades third-party and independent candidates have frequently siphoned support away from Republican and Democratic candidates in ways that helped secure a victory for the opposing major party. In 2000, for example, the Green Party attracted just enough support to play a role in placing the Republican Party's candidate in office.

Andrew Jackson (above, left) was the first President to campaign under the banner of the same Democratic Party that exists today.

Former Republican President Theodore Roosevelt tried to return to the White House as the nominee of the Progressive, or Bull Moose, Party. He finished second in the 1912 election, ahead of the sitting Republican President William Howard Taft. In no other presidential election has a third party surpassed one of the two major parties.

NATIONAL PROGRESSIVE PARTY
ROOSEVELT—JOHNSON

ULYSSES S. GRANT
18TH PRESIDENT OF THE UNITED STATES **1869–1877**

By the end of the Civil War, Ulysses Simpson Grant was the highest ranking U.S. general since George Washington. He was a national hero, too. Grant's popular appeal helped him become President in the first post–Civil War national election. Mastery of military tactics did not prepare him for the world of politics, however. His administration is remembered more for its scandals than for its accomplishments.

As a child Grant seemed an unlikely person to triumph on the battlefield. He disliked hunting, got sick in his father's leather tanning shop, and later resisted attending the U.S. Military Academy at West Point. Once there, however, Grant distinguished himself as a horseman and excelled at math. Within a few years Grant was on active duty in the Mexican War. His subsequent attempts at civilian life yielded little financial success, and

Birthplace of Ulysses S. Grant in Point Pleasant, Ohio. As a child Grant imagined becoming a farmer or a river trader.

he was happy to return to the military when the Civil War began.

Grant entered the fighting as a brigadier general of Illinois troops in Missouri. His aggressive assault on Fort Donelson, Tennessee, during February 1862, gave the Union its first notable victory in the Civil War. Citizens boasted that his initials stood for "Unconditional Surrender," the terms he had set for the Southern rebels at the fort. When Northerners learned he had smoked a cigar during the assault, they sent him as many as 10,000 boxes of them to help guarantee future victories. (Thus developed Grant's custom of smoking some 20 cigars a day, a habit that probably helped cause his death.) Some called him "Butcher Grant" for the casualties that came with his victories, but Abraham

NICKNAME
Unconditional Surrender Grant

BORN
April 27, 1822, in Point Pleasant, OH

POLITICAL PARTY
Republican

CHIEF OPPONENT
1st term: Horatio Seymour, Democrat (1810–1886); 2nd term: Horace Greeley, Democrat (1811–1872)

TERM OF OFFICE
March 4, 1869–March 3, 1877

AGE AT INAUGURATION
46 years old

NUMBER OF TERMS
two

VICE PRESIDENTS
1st term: Schuyler Colfax (1823–1885); 2nd term: Henry Wilson (1812–1875)

FIRST LADY
Julia Boggs Dent Grant (1826–1902), wife (married Aug. 22, 1848)

CHILDREN
Frederick, Ulysses, Ellen, Jesse

GEOGRAPHIC SCENE
37 states

NEW STATES ADDED
Colorado (1876)

DIED
July 23, 1885, in Mount McGregor, NY

AGE AT DEATH
63 years old

SELECTED LANDMARKS
Point Pleasant, OH (birthplace); Georgetown, OH (boyhood home); White Haven (home), St. Louis, MO; General Grant National Memorial, New York, NY (grave)

Grant (center, wearing hat) distinguished himself during the Civil War. By its end he was commander of all Union armies. The name of the nation's 18th President was accidentally changed from Hiram Ulysses Grant to Ulysses Simpson Grant when he was enrolled at the U.S. Military Academy. (His local congressman incorporated the maiden name of Grant's mother into his appointment recommendation by mistake.) Classmates nicknamed him "Uncle Sam," after the already popular patriotic character.

General Grant in 1863

> "No terms except an unconditional and immediate surrender can be accepted."
>
> Ulysses S. Grant, during the assault of Fort Donelson, Tennessee, February 16, 1862

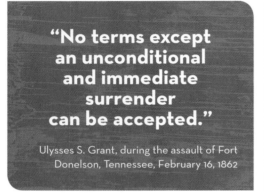

Passage of the 15th Amendment in 1870 permitted large numbers of African Americans to begin voting. In 1872 Victoria Claflin Woodhull became the first female presidential candidate. She suggested that Frederick Douglass, the former slave, run as her Vice President. He declined, and her third-party campaign fizzled.

Ulysses S. Grant was an expert handler of horses. While a student at West Point, he set a horse-jumping record that stood for 25 years. During his presidency, he was stopped for speeding in his horse-drawn carriage; Grant walked back to the White House after the officer confiscated his vehicle.

Lincoln was impressed. "I cannot spare this man—he fights," he said. Lincoln named him commander of all Federal troops in March 1864. Grant, who was superstitious about retracing his steps, did not like to retreat. He persisted on the battlefield, and, supported by Union commanders fighting aggressively elsewhere, he wore down the Confederate side until it was forced to surrender.

After the political infighting that filled Andrew Johnson's administration, voters were enthusiastic about electing Grant—the respected war hero—as their President. He was the only man to complete two presidential terms during the 76-year span between Andrew Jackson and Woodrow Wilson. Under Grant's leadership the government established the world's first national park (Yellowstone, founded in 1872), avoided war with Great Britain about Civil War damage claims, established the Department of Justice, and passed the 15th Amendment. This legislation granted voting rights regardless of "race, color, or previous condition of servitude" to all men. (Women did not gain voting rights until 1920.)

These accomplishments were overshadowed, however, by controversies. The federal government was unable to prevent white Southerners from using violence and political tricks to limit the rights of former slaves. The financial Panic of 1873 put millions of laborers out of work. Worst of all were

A scene from the second Inauguration of Ulysses S. Grant

Ulysses S. Grant retired after an administration tainted by scandal.

Grant found he had much in common with the Viceroy of China when they met during a world tour after his presidency (left). Both men liked to eat—the Viceroy hosted an eight-hour, 70-course dinner for his guest. Both leaders had defended their countries as generals during civil wars, too.

Missouri-born Julia Dent, the daughter of slave owners, married a Northern-born soldier even though none of their parents approved. Julia Grant was the first First Lady to write a memoir about her life.

the scandals of Grant's administration—from corrupt banking and currency deals to the stealing of federal liquor taxes by manufacturers and public officials. Although none of these crimes involved Grant directly, his reputation as a leader suffered.

Grant failed to win nomination for a third presidential term. (A constitutional amendment in 1951 limited a President to two elected terms of office, but no such barrier existed before then.) After leaving the White House, Grant, his wife, and their teenage son embarked on a 30-month tour of the world. Along the way he met Queen Victoria in England and became the first person ever allowed to shake hands with a Japanese emperor. In 1880 he failed yet again to win the Republican nomination for President. Grant invested in a family business venture during his retirement in New York City, but a dishonest business partner brought financial ruin to the project. Congress provided Grant with much needed income by putting him back on the Army payroll as a general, although he was not on active duty.

At the suggestion of author and publisher Mark Twain, Grant tried to make even more money by writing his autobiography. Grant raced to complete the book before his life could be claimed by throat cancer. He finished only days before his death. The book became a best seller and earned his family a small fortune. Grant and his wife, Julia, who died 17 years after him, are buried in the New York City landmark popularly known as Grant's Tomb.

RUTHERFORD B. HAYES
19TH PRESIDENT OF THE UNITED STATES 1877–1881

Rutherford Birchard Hayes started his administration amid controversy. Politicians argued about how to count the national election returns. In the end, Hayes won office by one electoral vote, the narrowest presidential victory in history. He went on to bring dignity, honesty, and reform to the government.

Hayes came to the White House with a solid background of service to his country. He was born in Delaware, Ohio, graduated from Kenyon College in Ohio, and earned a law degree from Harvard University. In 1861 Hayes interrupted law practice in his home state to join the Union Army. He rose to the rank of major general by the end of the Civil War and survived having four horses shot out from under him. Hayes declined to leave the battlefield after he was nominated for a seat in Congress. He wrote home that soldiers who campaigned for office "ought to be scalped" for deserting their posts. (These patriotic words ensured his election.) Later he served three terms as Ohio's governor.

Widespread ballot fraud, or illegal vote-casting, clouded the results of the popular and electoral voting in the 1876 presidential election. Victory belonged to the person with the greatest number of electoral votes, and Congress was left to determine the most accurate tally of them. The debate split along party lines and lasted for months. Finally, three days before the Inauguration, Congress confirmed Hayes as President. In exchange for these votes, Republicans

Lucy Hayes, with Fanny (above, right) and Scott and a friend, was the first First Lady to finish college. She was nicknamed "Lemonade Lucy" for supporting temperance by serving soft drinks instead of alcohol at the White House.

promised Democrats, who were concentrated in the South, that Reconstruction would end. The dealmaking earned Hayes the offensive nicknames of "His Fraudulency" and "Rutherfraud B. Hayes." As President, Hayes left scandal behind. He actually worked to increase the standards of behavior for civil servants, or government employees.

Alexander Graham Bell personally installed the first White House telephone while Hayes was President. Another inventor, Thomas Edison, visited the First Family to demonstrate his new phonograph. The Hayes family held the first public Easter Egg Roll on the White House lawn.

Having always planned to serve only one term, Hayes retired to Ohio where he took an active role in local and state causes. He died in 1893.

NICKNAME
His Fraudulency

BORN
Oct. 4, 1822, in Delaware, OH

POLITICAL PARTY
Republican

CHIEF OPPONENT
Samuel Jones Tilden, Democrat (1814–1886)

TERM OF OFFICE
March 4, 1877–March 3, 1881

AGE AT INAUGURATION
54 years old

NUMBER OF TERMS
one

VICE PRESIDENT
William Almon Wheeler (1819–1887)

FIRST LADY
Lucy Ware Webb Hayes (1831–1889), wife (married Dec. 30, 1852)

CHILDREN
Birchard Austin, Webb Cook, Rutherford Platt, Frances (Fanny), Scott, plus three sons who died young

GEOGRAPHIC SCENE
38 states

NEW STATES ADDED
none

DIED
Jan. 17, 1893, in Fremont, OH

AGE AT DEATH
70 years old

SELECTED LANDMARKS
Spiegel Grove National Historic Landmark, Fremont, OH (adult home, memorial library, museum, grave)

PRESIDENTIAL LANDMARKS
FROM LOG CABINS TO LIBRARIES

The presidency has led every Chief Executive to Washington, D.C. Even George Washington, who never lived there, visited the site of the nation's new capital as it was being planned and built. But all of the Presidents have left footprints in other parts of the country, too. Their birthplaces, homes, graves, museums, libraries, and memorials offer a trail of history for others to follow.

The oldest presidential landmarks lie along the eastern seaboard of the U.S. They remind us of the modest size of the new country and the role key states like Virginia and New York played in providing early national leaders. As citizens pushed the U.S. boundaries westward, new states, particularly in the Midwest, became an important home-base for Presidents. By the 20th century the West Coast had begun to foster future Presidents, too.

The lives of some Presidents are commemorated at multiple sites. Abraham Lincoln probably lays claim to having more memorials than any other President, in

GEORGIA 1776

WASHINGTON SLEPT HERE

"Monday, May 16th, 1791," wrote President George Washington in his diary as he recorded the date of his lodging in the Inn of Stephen Calfrey Pearce, 200 yards of this marker. Being forewarned, the Pearces had made lavish preparation for the entertainment of their distinguished guest and his party. Mrs. Pearce was famous for her cooking and Mr. Pearce for his story telling. The President enjoyed both immensely and praised gratefully the hospitality of the Inn Keepers who would accept no payment from the President of the United States.

The U.S. landscape is dotted with markers and landmarks connected to the personal histories of the U.S. Presidents.

part because he lived in and visited so many places during his lifetime. Other Presidents leave little more than a gravesite behind. Birthplaces, boyhood homes, even adult residences can fall into disrepair or give way to new construction before their value is ever recognized.

Some presidential landmarks are actually reproductions of original structures. They may even be located on different ground than the original buildings. Most log cabin homes are copies, for example. The furnishings in landmark buildings may not be original either, although they may mimic known pieces of furniture, wallpaper designs, and so on. Even with these modifications, the sites help visitors imagine what life might have been like for the Presidents.

In 1940, while still President, Franklin D. Roosevelt began the tradition of creating presidential libraries. These libraries, as well as one for FDR's predecessor, Herbert Hoover, are maintained in collaboration with the National Archives. Libraries for earlier Presidents have been developed, too, through the work of state and private sponsors.

Presidential libraries may be located near important home sites, at academic institutions, or in major cities of importance to the President. These sites hold the

THEY WHO SEEK TO ESTABLISH SYSTEMS OF GOVERNMENT BASED ON THE REGIMENTATION OF ALL HUMAN BEINGS BY A HANDFUL OF INDIVIDUAL RULERS... CALL THIS A NEW ORDER. IT IS NOT NEW AND IT IS NOT ORDER.

Even Fala, the President's dog, is commemorated at the Franklin Delano Roosevelt Memorial in Washington, D.C.

PRESIDENTIAL LANDMARKS

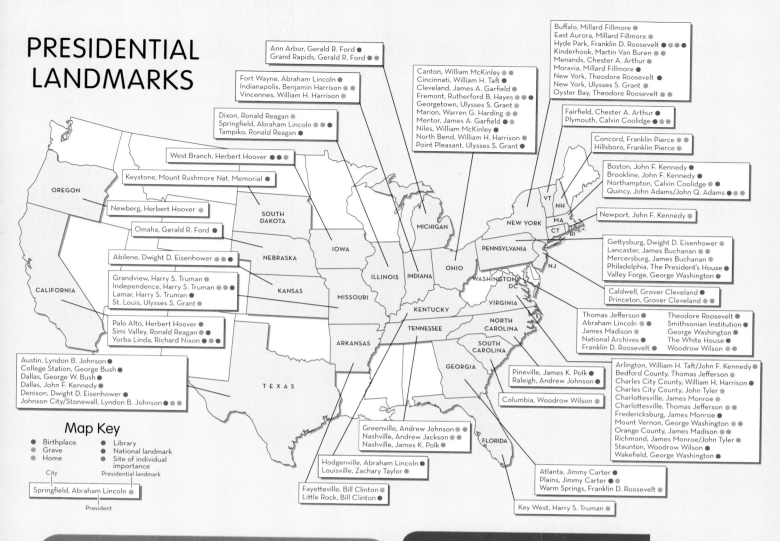

Ann Arbor, Gerald R. Ford ●
Grand Rapids, Gerald R. Ford ● ●

Fort Wayne, Abraham Lincoln ●
Indianapolis, Benjamin Harrison ● ●
Vincennes, William H. Harrison ●

Dixon, Ronald Reagan ●
Springfield, Abraham Lincoln ● ●
Tampiko, Ronald Reagan ●

West Branch, Herbert Hoover ● ● ●

Keystone, Mount Rushmore Nat. Memorial ●

Newberg, Herbert Hoover ●

Omaha, Gerald R. Ford ●

Abilene, Dwight D. Eisenhower ● ● ●

Grandview, Harry S. Truman ●
Independence, Harry S. Truman ● ●
Lamar, Harry S. Truman ●
St. Louis, Ulysses S. Grant ●

Palo Alto, Herbert Hoover ●
Simi Valley, Ronald Reagan ● ●
Yorba Linda, Richard Nixon ● ● ●

Austin, Lyndon B. Johnson ●
College Station, George Bush ●
Dallas, George W. Bush ●
Dallas, John F. Kennedy ●
Denison, Dwight D. Eisenhower ●
Johnson City/Stonewall, Lyndon B. Johnson ● ● ●

Canton, William McKinley ● ●
Cincinnati, William H. Taft ●
Cleveland, James A. Garfield ●
Fremont, Rutherford B. Hayes ● ● ●
Georgetown, Ulysses S. Grant ●
Marion, Warren G. Harding ●
Mentor, James A. Garfield ●
Niles, William McKinley ●
North Bend, William H. Harrison ●
Point Pleasant, Ulysses S. Grant ●

Buffalo, Millard Fillmore ●
East Aurora, Millard Fillmore ●
Hyde Park, Franklin D. Roosevelt ● ● ●
Kinderhook, Martin Van Buren ●
Menands, Chester A. Arthur ●
Moravia, Millard Fillmore ●
New York, Theodore Roosevelt ●
New York, Ulysses S. Grant ●
Oyster Bay, Theodore Roosevelt ● ●

Fairfield, Chester A. Arthur ●
Plymouth, Calvin Coolidge ● ● ●

Concord, Franklin Pierce ●
Hillsboro, Franklin Pierce ●

Boston, John F. Kennedy ●
Brookline, John F. Kennedy ●
Northampton, Calvin Coolidge ● ●
Quincy, John Adams/John Q. Adams ● ● ●

Newport, John F. Kennedy ●

Gettysburg, Dwight D. Eisenhower ●
Lancaster, James Buchanan ● ●
Mercersburg, James Buchanan ●
Philadelphia, The President's House ●
Valley Forge, George Washington ●

Caldwell, Grover Cleveland ●
Princeton, Grover Cleveland ●

Thomas Jefferson ● ●   Theodore Roosevelt ●
Abraham Lincoln ● ●   Smithsonian Institution ●
James Madison ●   George Washington ●
National Archives ●   The White House ●
Franklin D. Roosevelt ●   Woodrow Wilson ● ●

Pineville, James K. Polk ●
Raleigh, Andrew Johnson ●

Columbia, Woodrow Wilson ●

Arlington, William H. Taft/John F. Kennedy ● ●
Bedford County, Thomas Jefferson ●
Charles City County, William H. Harrison ●
Charles City County, John Tyler ●
Charlottesville, James Monroe ●
Charlottesville, Thomas Jefferson ● ●
Fredericksburg, James Monroe ●
Mount Vernon, George Washington ● ●
Orange County, James Madison ●
Richmond, James Monroe/John Tyler ●
Staunton, Woodrow Wilson ●
Wakefield, George Washington ●

Greenville, Andrew Johnson ●
Nashville, Andrew Jackson ● ●
Nashville, James K. Polk ●

Hodgenville, Abraham Lincoln ●
Louisville, Zachary Taylor ●

Fayetteville, Bill Clinton ●
Little Rock, Bill Clinton ●

Atlanta, Jimmy Carter ●
Plains, Jimmy Carter ● ●
Warm Springs, Franklin D. Roosevelt ●

Key West, Harry S. Truman ●

OREGON
SOUTH DAKOTA
MICHIGAN
NEBRASKA
IOWA
CALIFORNIA
ILLINOIS INDIANA OHIO
KANSAS
MISSOURI
KENTUCKY
TENNESSEE
ARKANSAS
TEXAS
PENNSYLVANIA
VT NH MA CT RI
NEW YORK
NJ
WASHINGTON DC
VIRGINIA
NORTH CAROLINA
SOUTH CAROLINA
GEORGIA
FLORIDA

Map Key

● Birthplace
● Grave
● Home
● Library
● National landmark
● Site of individual importance
Presidential landmark

City
Springfield, Abraham Lincoln ●
President

Presidential landmarks that may be visited by the public are shown on this map.

Landmarks may open long after a President's death (above, honoring Abraham Lincoln in Illinois, 2005).

James K. Polk and his wife, Sarah, are buried on the state capitol grounds in Nashville, Tennessee.

presidential papers, or the important documents of a leader's administration. Historians and other visitors study the thousands of pages of paper that make up each collection. The libraries acquire other material from the personal, professional, and family history of the Presidents, too. Collections include everything from Dwight D. Eisenhower's military souvenirs to Presidents' favorite artworks to official gifts received while in office to Herbert Hoover's fishing gear. Staff members use these extensive holdings to create exhibits for the general public about the Presidents' lives.

JAMES A. GARFIELD
20TH PRESIDENT OF THE UNITED STATES 1881

James Abram Garfield, like William Henry Harrison, barely had a chance to establish himself as President before death removed him from office. He was shot by an assassin early in his term and died 79 days later.

Garfield was the last President born in a log cabin. His election followed notable service as an educator, soldier, and statesman. A graduate of Williams College in Massachusetts, Garfield returned to his home state of Ohio to be a college professor. He had considered a career as a sailor until he fell overboard while working on a canal boat and caught a bad cold. A nonswimmer, he decided to teach instead. Later he became a lawyer, Ohio state senator, Civil War colonel, and U.S. congressman from his home state.

Garfield served 18 years in the House of Representatives before receiving his unexpected nomination for President in 1880. He became known as the "Preacher President" for his talents as a public speaker. Garfield was the nation's first left-handed President. He was actually ambidextrous, or able to write with either hand. Friends said he could write Latin with one hand and Greek with the other hand—at the same time!

As President, Garfield surprised legislators by how diligently he sought to end political corruption, or improper influence, especially among his own Republican Party. He refused to be bullied by powerful party leaders in the Senate when making political appointments; in the end, two senators resigned, and he got his way. Garfield fought similar battles on a smaller scale at the White House. The place swarmed with job hunters. People expected to be rewarded with posts in Garfield's administration because they had supported the Republican Party.

One disappointed and mentally ill job hunter shadowed Garfield and his staff for weeks. He shot the President at a Washington, D.C., train station on July 2, 1881. Although Garfield survived the initial wound, the bullet could not be found and removed. He died from complications two and a half months later. His assassin was tried and hanged. Reacting to Garfield's murder, lawmakers wrote new rules for how to fill many government posts. These jobs were to be given as a reward for talent and experience, not as political favors.

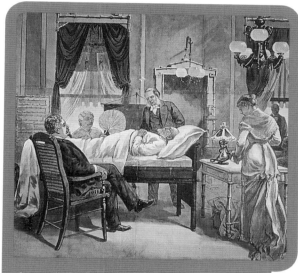

James A. Garfield became the second President to die by assassination, and the fourth to die in office. X-rays, surgery, and antibiotics might have saved him, had they been available.

NICKNAME
Preacher President

BORN
Nov. 19, 1831, near Orange, OH

POLITICAL PARTY
Republican

CHIEF OPPONENT
Winfield Scott Hancock, Democrat (1824–1886)

TERM OF OFFICE
March 4, 1881–Sept. 19, 1881

AGE AT INAUGURATION
49 years old

NUMBER OF TERMS
one (cut short by assassination)

VICE PRESIDENT
Chester A. Arthur (1829–1886)

FIRST LADY
Lucretia Rudolph Garfield (1832–1918), wife (married Nov. 11, 1858)

CHILDREN
Harry, James, Mary, Irvin, Abram, plus a son and a daughter who died young

GEOGRAPHIC SCENE
38 states

NEW STATES ADDED
none

DIED
Sept. 19, 1881, in Elberon, NJ

AGE AT DEATH
49 years old

SELECTED LANDMARKS
Lawnfield, Garfield National Historic Site, Mentor, OH (birthplace and replica homestead); Lake View Cemetery, Cleveland, OH

CHESTER A. ARTHUR
21ST PRESIDENT OF THE UNITED STATES **1881–1885**

Many citizens were as shocked at the thought of Chester Alan Arthur becoming President as they were by the shooting of his predecessor, James A. Garfield. Once again—as with John Tyler, Millard Fillmore, and Andrew Johnson—a Vice President chosen for political reasons instead of leadership skills became President.

Arthur had never been elected to public office until he became Garfield's Vice President. Born in Vermont, Arthur was a graduate of Union College in New York and an attorney. In 1871 he was made collector of the port of New York City and was responsible for collecting import fees for goods arriving at the nation's busiest harbor. Arthur built his personal and political fortune there by using the "spoils system" and "machine politics." He awarded jobs, raises, and favorable regulations (the spoils) to employees and businesses who supported his political candidates with their votes and donations (the vote-buying "machine" that influenced elections). This favoritism led the *New York Times* to call his pre–White House career a "mess of filth."

Arthur was deeply shocked that Garfield had been shot by someone caught up in the greed of machine politics. As President, he angered old friends and surprised the nation by supporting passage of the Pendleton Act. This legislation created a Civil Service Commission to oversee the government's

Chester A. Arthur (above, with daughter Nell) entered the White House a widower, his wife having died the previous year. His sister served as First Lady and helped him care for 13-year-old Nell. "Elegant Arthur" changed his clothes for each occasion of the day; he was said to own 80 pairs of pants.

civilian (nonmilitary) workers. It established procedures to ensure that a core of basic federal jobs were filled by competitive exam, not presidential appointment. It also protected these employees from being fired because of their political views.

After Arthur learned that he suffered from a fatal kidney disease, he did not care if he was renominated for a second term (he was not). Arthur retired to New York City. He died 20 months later.

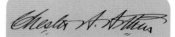

NICKNAME
Elegant Arthur

BORN
Oct. 5, 1829, in Fairfield, VT

POLITICAL PARTY
Republican

CHIEF OPPONENT
none; succeeded Garfield

TERM OF OFFICE
Sept. 20, 1881–March 3, 1885

AGE AT INAUGURATION
51 years old

NUMBER OF TERMS
one (partial)

VICE PRESIDENT
none

FIRST LADY
Mary Arthur McElroy (1842–1917), sister

WIFE
Ellen Lewis Herndon Arthur (1837–1880), married Oct. 25, 1859

CHILDREN
Chester, Ellen (Nell), plus a son who died young

GEOGRAPHIC SCENE
38 states

NEW STATES ADDED
none

DIED
Nov. 18, 1886, in New York, NY

AGE AT DEATH
57 years old

SELECTED LANDMARKS
Fairfield, VT (reconstructed birthplace); Albany Rural Cemetery, Menands, NY

Arthur visited Yellowstone National Park (seated, center) in 1883. Arthur modernized the U.S. Navy by ordering the construction of four steel warships.

GROVER CLEVELAND

22ND AND 24TH PRESIDENT OF THE UNITED STATES 1885–1889, 1893–1897

Grover Cleveland was the first Democrat to be elected President after the Civil War. Although he lost his reelection bid in 1888 to Benjamin Harrison, he returned to the White House four years later after winning a rematch in the 1892 election. Thus, Cleveland is the only President to serve two nonconsecutive terms of office. His disregard of popular and political opinion cost him reelection after each term.

Cleveland's political career developed rapidly; he went from county sheriff to U.S. President in only 11 years. Although born in New Jersey, he grew up in New York State, the son of a Presbyterian minister. His school years ended at age 16 with the death of his father. Eventually Cleveland studied law and entered into private practice in Buffalo, New York. His firm hand as the local sheriff led citizens to elect him mayor. Cleveland succeeded so well at ending corruption, waste, and scandal that he was nominated for governor of New York. He won by a landslide. His popularity in New York State made him a natural candidate for President in 1884.

Gossip and scandal fueled the presidential campaign. Republicans were delighted to discover that the bachelor Cleveland might have fathered a child. They chanted: "Ma, Ma, where's my Pa? Gone to the White House, ha, ha, ha!" However, the public seemed less concerned about Cleveland's private life than about the professional actions of his opponent. Democrats joked about "James Blaine, James Blaine, the continental liar from the state of Maine."

The Clevelands aboard the presidential train

Cleveland claimed "Public Office Is a Public Trust." Republican "Mugwumps" (an Indian word meaning "big chief") deserted their own party's candidate and favored him instead. Cleveland narrowly won the race.

Cleveland, who weighed 250 pounds, was nicknamed "Uncle Jumbo." He was the first President since the Civil War who had not fought in that conflict. Cleveland avoided military service then by paying a Polish immigrant $150 to take his place. Although this practice was legal, it was not considered admirable. As a presidential candidate, Cleveland was criticized for avoiding combat.

During his first administration, Cleveland vetoed more than twice as many pieces of legislation (413 total) as had all previous Presidents combined. As with Andrew Johnson two decades

NICKNAME
Uncle Jumbo

BORN
March 18, 1837, in Caldwell, NJ

POLITICAL PARTY
Democrat

CHIEF OPPONENTS
1st administration: James Gillespie Blaine, Republican (1830–1893); 2nd administration: President Benjamin Harrison, Republican (1833–1901)

TERM OF OFFICE
1st administration: March 4, 1885–March 3, 1889; 2nd administration: March 4, 1893–March 3, 1897

AGE AT INAUGURATION
1st administration: 47 years old; 2nd administration: 55 years old

NUMBER OF TERMS
two (nonconsecutive)

VICE PRESIDENTS
1st administration: Thomas Andrews Hendricks (1819–1885); 2nd administration: Adlai Ewing Stevenson (1835–1914)

FIRST LADIES
Rose Elizabeth Cleveland (1846–1918), sister; Frances Folsom Cleveland (1864–1947), wife (married June 2, 1886)

CHILDREN
Ruth, Esther, Marion, Richard, Francis

GEOGRAPHIC SCENE
1st administration: 38 states; 2nd administration: 44 states

NEW STATES ADDED
Utah (1896)

DIED
June 24, 1908, in Princeton, NJ

AGE AT DEATH
71 years old

SELECTED LANDMARKS
Caldwell, NJ (birthplace); Westland (home) and Princeton Cemetery, Princeton, NJ

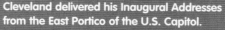
Cleveland delivered his Inaugural Addresses from the East Portico of the U.S. Capitol.

Grover Cleveland became the only President to marry at the White House when he wed Frances Folsom during his first administration. The couple changed their wedding vows so Frances could pledge to "love, honor, and keep" her husband instead of agreeing to "love, honor, and obey" him. Their first child, nicknamed "Baby Ruth," had a candy bar named after her. Their second child, Esther, was the only child of a President born in the White House.

earlier, critics called him the "Veto President." Children sang: "A fat man once sat in the President's chair, singing 'Ve-to,' 'Ve-to.'" Although Cleveland worked hard to hire loyal Democrats to fill government posts, other party members were often angered by his choices. He was more popular for his unexpected marriage, at age 49, to 21-year-old Frances Folsom, who was the daughter of a deceased friend.

During the election of 1888 Cleveland again won a greater share of the popular vote than his opponent. However, the presidency went to Benjamin Harrison because he earned the most votes in the Electoral College. The story goes that the departing First Lady assured the White House staff that she and her husband would return after the next election. They did. Cleveland won by a sizable margin in both popular and electoral voting when he faced Harrison in 1892.

Grover Cleveland campaigned on his party's ties to revered early Presidents, including Democrats Thomas Jefferson and Andrew Jackson as well as the nonpartisan George Washington. His two administrations were interrupted by Benjamin Harrison's single term.

Grover Cleveland hunted with a rifle he nicknamed "Death and Destruction." The President was forced to take a break from outdoor recreation in 1893 after developing mouth cancer. To avoid media attention, Frances Cleveland arranged for doctors to operate on the President aboard a private yacht. Doctors removed the tumor and part of Cleveland's jaw, then inserted a rubber shape to take the place of the missing bone. It left no visible scars. Some two dozen years passed before news of the operation leaked out.

"What is the use of being elected or reelected unless you stand for something?"

Grover Cleveland, 1887

Public support of Cleveland began to fall soon after his reelection, however, with the start of a new round of economic hard times. The Panic of 1893 lasted for the rest of Cleveland's presidency and brought widespread suffering. Cleveland argued with Congress over what, if anything, to do. Should the government issue more money, or less money, or should it do nothing? Should paper money continue to be worth a standard amount of gold? Should extra money be created in the form of silver coins? Was it better for the government to hoard precious metals or to share them? No one was quite sure how all the elements of national finance influenced one another, so it was hard to know what might help end the panic. Meanwhile, politicians gave little thought to the suffering of the nation's citizens. Some people joked that if a hungry man started eating grass on the White House lawn, Cleveland, instead of offering him food, would suggest he move to the backyard, where the grass was taller.

By the next election, Democrats were ready for a new candidate, and the public was ready for an entirely different party. Republicans, who had dominated the presidency since the Civil War, became the favored party again. Except for Cleveland and Woodrow Wilson, Republicans controlled the White House from 1861 until 1933.

Cleveland retired to New Jersey and became a lecturer and trustee for Princeton University. His dying words, 11 years after leaving the White House, were: "I have tried so hard to do right."

The Clevelands (from left to right: Esther, Francis, Mrs. Cleveland, Ruth, Richard, and the former President) posed for a family snapshot on the porch of the President's retirement home in New Jersey. Frances outlived her husband by 39 years. She became the first widow of a President to remarry when she wed a professor in 1913.

PRESIDENTIAL FACTS AND COMPARISONS

A LOOK AT THE STATS

Forty-four individuals have served their nation as President in 45 administrations. (Grover Cleveland is counted twice—once for each of his two separate presidencies.) The oldest President on taking office was Donald Trump, age 70; the youngest was Theodore Roosevelt, age 42. The President who served the shortest term in office—32 days—was William Henry Harrison. Franklin D. Roosevelt served the longest term; he was elected four times and was President for 12 years before dying in office at age 63.

Eight Presidents were born in Virginia, earning that state the nickname "Mother of Presidents." Many Presidents have come from Massachusetts, New York, and Ohio, too. In all, 24 Presidents were born in one of these four states. Some half a dozen Presidents were born in log cabins; Jimmy Carter was the first President born in a hospital. Carter, like many earlier Presidents, was the son of a farmer.

Nine Presidents have failed to complete their terms of office. Eight died on the job. One, Richard Nixon, resigned from office because of political scandal.

During the course of the nation's history the presidential salary has grown from $25,000 a year (for George Washington) to $400,000 a year today. Each President receives a significant expense allowance, too.

All but eight of the Presidents attended college; 32 were college graduates. More than half of all Presidents were members of the armed services, although not all witnessed combat. Eleven Presidents were former

George Washington tried false teeth of silver, ivory, cow's teeth, and more. Contrary to legend, wood was never used.

In 1974 Richard Nixon became the only U.S. President to resign from office.

William Howard Taft began a presidential tradition when he tossed out a ceremonial first pitch for the baseball season in 1910.

Gerald R. Ford (far left) is the only Eagle Scout to become a U.S. President. Folding the national flag was one of his duties while camping with other Boy Scouts during his youth.

generals. Fourteen Presidents were Vice Presidents of the country first. More than two dozen had served in the U.S. Congress. Seventeen were governors before becoming President. Twenty-six had studied law and become attorneys. Other prepresidential occupations include farmer, teacher, journalist, college professor, actor, engineer, and tailor.

Presidents have enjoyed hobbies including fishing, golf, and stamp collecting. Two played the piano (Harry S. Truman and Richard Nixon); two played the violin (Thomas Jefferson and John Tyler). Calvin Coolidge's instrument was the harmonica. Bill Clinton played the saxophone.

Most Presidents have been affiliated with Protestant churches, including 12 Episcopalians and 7 Presbyterians. Four Presidents, including Thomas Jefferson and Abraham Lincoln, listed no preferred religious affiliation. No one of non-Christian faith has yet served as President.

James K. Polk enjoyed the shortest retirement, 103 days. In 2012 Jimmy Carter surpassed Herbert Hoover's 31-year record for the longest retirement. Gerald R. Ford lived to be older than any other President: 93 years and 166 days. John F. Kennedy died at the youngest age: 46. Three Presidents died on the Fourth of July: John Adams, Thomas Jefferson, and James Monroe.

In the 19th century, members of Congress tried unsuccessfully to remove Andrew Johnson from office. Special tickets to his impeachment trial (above) allowed visitors to watch the proceedings at the U.S. Capitol.

Presidents have followed many pathways to the presidency. This chart makes it easy to follow the career paths of individuals or to study specific vocations and their evolving popularity over time.

PRESIDENTIAL CAREER PATHS

#	President	College Education	Graduate School	Military Service	Lawyer	Educator	State & Local Politics	House of Representatives	U.S. Senate	Governor	Diplomat	Cabinet Secretary	Vice President	Agriculture	Business
1.	George Washington			●			●								
2.	John Adams	●			●		●				●		●		
3.	Thomas Jefferson	●			●		●			●	●	●	●		
4.	James Madison	●	●	●			●	●				●			
5.	James Monroe	●		●	●		●		●	●	●	●			
6.	John Quincy Adams	●				●	●		●		●	●			
7.	Andrew Jackson			●	●		●	●	●	●					
8.	Martin Van Buren				●		●		●	●	●		●		
9.	William Henry Harrison	●	●	●			●	●	●	●	●				
10.	John Tyler	●			●		●	●	●	●			●		
11.	James K. Polk				●		●	●		●					
12.	Zachary Taylor			●											
13.	Millard Fillmore				●		●	●					●		
14.	Franklin Pierce	●			●		●	●	●						
15.	James Buchanan	●			●		●	●	●		●	●			
16.	Abraham Lincoln				●		●	●							●
17.	Andrew Johnson				●		●	●	●	●			●		
18.	Ulysses S. Grant	●		●											●
19.	Rutherford B. Hayes	●	●	●	●			●		●					
20.	James A. Garfield	●		●	●	●		●	●						
21.	Chester A. Arthur	●			●	●						●	●		
22. & 24.	Grover Cleveland				●		●			●					
23.	Benjamin Harrison	●		●	●				●						
25.	William McKinley			●	●			●		●					
26.	Theodore Roosevelt	●	●	●			●			●			●		
27.	William Howard Taft	●			●							●			
28.	Woodrow Wilson	●	●			●				●					
29.	Warren G. Harding						●		●						●
30.	Calvin Coolidge	●			●		●			●			●		
31.	Herbert Hoover	●										●			●
32.	Franklin D. Roosevelt	●	●		●		●			●					
33.	Harry S. Truman			●	●				●				●	●	
34.	Dwight D. Eisenhower	●	●	●		●									
35.	John F. Kennedy	●		●				●	●						
36.	Lyndon B. Johnson	●				●		●	●				●		
37.	Richard Nixon	●	●	●	●			●	●				●		
38.	Gerald R. Ford	●	●	●	●			●					●		
39.	Jimmy Carter	●		●			●			●				●	
40.	Ronald Reagan	●								●					
41.	George Bush	●		●				●			●		●		●
42.	Bill Clinton	●	●		●	●	●			●					
43.	George W. Bush	●	●	●						●					●
44.	Barack Obama	●	●		●	●	●		●						
45.	Donald Trump	●													●

BENJAMIN HARRISON
23RD PRESIDENT OF THE UNITED STATES 1889–1893

Benjamin Harrison's single term of office was sandwiched between the two presidential terms of Grover Cleveland. Harrison and Cleveland competed for the presidency in the consecutive elections of 1888 and 1892. In both cases Cleveland won the popular vote. However, Harrison was awarded the presidency in 1888 after receiving a majority of Electoral College votes.

Harrison grew up in the shadow of another resident of the White House—his grandfather. "Little Ben" was a seven-year-old boy living in Ohio when William Henry Harrison became President. The younger Harrison went on to graduate from Ohio's Miami University and become an attorney in Indiana. He served one term in the U.S. Senate before being nominated for President.

Harrison, as was customary at the time, chose to run a low-key campaign. He spoke only to the crowds who were encouraged to gather at his home in Indianapolis. For one campaign stunt,

Harrison facing the latest round of office seekers

40,000 drummers from 11 states were organized to visit him. Harrison's well-financed campaign earned him victories in enough key states so that he topped his opponent in the Electoral College. Cleveland's slim lead in popular votes—about 90,000—became irrelevant.

As President, Harrison authorized the first peacetime federal budget to reach the $1 billion mark. This money improved harbors, established naval fleets on both U.S. coasts, and helped pay the costs of building steamship lines. More states (six) were added to the nation during Harrison's single administration than during any other presidency.

Harrison's support of import tariffs cost him reelection when Cleveland mounted a bid to retake the White House. He returned to Indianapolis a widower, his wife having died of tuberculosis the previous year. He resumed his law practice and married his late wife's niece. He died of pneumonia five years later.

NICKNAME
Little Ben

BORN
Aug. 20, 1833, in North Bend, OH

POLITICAL PARTY
Republican

CHIEF OPPONENT
President Grover Cleveland, Democrat (1837–1908)

TERM OF OFFICE
March 4, 1889–March 3, 1893

AGE AT INAUGURATION
55 years old

NUMBER OF TERMS
one

VICE PRESIDENT
Levi Parsons Morton (1824–1920)

FIRST LADIES
Caroline Lavinia Scott Harrison (1832–1892), wife (married Oct. 20, 1853); Mary Scott Harrison McKee (1858–1930), daughter

SECOND WIFE
Mary Scott Lord Dimmick Harrison (1858–1948), married April 6, 1896

CHILDREN
Born to Caroline Harrison (first wife): Russell, Mary; born to Mary Harrison (second wife): Elizabeth

GEOGRAPHIC SCENE
38 states

NEW STATES ADDED
Montana, North Dakota, South Dakota, and Washington (1889); Idaho and Wyoming (1890)

DIED
March 13, 1901, in Indianapolis, IN

AGE AT DEATH
67 years old

SELECTED LANDMARKS
Indianapolis, IN (home); Crown Hill Cemetery, Indianapolis, IN

As a Union officer in the Civil War, Harrison fought in more battles in one month than his famous grandfather had in a lifetime. They are the only grandfather-grandson pair of Presidents.

AMERICA TAKES CENTER STAGE

1897–1933

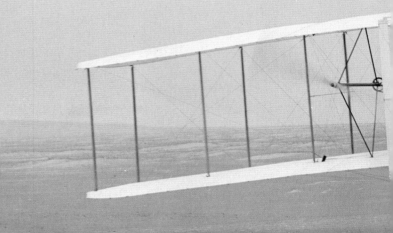

Presidents took firm control of the federal government at the start of the 20th century. They helped develop the United States into a global power, both economically and politically. The era featured fantastic advances in science, technology, transportation, and exploration. Leaders were challenged to expand the rights of citizens and curb the power of businesses. They struggled to cope with worldwide war and widespread economic suffering, too. Public opinion of federal policies played a central role in national elections.

CIRCA 1890s
By the late 19th century, labor-saving inventions such as the mechanical washing machine were changing the way families handled routine household chores.

1903
The Wright brothers (from left, Orville and Wilbur) revolutionized flight by soaring 120 feet on December 17. Only two dozen years later, Charles Lindbergh would fly solo across the Atlantic.

1906
On April 18 an earthquake and subsequent fires leveled much of San Francisco. Neighboring communities were hit, too; 50 miles away the Santa Rosa Courthouse (above) collapsed.

1912
The "unsinkable" *Titanic* went down on its first voyage after it struck an iceberg in the North Atlantic Ocean on April 14. More than 1,500 people died.

Wilbur (below, right) and Orville Wright made the first successful airplane flight—12 seconds long—on December 17, 1903, near Kitty Hawk, North Carolina (colorized image).

1913–1920
Women intensified their efforts to gain suffrage, or voting rights. In 1920 a constitutional amendment finally granted all female U.S. citizens the right to vote.

1914–1919
World War I had been raging for nearly three years when U.S. forces joined the fight in 1917. Their presence helped win the war. Nearly 10 million soldiers, including 100,000 Americans, died during the conflict.

1920s
People celebrated increased peace and prosperity during the Roaring Twenties. Flappers danced the Charleston (above) as fashions, behaviors, and outlooks changed.

1930s
A decade of economic suffering followed the stock market collapse of October 1929. Citizens who had lost their jobs and even their homes sought free food in breadlines.

WILLIAM McKINLEY
25TH PRESIDENT OF THE UNITED STATES 1897–1901

William McKinley was the last Chief Executive who fought in the Civil War. However, McKinley's witness of an earlier era did not stop him from pushing the nation and his office into modern times. He did everything from using telephones on a regular basis to expanding the political influence of the United States around the globe. Early in his second term, McKinley became the fifth President to die in office, and the third one to be assassinated.

The state of Ohio sent five of her sons, including McKinley, to the White House in 28 years. (Two more followed him over the next 24 years.) As a youth, McKinley played army games with friends or went fishing, ice-skating, and horseback riding. He attended public schools where he excelled at speechmaking, and he studied briefly at Allegheny College in Pennsylvania. He served in the Civil War under future President Rutherford B. Hayes. Despite four years of duty, he escaped all injury and illness. Twice he won promotions for acts of bravery. After the war McKinley took up the study of law and became an attorney. His final wartime rank of major remained his nickname among close friends for years.

"The Major" spent a dozen years in the U.S. House of Representatives and gained national notice for his McKinley Tariff legislation. Once implemented, however, this tax on imported goods brought unexpectedly high prices to consumer goods at home. Many Republicans, including McKinley and President Benjamin Harrison, lost their elected posts as a result. Nonetheless, McKinley persuaded Ohioans to elect him as their governor two years later. He served two terms before being nominated for President in 1896. McKinley defeated his opponent, William Jennings Bryan, in part because he spent five times as much money during the campaign as his rival. Bryan, a noted

When McKinley was Ohio's governor, each day at 3 p.m. he waved to his wife from his office window, and Ida McKinley waved back from their home across the street.

NICKNAME
Idol of Ohio

BORN
Jan. 29, 1843, in Niles, OH

POLITICAL PARTY
Republican

CHIEF OPPONENT
1st and 2nd terms: William Jennings Bryan, Democrat (1860–1925)

TERM OF OFFICE
March 4, 1897–Sept. 14, 1901

AGE AT INAUGURATION
54 years old

NUMBER OF TERMS
two (cut short by assassination)

VICE PRESIDENT
1st term: Garret Augustus Hobart (1844–1899); 2nd term: Theodore Roosevelt (1858–1919)

FIRST LADY
Ida Saxton McKinley (1847–1907), wife (married Jan. 25, 1871)

CHILDREN
two daughters who died young

GEOGRAPHIC SCENE
45 states

NEW STATES ADDED
none

DIED
Sept. 14, 1901, in Buffalo, NY

AGE AT DEATH
58 years old

SELECTED LANDMARKS
National McKinley Birthplace Memorial, Niles, OH; McKinley Museum and McKinley National Memorial (grave), Canton, OH

William McKinley was the only President between Andrew Johnson and Woodrow Wilson not to have facial hair. He liked to wear a red carnation in the buttonhole of his jacket. Ohio went so far as to make this bloom its official flower in honor of the "Idol of Ohio." McKinley liked cigars, too. Sometimes he broke one in two and chewed the halves instead of smoking the whole cigar.

William McKinley (seated, center), celebrated his second Inauguration in 1901 but did not live to complete his term.

orator, traveled 18,000 miles around the country during a three-month-long speaking tour. McKinley, as Benjamin Harrison had done in 1888, ran a "front porch" campaign from his home in Ohio and relied on others to campaign for him nationally.

As President, McKinley focused on U.S. relations with foreign countries. He started with Spain. This European nation still ruled Cuba and other Caribbean islands near the United States, as well as the Philippine Islands in the Pacific. Diplomatic talks gave way to war in 1898 after the suspicious destruction of the U.S. battleship *Maine* while it was anchored near Cuba. Future President Theodore Roosevelt rode to national fame as the head of the Rough Riders once the fighting began. Meanwhile, the U.S. Navy destroyed Spain's Atlantic and Pacific fleets during the four-month-long Spanish-American War.

Americans pledged to "Remember the *Maine!*" by going to war with Spain soon after the ship's destruction. William McKinley helped lead the United States to victory in the Spanish-American War of 1898.

McKinley proposed linking the Atlantic and Pacific Oceans by building a canal through Central America. He made full use of new technologies while in office. The President communicated with the war front by telegraph, kept in touch with newspaper editors by telephone, and established the first White House press room. He even had telegraph lines installed there so reporters could easily dispatch stories to their newspaper offices. He controlled the slant reporters gave to news by putting his own twist on details released to them. Sometimes he completely censored, or kept secret, certain facts.

Combat ended when Spain withdrew its claim to Cuba. Spain put Puerto Rico, Guam, and the Philippine Islands under U.S. control in exchange for a $20 million settlement. Guam and the Philippines gave the United States a Pacific base from which to influence Asian affairs, particularly in China. McKinley further increased the U.S. presence in the Pacific by annexing, or taking over, the Hawaiian Islands. In addition, he initiated plans to build the Panama Canal, linking the Atlantic and Pacific Oceans through Central America.

McKinley's first Vice President died in office. Theodore Roosevelt was nominated to fill the job during the election of 1900. Roosevelt talked himself hoarse while campaigning for "Four More Years of the Full Dinner Pail." Buoyed by a strong economy and public satisfaction with the outcome of the war, McKinley triumphed over Bryan again. This time he won by an even greater margin of support.

In the fall of 1901, barely six months into his second administration, McKinley attended the Pan-American Exposition in Buffalo, New York. During the events a lone assassin joined a crowd of spectators waiting to shake the President's hand. When McKinley reached out to greet him, the man fired two shots at the President from a hidden gun. McKinley died eight days later after developing gangrene from his wounds. The assailant, an unemployed laborer, said he was an anarchist, someone who believes all forms of government are tyrannical. He was convicted of murder and executed.

> "War should never be entered upon until every agency of peace has failed."
>
> William McKinley,
> Inaugural Address, March 4, 1897

William McKinley often charmed strangers by presenting them with the carnation he wore on his jacket. Once, when two brothers were introduced to him, he carefully replaced the flower in his buttonhole with a fresh one so each boy could receive a bloom from the President. McKinley had just presented his lapel flower to a young girl when he was shot (right). The President died eight days later.

THEODORE ROOSEVELT
26TH PRESIDENT OF THE UNITED STATES 1901–1909

Theodore Roosevelt took charge of the White House after the assassination of William McKinley. He filled it with his own personality and vision. He was the first "accidental" President to later win outright election to the office. During his tenure he expanded the reach of the U.S. government into such areas as industry, labor, the environment, consumer rights, and foreign affairs.

Few Presidents, if any, could compete with the unique background that Roosevelt brought to the White House. He was the son of a wealthy New York family. Sickly and asthmatic, he was schooled at home. Finally, "Teedie's" father encouraged him to improve his health through vigorous physical exercise. By the time he attended Harvard University, he was physically fit enough to compete in the campus boxing program. Roosevelt graduated with honors, married, and became a member of New York's state assembly.

Theodore Roosevelt wrote more than 30 books.

Then tragedy struck. Roosevelt's mother and wife both died from illnesses on Valentine's Day in 1884. Roosevelt took his grief to the western United States and worked as a cowboy and a rancher. Locals came to respect the eyeglasses-wearing "Four Eyes" as the East Coast "dude" whose strongest curse was "By Godfrey!" Roosevelt did not hesitate to punch out an offensive cowboy, fire a dishonest ranch hand, or capture thieves.

In the fall of 1886 Roosevelt returned to East Coast life. He remarried, took up

Not since Thomas Jefferson had a President enjoyed as many talents and diverse interests as Theodore Roosevelt. He loved being active outdoors. Roosevelt would swim through shark-infested waters to explore a shipwreck or lead cross-country hikes on an unwavering straight course, taking each obstacle as a fresh challenge. After being wounded by a would-be assassin during his 1912 presidential campaign, Roosevelt insisted on speaking for nearly an hour, dripping blood, before seeking medical care. The folded copy of his speech and his metal eyeglass case had slowed the path of the bullet and prevented the wound from being too severe.

Theodore Roosevelt

NICKNAME
T. R.

BORN
Oct. 27, 1858, in New York, NY

POLITICAL PARTY
Republican

CHIEF OPPONENTS
1st term: none, succeeded McKinley; 2nd term: Alton Brooks Parker, Democrat (1852–1926)

TERM OF OFFICE
Sept. 14, 1901–March 3, 1909

AGE AT INAUGURATION
42 years old

NUMBER OF TERMS
one, plus balance of William McKinley's term

VICE PRESIDENTS
1st term: none; 2nd term: Charles Warren Fairbanks (1852–1918)

FIRST WIFE
Alice Hathaway Lee Roosevelt (1861–1884), married Oct. 27, 1880

FIRST LADY
Edith Kermit Carow Roosevelt (1861–1948), second wife (married Dec. 2, 1886)

CHILDREN
Born to Alice Roosevelt (first wife): Alice; born to Edith Roosevelt (second wife): Theodore, Kermit, Ethel, Archibald, Quentin

GEOGRAPHIC SCENE
45 states

NEW STATES ADDED
Oklahoma (1907)

DIED
Jan. 6, 1919, in Oyster Bay, NY

AGE AT DEATH
60 years old

SELECTED LANDMARKS
New York, NY (birthplace); Sagamore Hill National Historic Site (homestead) and Young's Memorial Cemetery, Oyster Bay, NY; Theodore Roosevelt Island, Washington, DC; Mount Rushmore National Memorial, Keystone, SD

writing, and reentered public service. He worked on the U.S. Civil Service Commission for Benjamin Harrison, headed the New York City Police Board, and served as William McKinley's assistant secretary of the Navy. When the Spanish-American War broke out, Roosevelt recruited a volunteer company of cowboys, college football players, New York City police officers, and Native Americans. Roosevelt's "Rough Riders" became famous for their charge near San Juan Hill, in Cuba. Roosevelt was elected governor of New York after the

> ## "Speak softly and carry a big stick; you will go far."
>
> Theodore Roosevelt's version of an African saying

war. In 1901 Roosevelt became Vice President and then President. He won outright election to the post in 1904.

Roosevelt's political background as an administrator prepared him to take aggressive charge of the office. He expanded the role of the national government in protecting the lives of its citizens. He went head-to-head with large corporations that had formed monopolies—called trusts—in railroad, beef, oil, tobacco, and other industries. Trusts had become so powerful from lack of competition that citizens and workers were suffering from high prices, low wages, and poor working conditions. Roosevelt became known as a "trustbuster" for breaking up these monopolies.

In other domestic affairs Roosevelt forced coal mine owners to settle labor disputes with 150,000 striking miners by threatening to have the government take control of the mines. He set aside vast areas of the country for conservation and resource development. He increased safety standards for the preparation of meat, other food products, and medicine.

In foreign policy Roosevelt outlined what became known as "Big Stick Diplomacy." He declared that the United States would serve as "an

Theodore Roosevelt gained fame during the Spanish-American War as the commander of his fearless troop of Rough Riders.

Roosevelt's second wife, Edith (seated with their family), served as T.R.'s personal secretary during his presidency. Her research aided his Nobel Peace Prize–winning treaty negotiations.

Seven Rough Riders helped Theodore Roosevelt campaign to become governor of New York. At campaign stops, a bugler even sounded the cavalry charge.

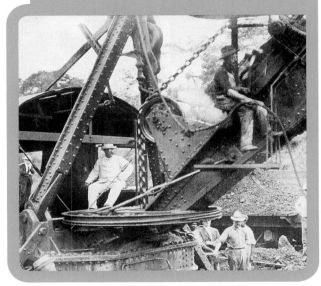

Theodore Roosevelt continued the work begun by his predecessor for the construction of a waterway connecting the Atlantic and Pacific Oceans across Central America. Roosevelt (in white suit) visited the Panama Canal construction site in 1906.

During his retirement years T.R. (above, far right) spent seven months exploring the River of Doubt in the jungles of Brazil. He suffered periodically from malaria and other ailments during the trip and for the rest of his life.

international police power" throughout the Western Hemisphere of the globe if it felt threatened by other nations. He proved an effective mediator in disputes among other nations, too. He won the Nobel Peace Prize in 1905 for his role in negotiating an end to the war between Russia and Japan.

Roosevelt, the youngest man ever to become President, was very much a family man when he entered the White House. His eldest daughter, Alice, was married there. His younger children grew up in its corridors and on its grounds. Once a son and his friends disrupted work at a nearby government building by using mirrors to bounce sunlight through the windows. When informed about the problem, Roosevelt, always playful, arranged for someone at the office building to send the boys a message with signal flags: "Attack on this building must immediately cease ..." A friend observed: "You must always remember that the President is about six."

Roosevelt left the White House in 1909. On an extended safari in Africa he collected hundreds of animals for the Smithsonian Institution. He made an unsuccessful attempt to regain the White House in 1912 by running as a third-party candidate for the Progressive, or Bull Moose, Party. Roosevelt's offer to raise a fighting force during World War I was refused, but all four of his sons joined the service. The combat death of his youngest son, Quentin, left Roosevelt shaken. With his health deteriorating, he died the following year.

Theodore Roosevelt (above, with envoys of Japan and Russia) is known for being first at many things, both great and trivial. He was the first President to travel by car and submarine while in office. During his retirement years, he became the first President to ride in an airplane. He was the first President to have his initials become his nickname. He made the first overseas trip by a sitting President (to Panama). He was the first President and first American to be awarded a Nobel Peace Prize. The teddy bear was named after Roosevelt by a toymaker who heard how he had spared the life of a bear cub during a hunting trip.

KIDS IN THE WHITE HOUSE
AT HOME IN THE SPOTLIGHT

The first residents of the White House—John and Abigail Adams—were also the first occupants to bring children to the President's home. Their four-year-old granddaughter, Susanna, traveled with her grandmother to stay at the residence in 1800. A parade of children has continued to live there off and on ever since.

In 1806 Thomas Jefferson's grandson James became the first baby born in the President's home. Grover Cleveland is the only President to have one of his own children born in the White House. His daughter Esther was born there in 1893.

In 1861 the Lincolns were the first family to have their own young children live in the White House. Among other antics, Tad Lincoln set up a White House refreshment stand, shot his toy cannon at the President's office door, and rode through an East Room tea party on a chair pulled by his pet goats.

Theodore Roosevelt brought six children with him to the White House in 1901. These youngsters roller-skated in the East Room, "sledded" down White House staircases on serving trays, and surrounded themselves with pets—including snakes, a badger, raccoons, pigs, parrots, baby bears, and a young lion. Their father noted: "I don't think that any family has ever enjoyed the White House more than we have."

The children of most Presidents are already grown up or are away in college by the time their parents move into the White House. Some of these young adults have been

Theodore Roosevelt's youngest sons, Archie (second from right) and Quentin, liked to join the daily roll call for the White House police. Willie and Tad Lincoln (above, left, seated between their parents) were an earlier pair of brothers who roamed freely in the President's home. They knew just how to cause chaos there by ringing various bells to call White House servants.

James A. Garfield's sons had pillow fights aboard velocipedes in the White House East Room.

Quentin Roosevelt rode his pony, Algonquin, while growing up in the Executive Mansion. Once he brought his pet on the White House elevator so the pair could visit his brother Archie, who was laid up with measles.

Malia Obama reads *Where the Wild Things Are* with her sister, Sasha, watching, as part of the White House Easter Egg Roll activities in 2011.

active campaigners for their fathers. In recent decades, five Presidents—John F. Kennedy, Jimmy Carter, Bill Clinton, Barack Obama, and Donald Trump—have brought younger children with them to the White House. As parents they sheltered their children from public attention while encouraging them to "just be kids" at home. Caroline Kennedy rode the grounds on her pony, Macaroni, and Amy Carter played in her own tree house, for example.

Since the days of Woodrow Wilson, Secret Service agents have acted as bodyguards for children of the Presidents— even out on dates! If the public spotlight ever gets too bright, presidential children can always find refuge back home in the White House.

John F. Kennedy, Jr., liked to hide under his father's desk in the Oval Office.

In 1971 Tricia Nixon became the eighth and most recent presidential daughter to marry at the White House. Maria Monroe was the first in 1820.

When the First Family includes pets, those animals can become famous, too. Barney (above) had his own website during the presidency of George W. Bush.

Chelsea Clinton accompanied her parents on some of their official trips abroad.

WILLIAM HOWARD TAFT
27TH PRESIDENT OF THE UNITED STATES 1909–1913

William Howard Taft was elected President in 1908 as Theodore Roosevelt's hand-picked successor. He lacked Roosevelt's charisma and administrative talent, however, and lost popularity as his term progressed. Taft was defeated during his reelection bid, a crowded and complex race that included a challenge by Roosevelt on a third-party ticket. Later, Taft served with distinction on the U.S. Supreme Court, making him the only person to be both a U.S. President and a Supreme Court justice.

Taft was the sixth Ohioan to become a U.S. President. His father, a lawyer and public servant, had served in the administrations of Ulysses S. Grant and Chester A. Arthur. Young Taft attended public schools and graduated second in his class from Yale University. By then "Big Bill" already weighed at least 225 pounds. Taft studied law, opened a practice, worked as a judge, and taught law.

In 1900 President William McKinley sent Taft to administer the Philippine Islands. He became governor of this new U.S. territory in the Pacific. Four years later Theodore Roosevelt made him secretary of war, responsible for the construction of the Panama Canal. Although Taft was eager to return to the bench as a judge, he turned down three opportunities to join the Supreme Court during these years. He felt he had to finish work assigned to him by Presidents instead.

Taft was encouraged by

William Howard Taft relaxed by playing golf.

his wife, Helen, and Roosevelt to run for President in 1908. With some hesitation, he did. He won election easily because of his association with Roosevelt. Taft tried to continue the progressive reforms begun by his predecessor. In his one term of office, he broke twice as many trusts as Roosevelt had done in eight years, including major monopolies in tobacco and petroleum. During Taft's administration, the federal government took control of railroad freight fares, established a parcel post delivery service, initiated a postal savings system,

NICKNAME
Big Bill

BORN
Sept. 15, 1857, in Cincinnati, OH

POLITICAL PARTY
Republican

CHIEF OPPONENT
William Jennings Bryan, Democrat (1860–1925)

TERM OF OFFICE
March 4, 1909–March 3, 1913

AGE AT INAUGURATION
51 years old

NUMBER OF TERMS
one

VICE PRESIDENT
James Schoolcraft Sherman (1855–1912)

FIRST LADY
Helen Herron Taft (1861–1943), wife (married June 19, 1886)

CHILDREN
Robert, Helen, Charles

GEOGRAPHIC SCENE
46 states

NEW STATES ADDED
New Mexico, Arizona (1912)

DIED
March 8, 1930, in Washington, DC

AGE AT DEATH
72 years old

SELECTED LANDMARKS
Cincinnati, OH (birthplace); Arlington National Cemetery, Arlington, VA

Baseball was one of William Howard Taft's childhood pastimes. However, "Big Lub," as children called the sizable Taft, was better at batting than at running bases. He struggled to reduce his weight for much of his adult life. Taft was the first President who played golf. He also rode horses, played tennis, and liked to dance. The "Taft March" (left) was written for his presidential campaign.

Taft (wearing dark jacket) served as governor of the Philippines for President William McKinley.

As Theodore Roosevelt's secretary of war, Taft (far right) supervised the construction of the Panama Canal.

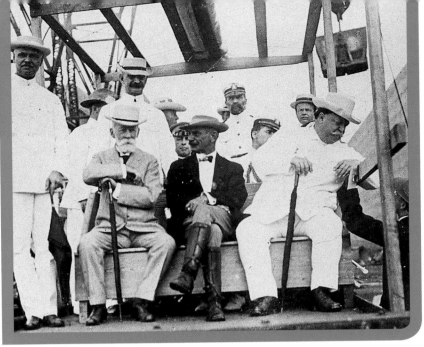

Taft, whose weight at times exceeded 330 pounds, was heavier than any other President. The story goes that he'd become stuck in the White House bathtub, and so a larger one was installed (left, workers fill the new tub). A careful review of the historical record reduces this story to an unfounded rumor, probably spread by political opponents.

created the Department of Labor, and added new lands to the federal conservation program. Congress passed two amendments to the Constitution, too. One created the structure for a federal income tax; the other called for the direct election of U.S. senators by citizens. (Previously, state legislatures had elected senators.) Taft was the first person to be President of all the lower 48 states. Nearly 50 years would pass before the nation added Alaska and Hawaii, its last two states.

These accomplishments were overshadowed in the minds of others by Taft's shortcomings. His efforts to reduce the tariff, or tax, on imports divided his party into warring factions. Many leaders at home and abroad disapproved of his "Dollar Diplomacy," a program that substituted "dollars for bullets" in an effort

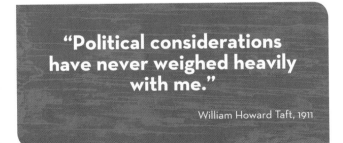

"Political considerations have never weighed heavily with me."

William Howard Taft, 1911

to influence foreign policy. He was ridiculed for trivial things such as not remembering names, needing an oversize bathtub, and falling asleep at awkward moments. (Once he even slept through his own parade while riding in an open car through the streets of New York City.) Voters rejected his reelection bid more firmly than that of any other major candidate in history. He won 23 percent of the popular vote, and just eight electoral votes. Even his former ally Roosevelt won more votes running on a third-party ticket.

After leaving the White House, Taft became a law professor at his alma mater, Yale University. Then, in 1921, President Warren G. Harding named him Chief Justice of the United States. Taft wrote 253 Court opinions during his nine years on the bench. Even more important than his rulings was the work he did persuading Congress to construct the Supreme Court building. (Previously, the Court met in a separate chamber of the U.S. Capitol Building.) Taft enjoyed his

"No one candidate was ever elected ex-President by such a large majority," joked William Howard Taft after losing his reelection bid to Woodrow Wilson. Taft and Wilson rode together to the U.S. Capitol when it was time for the new President to be inaugurated.

Taft was the first former Chief Executive to become a trustee of the National Geographic Society; he wrote more than a dozen articles for its magazine.

"I have tried to do in each case what seemed to me the wisest thing."

William Howard Taft, 1911

post so much that he remarked: "I don't remember that I ever was President."

Taft retired from the Supreme Court in 1930 when his health began to fail. He died a few weeks later. He was the first President to be buried in Arlington National Cemetery. His wife, Helen, was laid to rest beside him following her death 13 years later. John F. Kennedy and his wife, Jacqueline, are the only other presidential couple buried at Arlington.

As First Lady, Helen Taft coordinated the planting of ornamental Japanese cherry trees in the nation's capital. She took an active interest in government business, supported women's rights, and wrote a memoir about her years in the White House.

Helen Taft was the first President's wife to accompany her husband during his Inaugural Parade.

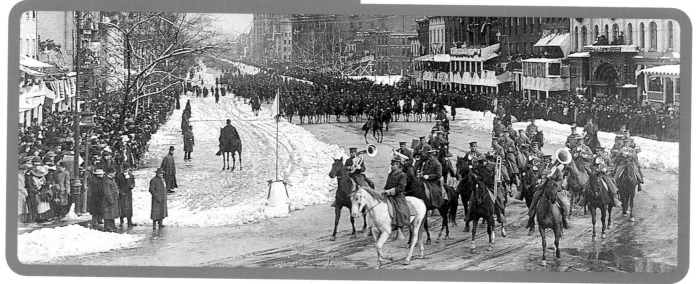

PRESIDENTS AND THE SUPREME COURT
A LEGACY THAT LASTS

The cry "Oyez! Oyez! Oyez!" opens each session of the U.S. Supreme Court. The President, with the approval of Congress, determines who will sit on the bench that holds the highest authority in the judicial branch of the U.S. government. Only 112 individuals have ever served on it. Because justices serve for life and are protected from firing and salary cuts, they are expected to weigh cases free from political pressures or other influences. Even so, they often reflect the beliefs and political backgrounds of the leaders who appoint them, giving Presidents a lasting legacy of influence long after they've retired from office.

The Supreme Court Building in Washington, D.C.

The size and composition of the Supreme Court (below, in 1892) has evolved since it formed in 1790 with six members. Membership ranged as high as 10 until Congress settled on its final size of nine members in 1869. The Court met for 177 years before anyone other than white men joined its bench.

When a vacancy occurs on the Supreme Court, either because of death or retirement, the President nominates someone to fill the space. Nominees typically have had extensive and distinguished experience as attorneys, judges, or in political office. The Senate Judiciary Committee decides whether or not to recommend approval of a nominee by the full Senate. Most nominees win Senate confirmation, but over the years about two dozen have not.

With the exception of Jimmy Carter and three 19th-century Presidents, all other Chief Executives have appointed someone to the Supreme Court. George Washington holds the record for appointing the most justices: 10. Franklin D. Roosevelt appointed almost as many—nine—during his lengthy presidency.

The Supreme Court opens its yearly term on the first Monday of October and continues to meet until early summer. It is asked to review some 10,000 cases each year; only about 100 are actually presented in front of the Court. Whenever the justices gather to undertake official

business, they shake hands as a reminder of their need to remain civil even when they disagree about the law.

The Supreme Court met inside the U.S. Capitol Building for most of the first 145 years of its history. After former President William Howard Taft became the Chief Justice in 1921, he persuaded Congress to construct the Court its own home. Taft died before he could see the opening of the Supreme Court Building in 1935.

In addition to issuing landmark decisions about the law, members of the Supreme Court have twice helped

When William Howard Taft joined the Supreme Court in 1921—the only former President to do so—he found two of the five justices he had appointed while Chief Executive still serving on the bench.

John Roberts (above, left, with President George W. Bush) became the court's newest Chief Justice in 2005. Of the 17 men who have served as Chief Justice, John Marshall held the post the longest: 34 years (1801–1835).

determine the outcome of presidential elections. A commission made up of five Supreme Court justices and 10 members of Congress voted 8 to 7 along party lines to hand victory to Republican candidate Rutherford B. Hayes following the election of 1876. More recently, in 2000, the Supreme Court ruled 5 to 4 in the case *Bush v. Gore*, also along party lines, in a decision that elevated George W. Bush to the presidency. The Court contributed to the ending of a presidency, too, when its 1974 ruling forced Richard Nixon to release secret recordings that tied him to the Watergate scandal. The President resigned later that year.

The Supreme Court holds the final say in government disputes. Its decisions can only be overcome in three ways: the passage of improved legislation that respects the Court's opinions, constitutional amendment, or future rulings by the Court.

When the Supreme Court convened in 2010 (below), three women sat on the bench simultaneously for the first time (from left, Sonia Sotomayor, Elena Kagan, and Ruth Bader Ginsburg). Presidents have appointed a total of four women and two African-American men to the nation's highest court. The first woman joined in 1981, 14 years after its first member of color.

WOODROW WILSON
28TH PRESIDENT OF THE UNITED STATES 1913–1921

As President, Woodrow Wilson ushered important legislation through Congress. However, World War I became the greatest challenge of his two terms in office. When he failed to keep the United States out of the conflict, he used the nation's resources to help win it. He sought to secure lasting peace afterward with a new international governing body called the League of Nations.

Wilson grew up in the shadow of an earlier war—the Civil War. He was born in Virginia and raised in Georgia and the Carolinas. His first childhood memory was of hearing in 1860 that a war would soon begin. He watched Confederate troops march off to battle; saw soldiers die from their wounds; and, after the war, glimpsed Confederate general Robert E. Lee march through town under Union guard. His Southern heritage contributed to his support for racial segregation.

Wilson struggled with dyslexia, a learning disorder that delayed his mastery of basic skills in reading, writing, and math. He went on to graduate from the College of New Jersey (later Princeton University). Wilson practiced law, earned a graduate degree from Johns Hopkins University, and became a college professor. (Hence, his nickname.) By 1902 he was president of Princeton. Wilson stepped from that post to the White House after

Wilson won reelection by being antiwar.

NICKNAME
Professor

BORN
Dec. 29, 1856, in Staunton, VA

POLITICAL PARTY
Democrat

CHIEF OPPONENTS
1st term: Theodore Roosevelt, Progressive (1858–1919), and President William Howard Taft, Republican (1857–1930); 2nd term: Charles Evans Hughes, Republican (1862–1948)

TERM OF OFFICE
March 4, 1913–March 3, 1921

AGE AT INAUGURATION
56 years old

NUMBER OF TERMS
two

VICE PRESIDENT
Thomas Riley Marshall (1854–1925)

FIRST LADIES
Ellen Louise Axson Wilson (1860–1914), first wife (married June 24, 1885); Margaret Woodrow Wilson (1886–1944), daughter; Edith Bolling Galt Wilson (1872–1961), second wife (married Dec. 18, 1915)

CHILDREN
Born to Ellen Wilson (first wife): Margaret, Jesse, Eleanor

GEOGRAPHIC SCENE
48 states

NEW STATES ADDED
none

DIED
Feb. 3, 1924, in Washington, DC

AGE AT DEATH
67 years old

SELECTED LANDMARKS
Staunton, VA (birthplace, library, and museum); Columbia, SC (boyhood home); The President Woodrow Wilson House (museum) and Washington National Cathedral (grave), Washington, DC

By 1917 intensified fighting in Europe had forced Woodrow Wilson to change his first-term antiwar stance and enter the United States into World War I. Within 18 months some two million U.S. soldiers had joined the front lines and helped turn the tide of the Great War.

Program for the Peace of the World
By PRESIDENT WILSON, January 8, 1918

The son of a Presbyterian minister, Woodrow Wilson thought it was God's will that he become President. He worked to end World War I as if he'd received a charge from heaven. His "Fourteen Points" for lasting peace (above, left), outlined in January 1918, formed the basis for the war's settlement, but Wilson wore himself out fighting for treaty ratification.

Wilson is credited with playing more golf than any other President, some 1,200 rounds.

brief service as governor of New Jersey. He was the top vote getter in the crowded presidential race of 1912 that included President William Howard Taft and former President Theodore Roosevelt.

Wilson was the first President to hold regular press conferences and to speak on the radio. He packed his first term with significant legislation that reduced import taxes, instituted wealth-based income taxes, created a Federal Trade Commission to monitor business practices, established a Federal Reserve system to manage the nation's money supply, supported the right of workers to strike, discouraged child labor, and promoted the eight-hour workday. Yet he also instituted racially biased policies, such as segregating the civil service. Wilson won reelection in part because, as his

campaign slogan put it, "He Kept Us Out of War." The Great War had begun in Europe in August 1914. The United States was drawn into the fight soon after Wilson's 1916 reelection. The war ended with a truce on November 11, 1918, a date celebrated in the U.S. as Armistice Day (and later renamed Veterans Day). All told, nearly 10 million soldiers died worldwide in the four-year conflict, including 100,000 Americans. During and after the war, his administration stifled dissent and stoked fears about immigration.

Wilson became the first U.S. President to visit Europe while in office when he traveled to Paris to help establish terms for peace. The final treaty supported Wilson's idea of creating a League of Nations that would settle future disputes using words and economic influence, not weapons. Wilson could not persuade Congress to accept his plan, though, and the League formed without support from the United States. Nonetheless, in 1919 Wilson earned the Nobel Peace Prize for his efforts. The United Nations took the place of the League after World War II.

Wilson had lived through the assassinations of three Presidents by the time he took office in 1913.

American cities across the country hosted victory parades (above) to honor soldiers returning home from World War I.

Woodrow and Edith Wilson set a positive example for nationwide rationing during the war by going without gas on Sundays, meat on Mondays, and wheat on Tuesdays. They even let sheep roam on the White House lawns so they could "mow" the grass naturally, saving gas and labor. Nationwide sacrifices helped make scarce resources available to U.S. soldiers overseas.

Wilson's first wife, Ellen, was a talented artist. As First Lady she worked to improve housing for residents in the nation's capital. Two of the Wilsons' three daughters were wed in White House ceremonies during his first term of office. Wilson was devastated when Ellen became ill and died in 1914. He even told friends he would welcome being assassinated. The following spring Wilson was introduced to a widow. He liked her so much at first sight that he invited her to stay for tea at the White House. He married his new friend, Edith, before the end of the year.

Wilson, who had suffered for years from minor strokes, had a major stroke in October 1919, which ended his campaign to win congressional support for the League of Nations. Edith took charge of her husband's recovery. She kept details of her husband's health a secret, overruled the idea that he should resign, and controlled what official business could be brought to his attention. Although her boldness drew criticism then—and still does among historians—it helped Wilson complete his presidency.

Wilson's retirement was relatively brief, and his health remained poor. He died in 1924, six months after the death of his successor, Warren G. Harding. Both Woodrow and Edith Wilson are buried at the Washington National Cathedral. He is the only President buried in the nation's capital.

> "The world must be made safe for democracy."
>
> Woodrow Wilson,
> request that Congress declare war
> on Germany, April 2, 1917

PRESIDENTS AT WAR
SERVING AS THE COMMANDER IN CHIEF

The role of Commander in Chief for the nation's armed forces takes on added weight for Presidents during wartime. Two of the country's earliest Presidents took this duty literally. During the Whiskey Rebellion of 1794, George Washington rode at the head of more than 10,000 soldiers to silence protests over a new federal tax on liquor. Likewise, when the British threatened the nation's capital near the end of the War of 1812, James Madison actually took command of scattered troops in an attempted defense.

Since then many wartime Presidents have visited troops near combat zones, even at the risk of being in harm's way. Most

George Washington led federal troops during the Whiskey Rebellion of 1794.

participate in debates about military strategy, too. All Presidents at least direct the nature of the fight by choosing military commanders. They often play a role in shaping the peacetime that follows war, too.

Ironically, some of the nation's most prominent wartime leaders had no personal combat experience themselves. Woodrow Wilson and Franklin D. Roosevelt, for example, grew up during peacetime. In all, 13 U.S. Presidents never served in the military. Others include John Adams and John Quincy Adams (who were foreign diplomats instead of soldiers during the Revolutionary War), Grover Cleveland (who paid someone else to take his place during the Civil War, a legal option at the time), and Bill Clinton (who pursued his education, not military service, during the Vietnam War). Even Abraham Lincoln, one of the most important Commanders in Chief, had served in the military for just a few months during a frontier Indian war.

Woodrow Wilson (above, at far right) worked with leaders from France, Great Britain, and Italy to draft the peace treaty that ended World War I.

During the Civil War of the 1860s, Abraham Lincoln began the practice of visiting battlefront troops.

Nonetheless, wartime service is often seen as a measure of fitness for presidential candidates. Those with little or no experience may be criticized, particularly if it appears that service was deliberately avoided. Those with more experience are often more favorably received. A number of Presidents have gained election, in part at least, because of famous military performances. They include George Washington, Andrew Jackson, Ulysses S. Grant, Theodore Roosevelt, and Dwight D. Eisenhower. Ironically, most of these leaders presided over periods of national peace after they were elected.

Presidential popularity tends to rise during times of national crisis. Approval ratings soared for Franklin D. Roosevelt after the bombing of Pearl Harbor, for Jimmy Carter during the early months of the Iran hostage crisis, and for George W. Bush following the 2001 terrorist attacks on U.S. soil. Such popularity inevitably falls if conflicts remain unresolved or if presidential leadership becomes questioned.

If presidential elections occur during times of war, voters often choose to "stay the course" instead of changing leaders. Such was the case for Franklin D. Roosevelt; he was reelected twice during World War II. George W. Bush also returned to the White House in 2004 with the help of wartime support. On the other hand, if a wartime leader is perceived to be failing as Commander in Chief, that issue alone can end a presidency. For example, the unpopularity of the Vietnam War forced Lyndon B. Johnson to cancel his 1968 reelection bid.

Wartime Presidents often choose to reduce constitutional freedoms in the name of national defense. At the outset of the Civil War, for example, Abraham Lincoln jailed potential traitors and restricted freedom of speech. During World War II, Franklin D. Roosevelt authorized the detention in restricted camps of 120,000 Japanese Americans, most of whom were U.S. citizens. Concerns over terrorist threats prompted George W. Bush to permit greater surveillance of U.S. residents. Not all Presidents have chosen this tack, however. James Madison insisted during the War of 1812 that civil liberties like free speech remain unchecked in order to demonstrate the nation's commitment to liberty.

Eleanor Roosevelt often visited World War II troops on behalf of her husband, FDR.

Vietnam antiwar protests affected the popularity of two U.S. Presidents, Lyndon B. Johnson and Richard Nixon.

Barack Obama visited troops overseas during wars in Iraq and Afghanistan (right, greeting soldiers in 2012).

WARREN G. HARDING
29TH PRESIDENT OF THE UNITED STATES **1921–1923**

When he was a young man, Warren Gamaliel Harding's friends thought he "looked like a President." Harding's presidential profile helped carry him to the White House, but it did not prepare him for the challenges of the job. Harding became the sixth President to die in office when his health failed him at midterm. His death came just as major scandals about his administration were coming to light.

Harding was born in Ohio. After graduating from Ohio Central College in Iberia, he became a newspaper publisher in the nearby town of Marion. He went on to serve in the state legislature, as lieutenant governor of Ohio, and as a U.S. senator during his climb to prominence in the Republican Party. His habit of changing his mind earned him the nickname "Wobbly Warren." Harding's nomination to the party ticket of 1920 followed much behind-the-scenes, late-night dealmaking by party leaders, many of whom were heavy smokers. This strategy became known as the "smoke-filled room" approach to politics.

Harding was elected President with the greatest landslide in a century. He earned 60 percent of the popular vote in the first election in which women were able to vote nationwide. The complex responsibilities of being President began to trouble Harding midway into his term. So did hints of illegal behavior within his administration. In early 1923 an important Harding appointee fled the country because of criminal activity on the job. One of the man's co-workers committed suicide soon afterward. Then the private

Warren G. Harding embraced new technology (above, with an early recording device). He was the first Chief Executive to travel by car to his Inauguration.

secretary of Harding's scandal-plagued attorney general killed himself over a different scheme. Speculation over these events was interrupted when Harding, his health already weakened, began a cross-country trip to visit the U.S. territory of Alaska. He died suddenly during the trip while staying in San Francisco.

Warren G. Harding's presidency is consistently ranked among the worst in U.S. history because of its widespread corruption. Most notably, apparently without Harding's knowledge, his secretary of the interior had been bribed to grant oil-drilling rights on Wyoming's Teapot Dome and other federal lands, a wrongdoing dubbed the Teapot Dome affair. Recent genetic testing validates another rumored scandal: Harding fathered a child born to Nan Britton out of wedlock in 1919.

NICKNAME
Wobbly Warren

BORN
Nov. 2, 1865, in Caledonia (now Blooming Grove), OH

POLITICAL PARTY
Republican

CHIEF OPPONENT
James Middleton Cox, Democrat (1870–1957)

TERM OF OFFICE
March 4, 1921–Aug. 2, 1923

AGE AT INAUGURATION
55 years old

NUMBER OF TERMS
one (cut short by death)

VICE PRESIDENT
Calvin Coolidge (1872–1933)

FIRST LADY
Florence Kling De Wolfe Harding (1860–1924), wife (married July 8, 1891)

CHILDREN
Born to Nan Britton: Elizabeth Ann Blaesing

GEOGRAPHIC SCENE
48 states

NEW STATES ADDED
none

DIED
Aug. 2, 1923, in San Francisco, CA

AGE AT DEATH
57 years old

SELECTED LANDMARKS
Harding Home and Museum and Harding Memorial (grave), Marion, OH

CALVIN COOLIDGE
30TH PRESIDENT OF THE UNITED STATES 1923–1929

Calvin Coolidge's high standard of conduct restored trust in the presidency following the sudden death of his predecessor, Warren G. Harding. Coolidge was a calm, frugal presence in the White House during the extravagance and waste of the Roaring Twenties.

The plain style of Coolidge's presidency had its roots in his simple New England childhood. His favorite chore, as a redheaded youth in rural Vermont, was making maple syrup. He went on to graduate from Amherst College, become a lawyer, and hold more than a dozen elected posts—including governor of Massachusetts—before rising from Vice President to President in 1923.

Coolidge cooperated with investigations into the Harding scandals. He removed corrupt staff members, and he chose reliable replacements for their posts. He followed a simple strategy: "When things are going along all right, it is a good plan to let them alone." This notion inspired the slogan "Keep Cool With Coolidge" during his successful election campaign in 1924.

Vermont-born Calvin Coolidge never lost his fondness for making maple syrup.

Coolidge was nicknamed "Red" (for his red hair), "Cal" (short for Calvin), and "Silent Cal" (because he spoke little). His habit of expressing himself with few words was famous. Once a dinner guest told Coolidge she had bet she could get three words of conversation out of him. All he replied was: "You lose." He advised his successor, Herbert Hoover, on how to handle talkative visitors: "If you keep dead still, they will run down in three or four minutes."

Coolidge retired to Massachusetts in 1929. He wrote, served as a trustee for the National Geographic Society, and worked in the insurance industry before his death in 1933. Frugal with words to the end, Silent Cal left behind a will to his estate that was only 23 words long.

NICKNAME
Silent Cal

BORN
July 4, 1872, in Plymouth, VT

POLITICAL PARTY
Republican

CHIEF OPPONENTS
1st term: none, succeeded Harding; 2nd term: John W. Davis, Democrat (1873–1955), and Robert M. La Follette, Progressive (1855–1925)

TERM OF OFFICE
Aug. 3, 1923–March 3, 1929

AGE AT INAUGURATION
51 years old

NUMBER OF TERMS
one, plus balance of Warren G. Harding's term

VICE PRESIDENT
1st term: none; 2nd term: Charles Gates Dawes (1865–1951)

FIRST LADY
Grace Anna Goodhue Coolidge (1879–1957), wife (married Oct. 4, 1905)

CHILDREN
John, Calvin

GEOGRAPHIC SCENE
48 states

NEW STATES ADDED
none

DIED
Jan. 5, 1933, in Northampton, MA

AGE AT DEATH
60 years old

SELECTED LANDMARKS
Plymouth, VT (birthplace, homestead); Northampton, MA (library, homestead); Plymouth Notch Cemetery, Plymouth, VT

Calvin Coolidge was the last President who met with everyone who visited the White House to see its chief resident. Several hundred people often called each day. He prided himself on his speed at working through a crowd. Once, he shook hands with 1,900 visitors in only 34 minutes.

YOU'VE GOT MAIL
SWAPPING LETTERS WITH THE PRESIDENT

Ever since John Adams moved into the White House, ordinary citizens have addressed letters to the President at the Executive Mansion and waited for a reply. Whereas early correspondents wrote with quill pens and trusted the delivery of their letters to horse power, presidential communication can now take place via email or be transported by jet plane. Regardless of format and delivery, individuals continue to write to the President—and anticipate a response.

The subjects of letters may change through the years, but the motivations that inspire them remain remarkably consistent. People may write to the President to express their opinions. They may complain, ask questions, or offer help. Some correspondents request favors. Others send words of praise, thanks, or advice.

In 1860 an 11-year-old girl wrote presidential candidate Abraham Lincoln and suggested that his chances of winning the election would improve if he grew a beard. Lincoln waited until after his election victory, but then he grew his signature whiskers. As a result, he became the nation's first bearded President.

Nearly a century later, long after presidential facial hair had gone out of fashion, Harry S. Truman reached the White House. A dip into his presidential mailbox illustrates the range of correspondence he received. For example, in 1948 a 13-year-old boy from Florida wrote with an offer to

At the age of 11, Grace Bedell of New York State wrote presidential candidate Abraham Lincoln (letter shown below) and suggested his chances of winning the 1860 election would improve if he grew a beard. Facial hair had become popular, and she observed that "you would look a great deal better for your face is so thin." The future President replied promptly but suggested that people might judge him negatively if he suddenly grew a beard. By the time he took office, though, Lincoln had shed his clean-shaven look (below, left, in 1860) for a bearded one (below, right, two years after taking office).

Sometimes Presidents meet their correspondents. Diego Diaz shared a letter—and a fist bump—with Barack Obama during a wished-for visit in 2011.

adopt a puppy the President had unexpectedly received. "If you don't keep him I sure would take good care of him," wrote Rusty Gilliland.

In contrast, citizens grew frustrated with Truman when a 1950 coal strike created a lack of coal fuel for home heating. They blamed the President for talking instead of acting to end the work stoppage. One wrote: "We are out of coal. Send some of your hot air out here." This correspondent, like many others, enclosed a bag of coal cinders, or ashes, with the letter.

The volume of mail sent to the White House has grown with the size and complexity of the country. By the 21st century, what was once a simple job for the President and his secretary had become a task undertaken by dozens of staffers and hundreds of volunteers. These workers process tens of thousands of emails every day plus thousands of pages of paper correspondence. Incoming mail goes through security screenings, too, to make sure no one is trying to sneak dangerous items or chemicals into the White House.

Most letters never actually reach the President today. There are just too many of them for one person to review. Even so, workers count and analyze the communication so that a President will have a sense of the public's opinions.

Mail still reaches the White House the old-fashioned way—by the sackful—but electronic methods work, too.

Workers answer all mail that merits a reply. These answers may be identical when addressing similar concerns or may be customized to match the specific content of the sender's message. Individual letters may appear to have been signed personally by the President but are actually signed by a machine that mimics the President's penmanship.

Each President chooses how to be kept informed about the mail received. Barack Obama, for example, decided early in his presidency that he wanted to personally read 10 letters every workday that, taken together, reflected the range of concerns addressed to his attention. His commitment to read—and in many cases respond with a handwritten reply—soon became a tradition of his presidency. Other Presidents follow similar patterns. Each Chief Executive chooses a specific color of paper for personal correspondence; no one else in the White House can use the same paper.

Anyone can email the President of the United States through the White House website: whitehouse.gov/contact. Or, just as citizens young and old have done for generations, anyone can put a postage stamp on an envelope and address it to: President of the United States, The White House, 1600 Pennsylvania Avenue NW, Washington, DC 20500.

HERBERT HOOVER
31ST PRESIDENT OF THE UNITED STATES 1929–1933

When the stock market crashed in October 1929 only a few months after Herbert Clark Hoover had taken office, the President found himself responsible for a different nation from the one he had planned to lead. The Great Depression that followed proved unstoppable and cost him the opportunity for a second term.

Hoover was a successful businessman, scientist, and public servant before becoming President. Born in Iowa and orphaned at age nine, he majored in geology at Stanford University. Hoover then began traveling the globe for the mining industry. While living in London, he received his first public service assignment—evacuating 120,000 Americans from Europe at the start of World War I. Later he helped direct relief efforts for European victims of the war. He went on to serve as secretary of commerce for Warren G. Harding and Calvin Coolidge.

Hoover carried 40 of the 48 states in the 1928 election. Although he had questioned some of the financial policies that led to the stock market crash of 1929, no one anticipated how serious the Great Depression that followed it would become. No economic collapse before or since has been so far-reaching, long lasting, or severe. A desperate public blamed Hoover for their troubles and, in 1932, voted in large numbers for the Democratic candidate, Franklin D. Roosevelt.

Herbert Hoover directed European relief efforts before and after his presidency (above, in Poland, 1946). During World War I, Finnish citizens used "hoover" as a new verb meaning "to help."

Two U.S. Presidents called Hoover back from retirement to perform national service. He organized post–World War II food relief in Europe for Harry S. Truman, and he evaluated government efficiency for Truman and again for Dwight D. Eisenhower. Hoover died in 1964 at age 90, 31 years after leaving office. In 2012 Jimmy Carter broke this record for the longest presidential retirement.

NICKNAME
Chief

BORN
Aug. 10, 1874, in West Branch, IA

POLITICAL PARTY
Republican

CHIEF OPPONENT
Alfred Emanuel Smith, Democrat (1873–1944)

TERM OF OFFICE
March 4, 1929–March 3, 1933

AGE AT INAUGURATION
54 years old

NUMBER OF TERMS
one

VICE PRESIDENT
Charles Curtis (1860–1936)

FIRST LADY
Lou Henry Hoover (1874–1944), wife (married Feb. 10, 1899)

CHILDREN
Herbert, Allan

GEOGRAPHIC SCENE
48 states

NEW STATES ADDED
none

DIED
Oct. 20, 1964, in New York, NY

AGE AT DEATH
90 years old

SELECTED LANDMARKS
Newberg, OR (boyhood home); Hoover Institution, Stanford University, Palo Alto, CA; Herbert Hoover National Historic Site (including birthplace, presidential library, museum, and grave), West Branch, IA

DAILY NEWS FINAL EDITION
NEW YORK'S PICTURE NEWSPAPER

WALL ST. CRASH

Herbert Hoover became a multimillionaire during his years as a geologist. He refused to be paid for his public service. Hoover acted more aggressively than any previous President to end hard times after the stock market crashed in 1929. Despite his efforts, suffering continued to spread.

SEEKING STABILITY IN THE ATOMIC AGE

1933–1981

The challenges faced by Presidents increased in complexity as the 20th century progressed. Leaders struggled to fight wars, end poverty, preserve democracy, extend equality, survive energy shortages, and heal national wounds. They led citizens through the tragedies of presidential deaths and scandals, too. Much of the era was dominated by the uneasy balance of power between the rivals of the atomic age—the United States and the Soviet Union. Presidents sought to offset the troubles of the times with hopes for a promising future.

1933
Germany revoked the citizenship of physicist Albert Einstein during his 1933 visit to the United States. Among the ideas proposed by this scientific genius was the concept of an atomic bomb.

1945
Japan, the final nation to surrender after World War II, formally acknowledged its defeat aboard the U.S.S. *Missouri* on September 2. U.S. general Douglas MacArthur (above) presided.

1946
The first programmable electronic computer weighed 30 tons and used some 18,000 bulky vacuum tubes to transfer information. By 1952 computers were calculating election results.

1957
Racial tensions mounted in Little Rock, Arkansas, after the governor ignored the 1954 Supreme Court ruling on the integration of public schools, *Brown* v. *Board of Education*.

destroyed Nagasaki, Japan, another atomic bomb. Nuclear weapons have never again been used in combat.

1967
Widespread protest of U.S. involvement in the Vietnam War developed during the late 1960s, particularly among young people (above, a protester fills gun barrels with flowers).

1969
On July 20, humans set foot on the moon for the first time. A series of six Apollo lunar missions carried 12 U.S. astronauts to the moon between 1969 and 1972.

1970s
After the first successful human heart transplant in 1967, scientists worked to perfect the procedure during the 1970s. Medical advances in the 1980s extended the survival rate of patients.

1976
U.S. citizens celebrated the 200th anniversary of the nation's Declaration of Independence with ceremonies, parades, and fireworks.

FRANKLIN D. ROOSEVELT
32ND PRESIDENT OF THE UNITED STATES 1933–1945

Not since the days of Abraham Lincoln did a President face such challenges as those met by Franklin Delano Roosevelt. During what became the longest presidency in U.S. history, Roosevelt led the nation out of the Great Depression and saw it safely through the darkest days of World War II. His wife, Eleanor, was an equal partner in his political career.

Franklin D. Roosevelt was the second member of his extended family to become President of the United States. His path to the White House included many of the same political and personal steps taken decades earlier by Theodore Roosevelt, a fifth cousin. Franklin was born at his family's estate in Hyde Park, New York. He called this spot home for most of his life. Roosevelt was his parents' only child. His mother and father took seven weeks to agree upon his name. As was the custom of the era, Roosevelt was clothed in dresses and kilts until age eight. His parents took him on extended trips abroad and had him tutored at home until his teen years.

After graduating from Harvard University in 1904, Roosevelt attended Columbia Law School. He passed the bar exam and took up the practice of law. By then he had

Franklin D. Roosevelt was the only person to serve three full terms as U.S. President and be elected to a fourth. He was encouraged during his childhood to pursue public service as an adult.

FDR began courting his distant cousin Eleanor Roosevelt while he was a student at Harvard University.

already married a distant relative, Anna Eleanor Roosevelt, known as Eleanor. The cousins had met for the first time in 1902, the year Eleanor turned 18 and Franklin was 20. At their wedding in 1905 the bride was given away by President Theodore Roosevelt, her uncle.

In 1910 Franklin D. Roosevelt joined the New York Senate. A few years later, Woodrow Wilson named him assistant secretary of the Navy. He ran unsuccessfully for the U.S. Senate in 1914 and left the Navy in 1920 to campaign as the running mate of the Democratic presidential nominee, James M. Cox. Illness sidelined his political career in 1921 when he was stricken suddenly with polio. Roosevelt went from being active and robust one day to being

NICKNAME
FDR

BORN
Jan. 30, 1882, in Hyde Park, NY

POLITICAL PARTY
Democrat

CHIEF OPPONENTS
1st term: President Herbert Hoover, Republican (1874–1964); 2nd term: Alfred Mossman Landon, Republican (1887–1987); 3rd term: Wendell Lewis Willkie, Republican (1892–1944); 4th term: Thomas Edmund Dewey, Republican (1902–1971)

TERM OF OFFICE
March 4, 1933–April 12, 1945

AGE AT INAUGURATION
51 years old

NUMBER OF TERMS
four (cut short by death)

VICE PRESIDENTS
1st & 2nd terms: John Nance Garner (1868–1967); 3rd term: Henry Agard Wallace (1888–1965); 4th term: Harry S. Truman (1884–1972)

FIRST LADY
Anna Eleanor Roosevelt Roosevelt (1884–1962), wife (married March 17, 1905)

CHILDREN
Anna, James, Elliott, Franklin, John, plus a son who died young

GEOGRAPHIC SCENE
48 states

NEW STATES ADDED
none

DIED
April 12, 1945, in Warm Springs, GA

AGE AT DEATH
63 years old

SELECTED LANDMARKS
Franklin D. Roosevelt National Historic Site (includes house that was birthplace, childhood, and adult home; presidential library; museum; grave), Hyde Park, NY; Little White House State Historic Site, Warm Springs, GA; FDR Memorial, Washington, DC

ABOLISH BREAD LINES VOTE FOR ROOSEVELT

Franklin D. Roosevelt had the longest presidency in U.S. history. He took office in 1933 after promising to end the Great Depression. When challenges continued at home and started abroad with World War II, voters were reluctant to switch leaders. He died in office in 1945. The 22nd Amendment, which became law in 1951, prohibits anyone from serving more than two terms as President. It was written by lawmakers who were uncomfortable with Roosevelt's extended term of office.

Join the march... to OLD AGE SECURITY

INFORMATION MAY BE OBTAINED AT ANY POST OFFICE

"While it isn't written in the Constitution, nevertheless it is the inherent duty of the federal government to keep its citizens from starvation," Roosevelt observed. As President he enacted sweeping legislation, including the Social Security Act of 1935 (being signed at right).

unable to walk two days later. Eleanor encouraged her husband to fight for his recovery. Although he never regained active use of his legs, Roosevelt learned how to stand on leg braces and take limited steps with the assistance of others. Within three years he was practicing law again. Before the decade was out, he had become governor of New York.

When Roosevelt ran for President in 1932, the nation was staggering under the burden of the Great Depression—the greatest economic crisis in its history. One-fourth of all workers were unemployed. Countless families had gone broke because of bank failures. More than a million homeless hoboes sought food and work as they roamed the country. Displaced families tacked together

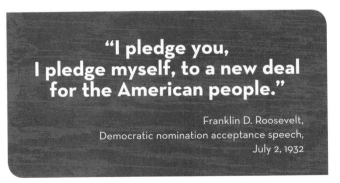

"I pledge you, I pledge myself, to a new deal for the American people."

Franklin D. Roosevelt, Democratic nomination acceptance speech, July 2, 1932

shacks in temporary settlements they nicknamed Hoovervilles—after President Herbert Hoover.

The grim national scene prompted voters to flock to Roosevelt and his promise of a "new deal for the American people." He earned 57 percent of the popular vote and won the electoral votes of all but six states. In the three presidential elections that followed, Roosevelt continued his streak of majority victories, earning 61 percent, 55 percent, then 53 percent of the vote.

As President, Roosevelt took charge of ending the Depression. Where Hoover had hesitated to interfere, Roosevelt plunged in. The beginning of his presidency was famous for its rush of legislation and was later

In 1943 the "Big Three" Allied leaders met in Tehran, Iran, for a wartime strategy session. Distrust ran high with Soviet Union leader Joseph Stalin (above, left). Roosevelt (above, center) won his cooperation in part by poking fun at fellow ally Winston Churchill, Prime Minister of Great Britain (above, right). He joked about the British, Churchill's cigars, even his moods. Soon the stern-faced Stalin was laughing along as Roosevelt teased the dictator and called him "Uncle Joe." Stalin betrayed the alliance by war's end.

Roosevelt used radio to connect with the American people in the days before television came into widespread use. His series of "fireside chats" (above), delivered in his reassuring voice, inspired the nation to face the day's challenges. He even used radio to build ties with French citizens. In 1942 he addressed them in their own language to announce the U.S. invasion of occupied French territories in North Africa. Roosevelt became the first President to appear on television with a 1939 broadcast from the New York World's Fair.

referred to as Roosevelt's Hundred Days. During this period, he signed 14 bills in all. Among other things, these new laws restored confidence in the banking industry, employed young men through a Civilian Conservation Corps, launched the construction of dams and power plants in the Tennessee River Valley, aided farmers, established loan programs, and improved working conditions. Later, Roosevelt established the Securities and Exchange Commission to help prevent future financial panics in the stock market. He also signed the Social Security Act of 1935, which established a series of cornerstone programs for public welfare that, among other benefits, ensured retirement incomes for senior citizens and temporary financial support for the unemployed. Many of these New Deal programs endure as essential elements of the American way of life.

In 1932 voters had been asked to "Kick Out Depression With a Democratic Vote." Four years later they agreed overwhelmingly to "Follow Through With Roosevelt." In

> ### "The only thing we have to fear is fear itself."
>
> Franklin D. Roosevelt,
> Inaugural Address,
> March 4, 1933

1940 they supported Roosevelt's third presidential campaign because he pledged that unless the U.S. was attacked, he would stay out of the war that was spreading around the globe. The next year Japan bombed U.S. naval bases at Pearl Harbor, Hawaii. Roosevelt predicted that the date, December 7, would "live in infamy," and he asked Congress to declare war on Japan. Declarations against Germany and Italy followed. For the rest of his life, the world would be at war.

Roosevelt took seriously his role as Commander in Chief during World War II. He plotted military strategy, appointed key field commanders, and authorized the secret development of the atomic bomb. He formed partnerships with Winston Churchill from Great Britain and, later, with Joseph Stalin of the Soviet Union. The "Big Three" discussed strategies for war and peace, including Roosevelt's idea for starting the United Nations. In 1944, with war raging full tilt, Roosevelt agreed to serve for a fourth term as President.

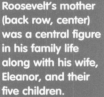

Roosevelt's mother (back row, center) was a central figure in his family life along with his wife, Eleanor, and their five children.

After her husband's death, Eleanor became known as the First Lady of the World for her work with the United Nations. She was part of the first U.S. delegation to that body, chaired its Commission on Human Rights, and helped write its International Declaration of Human Rights. She was the first President's wife to fly abroad.

Voters decided not to "change horses in midstream" and returned him to the White House once more.

During the early years of her husband's presidency, Eleanor Roosevelt tried to broaden the reach of the New Deal to African Americans, working women, children, labor unions, and immigrants. She wrote a daily national newspaper column and met weekly with women reporters. When war took center stage, she shifted her focus to it. Eleanor toured factories, launched battleships, and visited troops around the world. She represented her husband beyond the nation's capital, while he concentrated on military strategy.

In the spring of 1945 President Roosevelt made a visit to the "Little White House," his retreat at Warm Springs, Georgia. Twelve years had passed since his first Inauguration, and it was almost three months since his fourth. (Beginning in 1937, Presidents were inaugurated

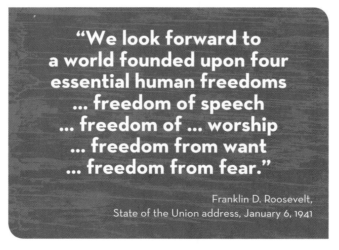

"We look forward to a world founded upon four essential human freedoms ... freedom of speech ... freedom of ... worship ... freedom from want ... freedom from fear."

Franklin D. Roosevelt, State of the Union address, January 6, 1941

on January 20 instead of March 4.) Other commitments kept Eleanor from making the trip, but among those joining the President was Lucy Page Mercer Rutherford. More than 30 years earlier, while she served as Eleanor's secretary, Lucy had fallen in love with Franklin. Although Franklin ended their affair after it was discovered by his wife, he and Lucy secretly renewed their friendship later on. During their visit to Georgia, Roosevelt suddenly fell ill while being sketched for a portrait. He reached for his head and observed: "I have a terrific headache." He was having a stroke. Roosevelt never spoke again and died within hours.

The nation was plunged into grief. Roosevelt was the only President whom many people had ever known, and he had helped them survive some of the country's toughest challenges. Roosevelt's combination as "Dr. New Deal" and "Dr. Win the War" had cured the Great Depression. Within months of his death, World War II would end, too. His pattern of federal involvement in national issues became the norm

U.S. soldiers fought battles around the globe after the United States joined the fighting of World War II in 1941. U.S. servicemen were part of the Allied forces who stormed the coast of Normandy, France, on D-Day, June 6, 1944 (above), in their march to free Europe from German control.

This musician wept as he played at Roosevelt's memorial service. Some of Roosevelt's wartime policies—such as the fear-based detention of 120,000 Japanese Americans, most of whom were U.S. citizens—have been discredited as mistakes, but he remains one of the nation's most acclaimed Presidents overall.

Conquest of Pacific islands, including Japan's Iwo Jima in early 1945, helped turn the tide of battle in the Pacific. Later this battle was recalled in the U.S. Marine Corps War Memorial (above).

for future leaders. In 1997 Roosevelt became the fourth President ever—and the only 20th-century one—to be recognized with a national monument in Washington, D.C. Eleanor Roosevelt is commemorated at the structure, too. Other memorials honor George Washington, Thomas Jefferson, and Abraham Lincoln.

THE FIRST LADIES
PARTNERS, HOSTESSES, AND ADVOCATES

The tradition of male Presidents being supported in their work by female partners is a custom that will invite reinvention when a woman becomes Chief Executive of the nation. New patterns will replace past practices when this collaborator is no longer a wife but a husband and the First Gentleman. In some administrations—either because of poor health or lack of interest or death—a President's spouse has been unable to play this role. In such cases, the President's grown child, another relative, or a family friend is asked to step in.

Early on, these presidential partners were addressed with titles such as "Lady," or "Mrs. President." The term "First Lady" became popular by the early 20th century; it

Edith Wilson stepped in to deal with administrative details in 1919 after a stroke left her husband partially paralyzed. Critics charged that she had become too involved in presidential matters, but her work helped her husband complete his term.

A variety of roles have occupied First Ladies during their partnerships with U.S. Presidents. Louisa Adams kept her husband, John Quincy Adams, company in 1828 by winding silk from her own silkworms while he worked nearby.

recalled a role for women in the home that was seen as first in importance to the nation.

For more than 100 years the chief duty of the First Lady was to serve as hostess at White House events. However, many of these women, such as Dolley Madison, were more than gracious entertainers; they were shrewd students of politics, too. They knew just how to soothe upset guests and encourage support of their husbands.

Entertaining was the focus for First Lady Martha Washington.

Early First Ladies came to the White House with the same background in domestic life as other women of their day. Until the mid-19th century, few had even attended school. Abigail Fillmore was the first President's wife to have held a job of her own (as a schoolteacher).

Eleanor Roosevelt expanded the role of the President's wife during her 12 years as First Lady. Because her husband's mobility was limited by polio, she traveled and spoke extensively on his behalf. She pursued her own interests, too—from civil rights to family welfare to benefits for laborers.

In recent decades, each First Lady has focused national attention on issues that might otherwise have been

Lucretia Garfield helping in the kitchen, 1881

Hillary Clinton proved that First Ladies could hold elected office by becoming a U.S. senator in 2000. Twice she ran for President (below, her 2016 bid). She is the first woman ever nominated for that office by a major party.

neglected. Jacqueline Kennedy restored historical spaces inside the White House, while her successor, Lady Bird Johnson, worked to beautify the exterior settings for landmarks in the nation's capital. Barbara Bush and her daughter-in-law Laura Bush each promoted the cause of literacy. First Ladies have frequently worked to improve public health and civic involvement, everything from increased volunteerism (Pat Nixon) to better care for hand-icapped children (Betty Ford) and the mentally ill (Rosalynn Carter) to avoidance of illegal drugs (Nancy Reagan) to streamlined delivery of health care (Hillary Clinton) and improved childhood nutrition (Michelle Obama).

Jacqueline Kennedy, who revived interest in White House history, poses in the newly restored residence.

Laura Bush stands shoulder to shoulder with members of the armed services in a show of wartime support.

Fitness advocate Michelle Obama leads hundreds of children in jumping jacks on the way to setting a new Guinness world record.

Eleanor Roosevelt visits with mine workers.

151

HARRY S. TRUMAN
33RD PRESIDENT OF THE UNITED STATES 1945–1953

When Harry S. Truman became President after the sudden death of Franklin D. Roosevelt, he was stunned. "I felt like the moon, the stars, and all the planets had fallen on me," he said. Issues such as the use of atomic weapons, tensions with the Soviet Union, and war in Korea dominated his administration.

Truman was no stranger to challenge when he became President. He grew up on a farm in Missouri, and tight family finances made him the only 20th-century President who did not attend college, although he later went to law school. Truman's meandering career included work as a railroad timekeeper, a farmer, a World War I artillery captain, and a clothing store owner. He entered politics in 1922 as a local administrator; eventually he spent 10 years in the U.S. Senate.

Harry S. Truman's whistle-stop campaign of 1948

In 1944 President Franklin D. Roosevelt persuaded Senator Truman to join his fourth-term reelection ticket.

Only months after becoming Vice President, Truman found himself taking the presidential oath of office because President Roosevelt had died. Soon after that, World War II ended in Europe. Truman decided to use a secret weapon—the atomic bomb—to stop the intense fighting that continued with Japan. He hoped this plan would spare the lives of U.S. troops by ending the war quickly and avoiding the need to invade Japan. More than 200,000 Japanese died instantly in

Truman married Elizabeth "Bess" Wallace when he was 35; the couple met in Sunday school when he was six. Truman's middle initial did not stand for a middle name; his parents used the letter to honor their own fathers, each of whom had a name that started with S.

NICKNAME
Give 'Em Hell Harry

BORN
May 8, 1884, in Lamar, MO

POLITICAL PARTY
Democrat

CHIEF OPPONENT
1st term: none, succeeded Roosevelt; 2nd term: Thomas Edmund Dewey, Republican (1902–1971)

TERM OF OFFICE
April 12, 1945–Jan. 20, 1953

AGE AT INAUGURATION
60 years old

NUMBER OF TERMS
one, plus balance of Franklin D. Roosevelt's term

VICE PRESIDENT
1st term: none; 2nd term: Alben William Barkley (1877–1956)

FIRST LADY
Elizabeth (Bess) Virginia Wallace Truman (1885–1982), wife (married June 29, 1919)

CHILDREN
Margaret

GEOGRAPHIC SCENE
48 states

NEW STATES ADDED
none

DIED
Dec. 26, 1972, in Independence, MO

AGE AT DEATH
88 years old

SELECTED LANDMARKS
Lamar, MO (birthplace); Grandview, MO (family farm); Key West Little White House Museum, Key West, FL; Harry S. Truman National Historic Site (adult home) and Harry S. Truman Library and Museum (and grave), Independence, MO

nuclear attacks at Hiroshima and Nagasaki before Japan surrendered. Worldwide casualties by the end of the war topped 10 million people, including more than 400,000 Americans.

International events dominated Truman's presidency. He supported the creation of the United Nations and favored the formation of Israel. He used the Marshall Plan to rebuild war-torn Europe and helped

Harry S. Truman took delight in an election-eve headline that mistakenly announced the victory of his opponent in 1948. His whistle-stop campaign effort helped clinch his victory. It took him to six million people during a 31,000-mile train journey. "Give 'em hell, Harry!" yelled supporters when Truman criticized the uncooperative Congress.

form the North Atlantic Treaty Organization (NATO) to fortify the security of Western Europe, the United States, and Canada. In particular, he sought to discourage the expanding influence of the Soviet Union and its political system of communism. Communism—a program of government control over citizens, industries, and finances—was at odds with the U.S. system of democracy, freedom, and market-based capitalism. A Cold War—one with limited fighting but much hostility, mistrust, and stockpiling of nuclear weapons—developed between the United States, the Soviet Union, and their allies.

As tensions grew between the two "blocs" of countries, Truman committed the United States to "support free peoples who are resisting" conquest. When the Soviet Union restricted access to West Berlin, Truman organized a massive airlift of supplies into the city. When war broke out between communist North Korea and independent South Korea in 1950, Truman developed an international army through the United Nations to "contain" the spread of communism. When anticommunist citizens asked for U.S. assistance in Vietnam, Truman sent aid.

A fear of communism at home developed at the same time as these international worries. U.S. senator Joseph McCarthy exploited this anxiety by conducting congressional investigations of suspected communists. Among those who eventually joined his efforts was a future President, Senator

Truman met with Allied leaders in July 1945.

The nation enjoyed a postwar boom during Truman's presidency. Thousands of returning veterans earned free college education through the G.I. Bill of Rights. Couples who had put off marriage during the war were wed in record numbers and started a "baby boom" of soaring births.

Richard Nixon. McCarthy's Red Scare (named after the symbolic communist color) lasted until 1954, when other senators shut down his hearings.

Truman won election in his own right in 1948. As President he tried to extend Roosevelt's New Deal of federal programs with his own 21-point Fair Deal, but most proposals failed to take hold. His efforts to integrate all races in the armed forces met with both favor and controversy.

"The buck stops here."

Motto on Harry S. Truman's desk

Challenged by so many difficult issues, Truman left the White House with the lowest approval rating for a President up to that time. In later years, respect for Truman's handling of tough times increased; since 1962 historians have consistently ranked him among the top 10 Presidents.

Truman and his wife retired to Independence, Missouri. Bess Truman lived to age 97—longer than any other First Lady. She died in 1982, 10 years after her husband.

After World War II, Germany and its capital city of Berlin were divided in half; the Soviet Union assumed control over eastern sections, and the United States, France, and Great Britain oversaw western territories. When the Soviet Union cut off access to West Berlin in June 1948, Western allies delivered necessary supplies to stranded residents (left). Planes landed as often as every few minutes during the Berlin airlift. The Soviet blockade lasted until May 1949.

Harry S. Truman knew nothing about the development of the atomic bomb until after he became President near the end of World War II. As President he followed the war's progress by visiting the White House Map Room (left).

After the war Truman supported the European recovery plan devised by Secretary of State George C. Marshall (far right). The Marshall Plan shared $12 billion over three years with such countries as Great Britain, France, and West Germany. It boosted the American economy and helped create democracies throughout Europe. "Peace, freedom, and world trade are indivisible," noted Truman.

POLLSTERS AND POLLING
SIZING UP PUBLIC OPINION

One of the first recorded public opinion surveys—conducted in 1824 by a newspaper in Pennsylvania—suggested that Andrew Jackson would win the election. He did not. (His strong showing among voters failed to earn him the support he needed in the Electoral College.) Informal measures of public opinion, often called straw polls, continue to this day. So do complex polls conducted by professional researchers, although even these efforts can lead to false predictions.

The scientific research methods used by modern pollsters originated in 1935 through the work of statisticians such as George Gallup and Elmo Roper. They competed in 1936 with *Literary Digest*, a magazine known for its respected polls, to predict whether or not Franklin D. Roosevelt would be reelected for a second term of office. Gallup and Roper each predicted victory for Roosevelt, while *Literary Digest* forecast that Alfred Landon would win. Landon, in fact, lost decisively, establishing Gallup and Roper's reputations as pollsters.

Analysis of the *Literary Digest* poll revealed unintended bias in the magazine's choice of whom to survey. By targeting people listed as owners of cars and telephones, they had inadvertently surveyed individuals who matched the more affluent background of Republican voters. Instead, Gallup and Roper deliberately had interviewed people chosen to represent the mix of the overall population.

Over the years pollsters have worked to improve

the accuracy of their results. They learned to survey a large number of people, often 1,000 or more individuals. They worked to create questions free from unintended pressures on how best to answer them. Pollsters tried to account for people who might give misleading answers, too. Someone who objected to candidates for personal reasons—such as their gender or race—might be reluctant to admit that prejudice to an interviewer, for example. Polling results typically include a margin of error percentage that can be applied to the survey's results.

Even so, pollsters make mistakes. In 1948 they failed to predict the victory of Harry S. Truman over Republican challenger Thomas E. Dewey. Polling firms concluded they had missed late-breaking trends by discontinuing their surveys several weeks before Election Day. More recently, Donald Trump likewise upset the projections of pollsters in 2016 by defeating Democratic rival Hillary Clinton. Flawed data and faulty models for interpreting it contributed to the error.

George Gallup, political pollster

In an effort to make accurate predictions, some organizations conduct daily tracking polls to chart a candidate's level of support over time. Other polls measure voter opinions at specific moments during the campaign season, such as after a presidential debate or major political event. Polling continues even on Election Day with interviews of voters. These so-called exit polls help news organizations predict the outcome of the day's results even as the ballots are still being counted. Only after reviewing the final tallies can pollsters breathe a sigh of relief or—as they did after the 2016 election—determine what went wrong and identify better methods for use during the next election season.

Pollsters use written questionnaires (above, a 1944 Gallup survey), make phone calls, and stop people on the street in their efforts to predict support for presidential candidates. The accuracy of polls is put to the test on Election Day (left, citizens cast their ballots) when these forecasts are measured against the final results.

DWIGHT D. EISENHOWER
34TH PRESIDENT OF THE UNITED STATES 1953–1961

Like Generals George Washington and Ulysses S. Grant, Gen. Dwight David Eisenhower became President thanks to his popularity as a war hero. Eisenhower—the man who helped bring victory to Europe during World War II—sought to keep peace at home and abroad after becoming President. His moderate political views earned the Republican Party new respect.

Although born in Texas, Eisenhower was raised in Abilene, Kansas, where his father worked in a creamery. He learned lessons about war and peace at an early age while growing up there with five brothers. The boys, all of whom took turns using the nickname "Ike," never hesitated to come to blows among themselves or with others when arguments arose. Even as a youngster, Eisenhower enjoyed studying military history. He went on to graduate from the U.S. Military Academy at West Point and take up a

The Eisenhowers on their wedding day

career in the Army. Later that year he met Marie "Mamie" Doud; the couple married soon afterward.

For the next 26 years, Eisenhower's Army duties took him to bases throughout the United States as well as to the Panama Canal Zone and the Philippines. Along the way he finished first in his class at officer training school and did desk duty at war offices in Washington, D.C. Much to his regret he missed out on World War I combat; he was instead assigned to train others to fight.

By the time of World War II, however, Eisenhower's leadership skills and organizational talents earned him key military appointments. He commanded the combined Allied forces that overran enemy

Dwight D. Eisenhower played football at West Point until a knee injury ended his athletic career. His skills as a military leader helped carry him to the White House years later.

NICKNAME
Ike

BORN
Oct. 14, 1890, in Denison, TX

POLITICAL PARTY
Republican

CHIEF OPPONENT
1st and 2nd terms: Adlai Ewing Stevenson, Democrat (1900–1965)

TERM OF OFFICE
Jan. 20, 1953–Jan. 20, 1961

AGE AT INAUGURATION
62 years old

NUMBER OF TERMS
two

VICE PRESIDENT
Richard Nixon (1913–1994)

FIRST LADY
Marie (Mamie) Geneva Doud Eisenhower (1896–1979), wife (married July 1, 1916)

CHILDREN
John, plus a son who died young

GEOGRAPHIC SCENE
48 states

NEW STATES ADDED
Alaska, Hawaii (1959)

DIED
March 28, 1969, in Washington, DC

AGE AT DEATH
78 years old

SELECTED LANDMARKS
Eisenhower Birthplace State Historic Site, Denison, TX; Eisenhower National Historic Site, Gettysburg, PA (retirement home); Eisenhower Center (including presidential library, museum, family home, and grave), Abilene, KS

General Eisenhower served as supreme commander of all Allied forces during the World War II campaigns that liberated North Africa and Europe from German and Italian occupation forces. In June 1944 Eisenhower urged members of the U.S. 101st Airborne Division (left) to accomplish their mission during the impending D-Day invasion of France. Later on, Eisenhower toured so many countries as President—27 in all—that his travels were written up in *National Geographic*.

Republicans reclaimed the White House after a 20-year absence thanks to the popular appeal of party nominee Dwight D. Eisenhower. During his presidency, "Ike" authorized construction of the nation's interstate highway system and collaborated with Canada to create the St. Lawrence Seaway linking the Great Lakes with the Atlantic Ocean. By the end of his administration, citizens could chant: "Ike is nifty, Ike is nifty; started out with 48; ended up with 50," because Alaska and Hawaii had joined the Union.

Broadway songwriter Irving Berlin wrote a catchy tune to popularize Eisenhower's 1952 campaign slogan.

troops in North Africa, Sicily, Italy, and northern Europe. Before the end of the war he had risen to the Army's highest rank—five-star general. One soldier who spotted the rows of stars on Eisenhower's uniform exclaimed: "Cripes! The whole Milky Way!"

After the war Eisenhower served as chief of staff for the Army, president of Columbia University, and commander of international troops in Europe. As early as 1943 people had suggested that

> **"What counts is not necessarily the size of the dog in the fight—it's the size of the fight in the dog."**
>
> Dwight D. Eisenhower, January 31, 1958

Eisenhower run for President with either political party. Happy with Army life, he dismissed the idea.

Finally, in 1952, he agreed to run for President as a Republican. Eisenhower faced the same opponent that year and four years later—Adlai Stevenson. Eisenhower's signature grin, victory wave, and record of wartime service encouraged voters to proclaim: "We like Ike!" They proved it by awarding Eisenhower a sizable majority of votes in each election.

Challenges from the Truman Administration carried over into Eisenhower's presidency. Peace talks finally ended the fighting in Korea in 1953. The conflict had killed or wounded more than three million people, including 34,000 Americans. Relations with the Soviet Union remained tense. Although Eisenhower urged the Soviets to consider nuclear disarmament, or the reduction of atomic weapons, neither

President-elect Eisenhower (far left) visited U.S. troops in Korea during 1952 as part of his efforts to end U.S. military involvement there.

Dwight and Mamie Eisenhower were a popular presidential couple. Mamie acted as a traditional hostess during her years as First Lady. She restored the custom, discontinued during World War II, of holding an annual White House Easter Egg Roll. Eisenhower changed Franklin D. Roosevelt's name for the presidential retreat in Maryland from Shangri-La to Camp David in honor of their grandson.

Senator Joseph McCarthy continued to inflame U.S. fears of communism at home until fellow senators shut down his high-profile congressional hearings (above) in 1954. The domino theory—the idea that communism could spread from one vulnerable country to the next like a row of tumbling dominoes—led the President to develop his Eisenhower Doctrine. This policy fostered increased U.S. assistance for anticommunist efforts in Vietnam during his administration.

side seemed willing to trust the other. In 1957 the Soviets launched the world's first satellite, Sputnik. Americans feared it might be armed with nuclear weapons. Three years later, the Soviets were equally alarmed when they captured a U.S. pilot flying a U-2 spy plane over their country.

Although Eisenhower didn't consider ending segregation in the United States a priority, he took modest steps to advance racial integration. When laws changed, he considered it his constitutional duty to uphold them. The President sent federal troops to Little Rock, Arkansas, to enforce the Supreme Court's *Brown* v. *Board of Education* ruling. This landmark decision called for public schools to be desegregated, or open to children of all races. He also bolstered civil rights by signing new voting laws.

In 1961 Eisenhower and his wife retired to a farm they had purchased in 1950 near Gettysburg, Pennsylvania. Because Eisenhower's career had kept them forever on the go (they moved 28 times during their marriage), this was the first home they ever owned. Although several heart attacks threatened the former President's health, he enjoyed writing his memoirs, playing golf, painting landscapes, and keeping a finger in politics. He died in 1969. Mamie died 10 years later.

When Dwight D. Eisenhower became President, black children and white children in the United States were routinely educated in separate schools. The Supreme Court ruled such segregation illegal in 1954.

JOHN F. KENNEDY
35TH PRESIDENT OF THE UNITED STATES **1961–1963**

John Fitzgerald Kennedy was elected by the narrowest popular voting margin in history and served as President for only about 1,000 days before he was assassinated. Yet he remains a central figure of the American presidency. His eloquent calls for peace, justice, and national service inspired action among countless citizens during his lifetime and continue to influence others today.

After his death, the Kennedy Administration was compared to Camelot, the legendary ancient realm of the fair-minded King Arthur. Kennedy's birth to a privileged family was the perfect place to begin the comparison. His father hoped one of his four sons would become President; eventually three of them campaigned for that office. John (nicknamed Jack, and later JFK) attended prestigious schools and graduated with honors from Harvard University. Although plagued by a string of childhood illnesses, he was athletic, playful, and handsome.

John F. Kennedy (perched on a scooter) with his mother, Rose, and siblings (left to right) Eunice, Kathleen, Rosemary, and Joe, Jr.

A decorated World War II naval officer, Kennedy took up the family's presidential hopes after his older brother, Joseph, died in combat.

NICKNAME
JFK

BORN
May 29, 1917, in Brookline, MA

POLITICAL PARTY
Democrat

CHIEF OPPONENT
Richard Nixon, Republican (1913–1994)

TERM OF OFFICE
Jan. 20, 1961–Nov. 22, 1963

AGE AT INAUGURATION
43 years old

NUMBER OF TERMS
one (cut short by assassination)

VICE PRESIDENT
Lyndon B. Johnson (1908–1973)

FIRST LADY
Jacqueline Lee Bouvier Kennedy (1929–1994), wife (married Sept. 12, 1953)

CHILDREN
Caroline, John, plus a daughter and son who died young

GEOGRAPHIC SCENE
50 states

DIED
Nov. 22, 1963, in Dallas, TX

AGE AT DEATH
46 years old

SELECTED LANDMARKS
Brookline, MA (birthplace); Hammersmith Farm, Newport, RI ("summer White House"); Sixth Floor Museum, Dallas, TX; John F. Kennedy Library and Museum, Boston, MA; Arlington National Cemetery, Arlington, VA

Kennedy (above) became a World War II hero after the patrol torpedo boat (PT-109) under his command was destroyed by a Japanese warship (left). Kennedy swam with the surviving crew members to safety several miles away, towing one injured sailor by clamping the man's life jacket strap in his teeth. When asked later how he became a hero, Kennedy replied: "It was easy—they sank my boat."

Jacqueline Kennedy was an active First Lady while mothering the Kennedys' young children, Caroline and John, Jr. (below, with John F. Kennedy on vacation in Hyannisport, Massachusetts).

Kennedy (above, right, as a U.S. senator in 1957 with his younger brother Robert), brought Bobby into his administration as a close adviser and as his attorney general.

Cold War tensions were reduced shortly before Kennedy's death when the U.S. signed a nuclear test ban treaty with the Soviet Union and the United Kingdom, outlawing atomic explosions in the atmosphere, in space, and underwater.

Military arsenals for the Soviet Union and the United States grew in the 1960s (above, Kennedy reviews the preparedness of U.S. ally West Germany).

Kennedy met Jacqueline Bouvier during his six years as a U.S. congressman from Massachusetts. Jackie was sophisticated, charming, and beautiful. The pair were married in 1953, soon after he became a U.S. senator. Kennedy sought the Democratic presidential nomination in 1960. "We stand today on the edge of a New Frontier," he proclaimed after winning the nomination. Kennedy narrowly defeated Richard Nixon in a tight race. A surge in support among African Americans in key states like Texas and Illinois may have helped seal his victory. Kennedy is the only Catholic to be elected President.

Conflicts in the Cold War dominated much of Kennedy's presidency. First, the U.S. government secretly tried to overthrow Cuba's new communist dictator, Fidel Castro, by helping Cuban exiles invade their homeland at the Bay of Pigs. U.S. involvement proved embarrassing when the mission failed. Then tensions flared when the Soviet Union built a wall dividing East and West Berlin in Germany. Next the two superpowers narrowly avoided nuclear war during the Cuban missile crisis, a tense standoff resulting from the U.S. discovery of Soviet warheads in Cuba. Secretly, Kennedy fought the spread of communism elsewhere by continuing U.S. support of anticommunists in Vietnam. Publicly he urged Americans to win the "space race" against the Soviets by sending astronauts to the moon and back. Cold War tensions eased somewhat in 1963 after the two nations signed a treaty banning most nuclear testing.

JFK visited coal miners as part of his presidential campaign in 1960.

Near the end of the Kennedy Administration, more than 200,000 people took part in a March on Washington for Jobs and Freedom that coincided with the 100th anniversary of Abraham Lincoln's Emancipation Proclamation. Martin Luther King, Jr., delivered his famous "I Have a Dream" speech from the steps of the Lincoln Memorial during the massive gathering.

John F. Kennedy was the youngest man ever elected President. (Teddy Roosevelt was the youngest President by succession, not election.) Kennedy was also the youngest one to die, when an assassin shot him in a motorcade just three years after his election. Jacqueline Kennedy modeled her husband's funeral after Abraham Lincoln's. Kennedy's casket even lay in state at the U.S. Capitol on the same platform that was used for Lincoln.

Civil rights, including the freedom for all citizens regardless of race to vote, was a dominant issue, too. At first Kennedy relied on the Justice Department, headed by his younger brother Robert, to aid this cause. Later the President publicly supported racial equality. Much of the civil rights legislation Kennedy favored became law in tribute to him after his assassination.

Kennedy was shot and killed on November 22, 1963, while touring Dallas, Texas, in a presidential motorcade. More than a hundred nations sent representatives to his funeral in Washington, D.C. Anyone who could find a television "attended" the event, too. All were moved

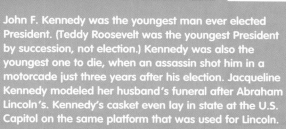

"Ask not what your country can do for you—ask what you can do for your country."

John F. Kennedy, Inaugural Address, January 20, 1961

by the solemn processions, by Jackie's dignity, and by the composure of their children. Hearts broke as three-year-old John-John saluted his father's coffin.

The identity of Kennedy's assassin remains a subject of speculation. Gunman Lee Harvey Oswald was charged with the death but was himself murdered before he could be tried. Repeated investigations have failed to confirm theories that others may have helped Oswald kill the President.

Kennedy's presidency remains highly ranked despite facts that have emerged in the years since (such as the extent of the covert, or secret, support his administration gave to anticommunists in Vietnam, and his extramarital affairs while in office). The President's brother Bobby became a U.S. senator; he was assassinated in 1968 while running for President. His youngest brother, Edward, served five decades as a U.S. senator; he sought his party's nomination for President in 1980. Jackie remarried five years after her husband's death. She died from cancer in her mid-60s and was buried beside her husband at Arlington National Cemetery.

PRESIDENTS WHO DIED IN OFFICE
THE MYSTERIOUS 20-YEAR CURSE

Eight of the nation's Presidents have died before completing their terms of office. Half of these men were victims of illnesses; the others were assassinated. Oddly, seven of these deaths have occurred in a regular pattern. The winner of every fifth election from 1840 to 1960 has died before completing his final term. This circumstance has been called the 20-year jinx or the 20-year curse.

The first President to die in office was William Henry Harrison. He became ill after his Inauguration and died one month later on April 4, 1841. Abraham Lincoln's first term began 20 years after Harrison's. Lincoln died on April 15, 1865, within a week of the end of the Civil War, after being shot by a supporter of the defeated South.

Twenty years after Lincoln's first election, James A. Garfield took office. Garfield was shot on July 2, 1881, by a deranged former political supporter. He died two and a half months later.

President William McKinley was shot 20 years afterward. Early in his second term, a disgruntled factory worker fired on him

in a receiving line. McKinley died eight days later, on Sept. 14, 1901.

The next two sitting Presidents to die five terms apart were victims of natural causes. Warren G. Harding died suddenly on Aug. 2, 1923. Doctors think he may have had a heart attack. Franklin D. Roosevelt was killed by a stroke, a brain injury caused by improper blood flow in the head. He died a few months into his fourth term of office on April 12, 1945.

President Kennedy lies in state, 1963.

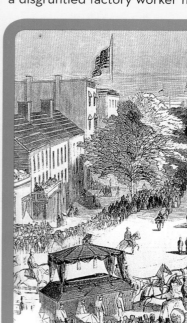

Mourners hung ribbons (far left) in their windows following the assassination of Abraham Lincoln. Future President Theodore Roosevelt, as a child in New York City, was among the countless citizens who viewed Lincoln's coffin when it traveled through key cities (left, Washington, D.C.) on its way to burial in Illinois.

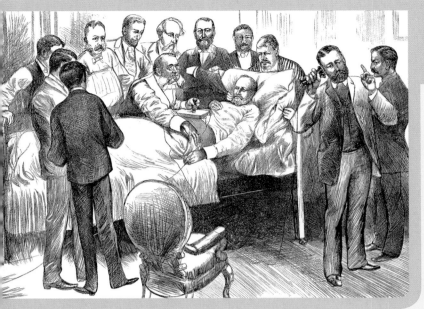

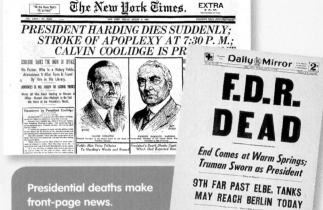

In 1881 Alexander Graham Bell tried to find the bullet lodged in James A. Garfield by an assassin's gun. Bell's early metal detector failed, and Garfield died of blood poisoning.

Presidential deaths make front-page news.

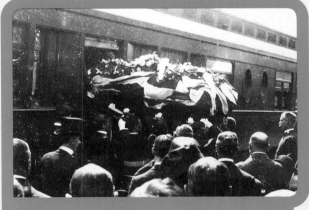

The death of a President brings shock and sorrow to the entire nation, not just to relatives. Mourners bade farewell to William McKinley as his coffin was loaded onto his funeral train.

John F. Kennedy's family observed his funeral procession while millions of citizens watched via live television broadcast.

John F. Kennedy, the last President to die in office, and on a 20-year cycle, was assassinated on November 22, 1963, in Dallas, Texas.

Zachary Taylor was the only President who died in office outside of the 20-year death cycle. He died after a short illness on July 9, 1850.

Ronald Reagan finally broke the 120-year history of cyclical presidential deaths. Even so, his life was threatened by an assassination attempt in 1981. Prompt modern medical attention saved his life.

Other assassination attempts were made against Presidents Andrew Jackson, Harry S. Truman, and Gerald R. Ford. An assassin threatened President-elect Franklin D. Roosevelt, too. No Vice Presidents have been assassinated, but seven have died in office.

Often the bodies of fallen Presidents—even those who die after their terms are over—"lie in state." During this honor, the coffin of the deceased is temporarily displayed on a platform, and visitors file past the casket in tribute. Sometimes the coffin lid is open to show the body inside; other times it is closed and covered with the U.S. flag. Seven Presidents have lain in state in the White House East Room; 10 others have rested in the rotunda of the U.S. Capitol. Ronald Reagan was the first President to receive this honor (in 2004) since the death of Lyndon B. Johnson in 1973.

LYNDON B. JOHNSON
36TH PRESIDENT OF THE UNITED STATES **1963–1969**

Lyndon Baines Johnson channeled energy from the nation's grief over the sudden death of John F. Kennedy into the creation of a living memorial to the slain leader. Johnson called this legacy the Great Society. He envisioned a nation that offered opportunity, prosperity, and fairness to all citizens. His tireless efforts for this cause brought considerable improvement to the lives of racial minorities and the poor. These accomplishments became overshadowed, however, by escalating U.S. involvement in an increasingly controversial war in Vietnam.

"No words are sad enough to express our sense of loss," President Johnson observed two days after the funeral of John F. Kennedy. "No words are strong enough to express our determination to continue the forward thrust of America that he began." Johnson, a veteran politician, was uniquely prepared to lead that effort.

LBJ and Lady Bird by the U.S. Capitol

The son of a farmer and legislator, Johnson grew up in rural Texas. His childhood mixed hard times with breaks for marble games, and endless chores with a memorable visit to the Alamo. After finishing high school, he drifted around California for two years doing odd jobs. Later he enrolled at Southwest Texas State Teachers College; he graduated in

Lyndon B. Johnson became the only U.S. President to take the oath of office on an airplane when he was sworn in aboard Air Force One two hours after the assassination of John F. Kennedy. The plane was preparing to take him back to Washington, D.C., along with Kennedy's body. Johnson was flanked by his wife (on his right) and Kennedy's widow. Jacqueline Kennedy still wore the clothes stained during the shooting of her husband.

NICKNAME
LBJ

BORN
Aug. 27, 1908, near Stonewall, TX

POLITICAL PARTY
Democrat

CHIEF OPPONENT
1st term: none, succeeded Kennedy; 2nd term: Barry Morris Goldwater, Republican (1909–1998)

TERM OF OFFICE
Nov. 22, 1963–Jan. 20, 1969

AGE AT INAUGURATION
55 years old

NUMBER OF TERMS
one, plus balance of John F. Kennedy's term

VICE PRESIDENT
1st term: none; 2nd term: Hubert Horatio Humphrey (1911–1978)

FIRST LADY
Claudia Alta (Lady Bird) Taylor Johnson (1912–2007), wife (married Nov. 17, 1934)

CHILDREN
Lynda, Luci

GEOGRAPHIC SCENE
50 states

DIED
Jan. 22, 1973, near San Antonio, TX

AGE AT DEATH
64 years old

SELECTED LANDMARKS
Lyndon B. Johnson National Historical Park, Stonewall, TX, and Johnson City, TX (includes visitor center, reconstructed birthplace, school, boyhood home, Johnson Settlement, "Texas White House," LBJ Ranch, and grave); Lyndon Baines Johnson Library and Museum, University of Texas, Austin, TX

As President, Johnson declared a "war on poverty." He worked two shifts a day, sleeping a few hours at night and napping in his pajamas between shifts during the day. Johnson was famous for giving "the treatment"—intense verbal and physical communication—to anyone whose support he needed. "You really felt as if a St. Bernard had licked your face for an hour, had pawed you all over," explained one recipient. Few could resist his pitch.

Johnson's Southern background helped secure their victory that fall.

After Kennedy was assassinated three years later, Johnson suggested the nation create an improved Great Society as a way of commemorating the slain President. Using skills from his years as a powerful U.S. senator, Johnson influenced Congress to pass sweeping laws. Among other things, this legislation secured fair voting rights for minorities, funded education programs, battled poverty and crime, encouraged fair housing practices, strengthened access to health care, aided environmental cleanup and conservation, and established federal services such as the Public Broadcasting Service. No President has ever been more successful at ushering legislation through Congress.

Johnson won outright election to the presidency in the midst of this burst of legislation. Voters agreed to go "All the Way With

1930. Johnson met his future wife, Claudia "Lady Bird" Taylor, while working for a U.S. congressman. Her nickname gave the couple the same initials after they were married. In future years, their daughters, their Texas ranch, and even a family dog bore names that yielded the trademark LBJ initials.

Johnson was elected to the House of Representatives six consecutive times beginning in 1937. He received a Silver Star for World War II service while on leave from Congress. He earned the nickname "Landslide Lyndon" in 1948 when he won his first U.S. Senate seat by nothing like a landslide—just 87 votes. He was reelected overwhelmingly six years later. In 1960 Kennedy asked the influential senator to be his running mate. (He had just defeated Johnson in a spirited contest for their party's presidential nomination.)

> "Let this session of Congress be known as the session which did more for civil rights than the last hundred sessions combined."
>
> Lyndon B. Johnson,
> State of the Union address, January 8, 1964

LBJ" in 1964. He truly was "Landslide Lyndon" by then, earning 16 million more votes than his opponent. This edge gave him 61 percent of the popular vote.

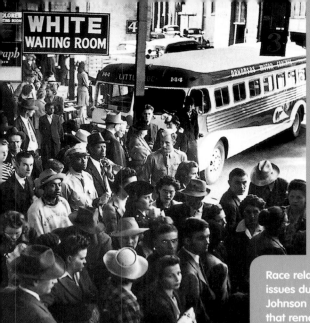

WHITE
WAITING ROOM

LBJ appointed the first African American to the Supreme Court in 1967—Thurgood Marshall. LBJ's commitment to civil rights led many Southern whites to abandon the Democratic Party.

Race relations and civil rights were dominant issues during the presidency of Lyndon B. Johnson. Johnson sought to end practices of discrimination that remained in schools, waiting rooms, and other public areas (left) by signing legislation to protect human rights regardless of race (above).

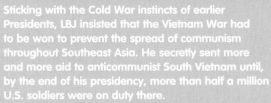

Sticking with the Cold War instincts of earlier Presidents, LBJ insisted that the Vietnam War had to be won to prevent the spread of communism throughout Southeast Asia. He secretly sent more and more aid to anticommunist South Vietnam until, by the end of his presidency, more than half a million U.S. soldiers were on duty there.

The Johnsons enjoyed the beauty of the Hill Country in their native Texas. During their years together in the White House, Lady Bird promoted legislation to limit unsightly billboards along highways, and she encouraged better land-scaping of public areas in the nation's capital and elsewhere. Later she promoted the study and cultivation of wildflowers around the country.

The Vietnam War undercut Johnson's domestic triumphs. Before his administration was over, the United States had dropped more tons of bombs over the divided countries of North and South Vietnam than it had used in Europe during all of World War II. Yet, despite these efforts, North Vietnamese communists were more committed than ever in the fight to reunite North with South. Widespread opposition developed to the war among U.S. citizens, particularly as the growing level of their nation's involvement became fully known.

Public protests about the Vietnam War forced Johnson to abandon thoughts of running for reelection in 1968. Instead, he pledged to seek peace between the North and South Vietnamese. His efforts were unsuccessful; the two sides had difficulty even agreeing what shape to make their negotiating table.

In 1969 Johnson retired with Lady Bird to the LBJ Ranch near Johnson City, Texas. He wrote his memoirs, managed his farm, and regretted the bitter end of his presidency. Johnson had had a severe heart attack years earlier while a U.S. senator; he suffered two more during his retirement. The last one proved fatal. After lying in state at the U.S. Capitol, President Johnson's body was buried at his family ranch. In the decades following her husband's death, Lady Bird Johnson worked tirelessly for her favorite causes. She died in 2007 at the age of 94.

RICHARD NIXON
37TH PRESIDENT OF THE UNITED STATES **1969–1974**

Richard Milhous Nixon was forced to resign from office after the public learned how he had encouraged the use of illegal activity to support his administration. He is the only U.S. President to resign, and the only one to leave office alive without completing his term. The importance of Nixon's official accomplishments in office are diminished by his serious abuses of presidential power.

Throughout his long political career, Nixon made much of his humble origins. He grew up in Southern California, where his family struggled against poverty and ill health. Two of his four brothers died by the time he was 20. Nixon paid for his education at nearby Whittier College by working long hours as manager of the vegetable section in his father's grocery store. Later he graduated from Duke University Law School in North Carolina and opened a law practice back home. He met his future wife, Thelma "Pat" Ryan, when they acted together in a local play. He served as a noncombat naval officer in the Pacific during World War II.

Richard Nixon vacationed in Florida with his wife, daughters, and future son-in-law before embarking on his 1968 presidential campaign.

Nixon won seats in the U.S. House in 1946 and the U.S. Senate in 1950. By then, people were calling him "Tricky Dick" because of "dirty tricks" (including illegal campaign funding and sensational character attacks) he used to get elected. He won notice for his part in Senator Joseph McCarthy's "Red Scare" search for communists. Then Nixon became Dwight D. Eisenhower's Vice President. He lost the 1960 presidential race to John F. Kennedy and the 1962 California governor's race before being elected President in 1968.

In the White House at last, Nixon was eager to mark his place in history. At home he tried to improve welfare, protect the environment, and reduce crime. He fought double-digit inflation caused by large military budgets and shortages in oil and gas. He

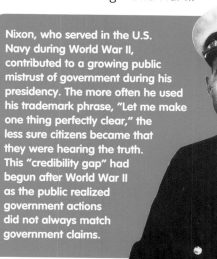

Nixon, who served in the U.S. Navy during World War II, contributed to a growing public mistrust of government during his presidency. The more often he used his trademark phrase, "Let me make one thing perfectly clear," the less sure citizens became that they were hearing the truth. This "credibility gap" had begun after World War II as the public realized government actions did not always match government claims.

NICKNAME
Tricky Dick

BORN
Jan. 9, 1913, in Yorba Linda, CA

POLITICAL PARTY
Republican

CHIEF OPPONENTS
1st term: Hubert Horatio Humphrey, Democrat (1911–1978), and George Corley Wallace, American Independent (1919–1998); 2nd term: George Stanley McGovern, Democrat (1922–2012)

TERM OF OFFICE
Jan. 20, 1969–Aug. 9, 1974

AGE AT INAUGURATION
56 years old

NUMBER OF TERMS
two (cut short by resignation)

VICE PRESIDENTS
1st term & 2nd term (partial): Spiro Theodore Agnew (1918–1996); 2nd term (balance): Gerald R. Ford (1913–2006)

FIRST LADY
Thelma Catherine (Pat) Ryan Nixon (1912–1993), wife (married June 21, 1940)

CHILDREN
Patricia, Julie

GEOGRAPHIC SCENE
50 states

DIED
April 22, 1994, in New York, NY

AGE AT DEATH
81 years old

SELECTED LANDMARKS
Nixon Presidential Library and Museum (includes birthplace and grave), Yorba Linda, CA

Richard Nixon spoke with U.S. astronauts in space after their successful landing on the moon on July 20, 1969.

Nixon toured the country with enthusiasm whether he was campaigning or appearing as President. Nixon appeared on 54 covers of *Time* magazine, more than anyone else in history. During his administration the nation's voting age was lowered from 21 to 18 by constitutional amendment.

In 1972 Richard Nixon became the first sitting U.S. President to visit China. Nixon helped dissolve hostilities between the two nations by meeting with communist leaders and visiting landmarks like the Great Wall (right). Three months later he met with communist leaders in the Soviet Union.

often ignored or stretched laws that met with his disapproval (from those that regulated wiretapping procedures to those that funded Native American education programs). Federal courts often overruled him.

Abroad, Nixon improved relations between the United States and the communist nations of China and the Soviet Union. He made celebrated trips to each country, and he signed new agreements limiting the spread of nuclear weapons. Although Nixon entered the White House with a pledge to end the Vietnam War, the task proved difficult. Even as he brought more troops home, fighting spread to nearby countries. North Vietnam took control of South Vietnam in 1975, two years after the nations made "peace" and U.S. troops had withdrawn. Many Americans were bitter about the war's costs: 58,000 U.S. lives and $110 billion since America joined the effort in 1956.

Nixon expanded on his use of "dirty tricks" while President. He and other staff members broke laws in their efforts to discover embarrassing information about his rivals and enemies (a list of more than 40,000 names). They hired people to commit burglaries and tap phones in their search for "dirt." They silenced their helpers with "hush money," spent federal campaign funds improperly, made illegal use of government records, and filed false income tax reports.

In 1972 Nixon's associates hired men to burglarize Democratic Party offices at the Watergate building

in Washington, D.C. (They hoped to gain insider information there that would help Nixon be reelected later that year.) The Watergate scandal that ended Nixon's presidency began after the burglars were caught. The investigation of the break-in did not progress quickly enough, though, to prevent Nixon's landslide reelection in 1972.

For more than two years, Nixon and others tried to hide their involvement in the crime. They denied that Nixon was involved in planning the caper or its cover-up. Newspaper reporters and members of Congress led increasingly intense investigations into possible crimes. Eventually the Supreme Court forced Nixon to release secret tape recordings he had made of his White House conversations. The tapes confirmed that Nixon had lied about his innocence in planning illegal activities and covering them up.

> "Those who hate you don't win unless you hate them. And then you destroy yourself."
>
> Richard Nixon, parting speech, August 9, 1974

On August 9, 1974, Nixon resigned from office. Otherwise he faced the likelihood of impeachment by the House of Representatives and removal from office through a trial in the U.S. Senate. More than 20 other people, including top White House staff members, a former attorney general, and a former secretary of commerce were found guilty of crimes, fined, and/or sent to jail. Nixon's first Vice President, Spiro Agnew, had resigned from office in an earlier scandal involving bribery and income tax evasion. After Agnew's successor, Gerald R. Ford, became President, he spared Nixon from prosecution by pardoning him for any crimes he may have committed.

Nixon lived another two decades. He and his wife eventually settled in the New York City area. He died in 1994. Historians have rated Nixon's presidency as one of the worst in U.S. history. Classified documents from his administration continue to be made public, allowing scholars to further evaluate his reputation and legacy.

"Pat" Nixon earned her nickname for being born near St. Patrick's Day. As First Lady she traveled widely and promoted volunteer work. She is shown here with daughters Julie (far left) and Tricia.

Richard Nixon announced his plans to resign from office during a televised address in August 1974 (below).

Scandals resulting from the bungled 1972 burglary of Democratic Party offices in the Watergate building (left) eventually led to calls for Nixon's removal from office (above, left). Nixon had defused an earlier scandal with another emotional television appearance. In 1952 he preserved his spot as Vice President on Dwight D. Eisenhower's ticket by denying, during a televised speech, his illegal use of campaign funds. His remarks became known as the "Checkers speech" because he admitted that the family dog, Checkers, had been a political gift.

GERALD R. FORD
38TH PRESIDENT OF THE UNITED STATES **1974–1977**

Gerald Rudolph Ford is the only President never elected to the offices of President or Vice President. He was promoted to both roles during the turbulent political changes of the early 1970s. In the wake of President Richard Nixon's resignation, Ford worked to restore the confidence of citizens in their Chief Executive.

Ford came to the presidency after serving 25 years as one of Michigan's representatives to Congress. A native of Nebraska, he was a graduate of the University of Michigan and Yale University Law School. During World War II, he earned 10 battle stars for combat duty in the Navy. "Jerry" Ford married Elizabeth "Betty" Bloomer Warren, a former professional dancer, in 1948.

Ford, who joined Congress in 1949, became Vice President in 1973. He was appointed to the post by then President Nixon after Vice President Spiro T. Agnew was forced by scandals to resign from office. When the scandal-plagued Nixon himself resigned in disgrace some eight months later, Ford became President. "This is an hour of history that troubles our minds and hurts our hearts," Ford noted. Yet he praised the soundness of the nation for its successful transfer of power from Nixon to himself. "Our Constitution works; our great Republic is a government of laws and not of men. Here the people rule," he said.

With words like these and with honest behavior, Ford began restoring citizen trust in the government. His efforts to resolve other challenges—such as double-digit inflation, high unemployment, and economic recession—were less successful. Ford drew criticism, too, for granting Nixon a full pardon for crimes committed while President. In a close contest in 1976, Ford lost his chance to gain outright election. He went on to live longer than any other President.

Gerald R. Ford rejected offers to play professional football after college and went to law school instead. Years later, Lyndon B. Johnson joked that Ford had "played football too long without a helmet." Ford replied by showing up at a public event with an old helmet that no longer fit. "Heads tend to swell in Washington," he joked.

Gerald R. Ford

NICKNAME
Jerry

BORN
July 14, 1913, in Omaha, NE

POLITICAL PARTY
Republican

CHIEF OPPONENT
none; succeeded Nixon

TERM OF OFFICE
Aug. 9, 1974–Jan. 20, 1977

AGE AT INAUGURATION
61 years old

NUMBER OF TERMS
one (partial)

VICE PRESIDENT
Nelson Aldrich Rockefeller (1908–1979)

FIRST LADY
Elizabeth (Betty) Bloomer Warren Ford (1918–2011), wife (married Oct. 15, 1948)

CHILDREN
Michael, John, Steven, Susan

GEOGRAPHIC SCENE
50 states

DIED
Dec. 26, 2006

AGE AT DEATH
93 years old

SELECTED LANDMARKS
Omaha, NE (birthplace); Gerald R. Ford Library, Ann Arbor, MI; Gerald R. Ford Museum (and grave), Grand Rapids, MI

THE QUESTION OF THE WEEK
MR. PRESIDENT:
WHAT CAN WE BELIEVE?

Public distrust of the presidency carried over from Nixon's term in office to Ford's.

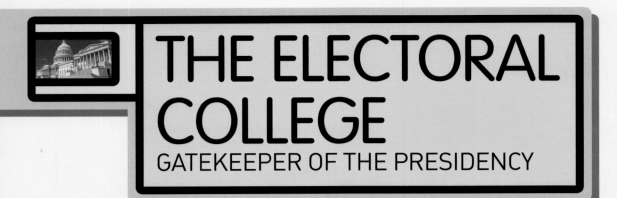

THE ELECTORAL COLLEGE
GATEKEEPER OF THE PRESIDENCY

In most countries, national elections are straight-forward affairs. Eligible voters have the opportunity at a specified time to mark their preference on a ballot of various choices. Victors are declared based on the tabulated results.

Citizens of the United States participate in a more complex, two-step process. The outcome of the presidency rests not, as is often thought, with the votes cast on Election Day. In fact, these votes only determine the membership of an Electoral College that is charged by the U.S. Constitution with selecting the President and Vice President of the United States.

Each state has as many members in the Electoral College as it has U.S. senators and representatives (see map). The District of Columbia has electoral votes, too, even though it lacks full representation in Congress. The first Electoral College had 69 members. Today, there are 538. In order to become President, a candidate must win a majority, at least one more than half, of all electoral votes, or 270.

The Founding Fathers established the Electoral College to ensure that the President and Vice President would be selected by an elite group of learned and well-qualified individuals, fairly distributed among the states. At the time, few people had the right to vote, and members of the Electoral College were either appointed by governors or selected by state legislatures. The earliest members of the Electoral College voted independently, based on their individual judgments.

ELECTORAL VOTES BY STATE

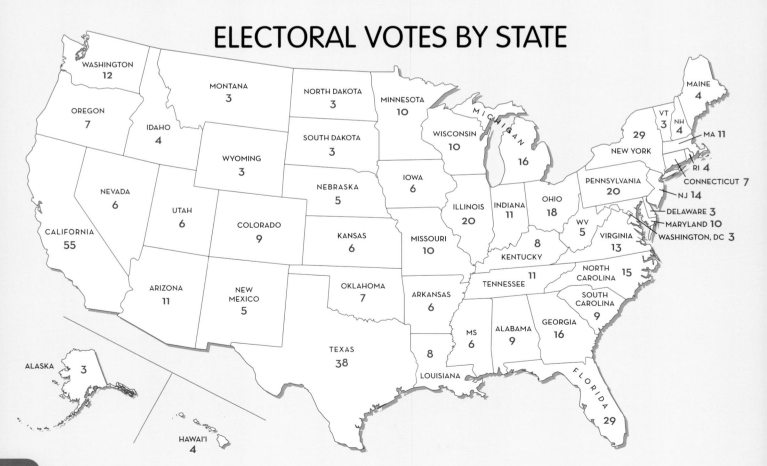

During the 1820s, as voting rights began to expand, states started to entrust citizens with the selection of electors. Then as now, voters expressed preferences for their state's electors (who usually go unnamed) by their selection of a presidential candidate. Victory within each state goes to the electors who represent the political party of the victorious candidate. This "winner-take-all" formula is used today by most states and the District of Columbia. Exceptions include Maine and Nebraska, which allocate electoral votes in proportion to the support received by various candidates within each congressional district.

Members of the Electoral College vote during separately held state meetings on an appointed day in December, and their votes are tabulated in front of a joint session of Congress in early January. If controversies arise when votes are tallied, Congress is empowered to intervene. Otherwise the selection process for President and Vice President is complete.

Thus every presidential election has two sets of results, the popular vote and the Electoral College vote. In most cases, the winner of the popular vote is victorious

The states' share of Electoral College votes is reviewed every 10 years based on changes in the U.S. Census (see map opposite for the latest allocation). The contested election of 2000 (above) sparked the bipartisan National Popular Vote effort to circumvent the Electoral College through the actions of state legislatures; so far about a dozen states have signed on to the plan.

in the Electoral College, as well. However, five of the nation's presidential elections have brought victory to candidates who failed to win the popular vote.

Three of these elections occurred during the 19th century. Inconclusive voting by the Electoral College in 1824 prompted the House of Representatives to award the presidency to John Quincy Adams. Rutherford B. Hayes became President following the election of 1876 when disputes over the selection of electors forced Congress to refer the decision to a special commission. In 1888 Benjamin Harrison defeated Grover Cleveland without dispute in the Electoral College yet failed to win a majority of popular votes.

The long absence of further discrepancies between popular and electoral voting led many to view the Electoral College as a largely ceremonial body. Then, unexpectedly, two of the first five elections of the 21st century resulted in Electoral College victories without majority support in the popular vote. In each case Republicans triumphed over Democrats, first in 2000 with the victory of George W. Bush and then in 2016 with Donald Trump's election win.

JIMMY CARTER
39TH PRESIDENT OF THE UNITED STATES **1977–1981**

James Earl Carter, Jr., was the first person elected President from the Deep South since Zachary Taylor in 1848. Economic troubles at home combined with other challenges from abroad (including citizens being taken hostage in Iran) cost him his bid for a second term of office. Carter returned to the world stage after his presidency ended, serving as an advocate for international peace. In 2002 he became the third U.S. President to win a Nobel Peace Prize.

Carter liked his nickname, "Jimmy," so much that he was sworn in as President by that name. As a child growing up in Georgia, Carter had been known by another nickname, too: "Hot," short for "Hot Shot." Carter helped with chores on his father's sizable peanut farm, attended schools segregated by race, and played with children both black and white. He graduated 59th out of the 820 students in his class at the U.S. Naval Academy

The Carters on their wedding day

at Annapolis. He married the best friend of one of his sisters and took up a career in the U.S. Navy.

After his father's sudden death in 1953, Carter left the Navy and his post as a nuclear submarine engineer to manage the family farm. Later he served in the Georgia Senate. As governor of the state

Jimmy Carter [signature]

NICKNAME
Jimmy

BORN
Oct. 1, 1924, in Plains, GA

POLITICAL PARTY
Democrat

CHIEF OPPONENT
President Gerald R. Ford, Republican (1913–2006)

TERM OF OFFICE
Jan. 20, 1977–Jan. 20, 1981

AGE AT INAUGURATION
52 years old

NUMBER OF TERMS
one

VICE PRESIDENT
Walter Frederick (Fritz) Mondale (1928–present)

FIRST LADY
Rosalynn Smith Carter (1927–present), wife (married July 7, 1946)

CHILDREN
John, James, Donnel, Amy

GEOGRAPHIC SCENE
50 states

SELECTED LANDMARKS
Plains Nursing Center, Inc., Plains, GA (birthplace); Jimmy Carter National Historic Site, Plains, GA; the Carter Center and the Jimmy Carter Library, Atlanta, GA (includes a museum)

Jimmy Carter (shown with his wife, Rosalynn) was nicknamed "Jimmy Cardigan" after he wore a sweater instead of a suit when he addressed the nation during a televised fireside chat in 1977. Carter dispensed with other formal precedents, too. Bands stopped playing "Hail to the Chief" for his public entrances. He sent his daughter, Amy, to public schools. Sometimes he even carried his own suitcase and stayed at private homes when he traveled.

Jimmy Carter broke with precedent during his Inaugural Parade in 1977. Instead of riding in a motorcade, he walked from the U.S. Capitol toward the White House with his daughter, Amy; his wife, Rosalynn; and other family members. As First Lady, Rosalynn sat in on Cabinet meetings, represented the nation abroad, and spoke out in favor of mental health care.

The popularity of nuclear energy suffered during the Carter presidency after a serious accident occurred in 1979 at the Three Mile Island nuclear power plant near Harrisburg, Pennsylvania (left). Carter encouraged scientists to develop new forms of energy using such renewable resources as the sun and the wind.

during the early 1970s Carter criticized racial discrimination, the practice of favoring whites over blacks and other races. Carter entered the presidential race of 1976 almost completely unknown to the rest of the country. His tireless campaigning won him the Democratic Party nomination and, in what became a tight race, the presidency.

Carter was elected in part because voters liked the fact that he was an "outsider"—someone who was not part of national politics and the recent Watergate scandal. Being an "outsider" turned into a drawback after Carter became President. Because he ignored the political strategies of Congress, legislators on Capitol Hill regularly refused to pass his bills. The economy did not cooperate either. Years of extravagant government spending and a new wave of energy shortages sent prices higher than ever. Citizens were literally stranded at empty gas pumps in their search for gasoline.

Although these issues proved troublesome to solve, Carter took other significant actions. He pardoned citizens who had illegally avoided fighting in the Vietnam War, appointed people from diverse backgrounds to key posts, reduced the rules that governed national

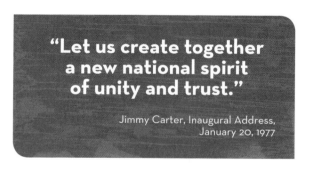

"Let us create together a new national spirit of unity and trust."

Jimmy Carter, Inaugural Address,
January 20, 1977

transportation systems, increased protection of the environment, and promoted research into alternative forms of energy. He also established a Department of Energy and a separate Department of Education.

Carter emphasized respect for human rights in his relations with other nations. He withheld U.S. foreign aid from countries with unjust governments. Carter arranged for Panama to assume control of the canal that the United States had built through its territory years before. He expanded relations with China. He tried to further limit the spread of nuclear weapons. He organized international protests, including a controversial boycott of the 1980 Summer Olympics in Moscow, after the Soviet Union invaded nearby Afghanistan.

Carter's greatest foreign policy challenge began in 1979 when angry Iranians stormed the U.S. Embassy in Tehran and began holding 52 captured Americans hostage. All efforts to free the prisoners failed during Carter's administration, including an attempted military rescue. Only after he left office were the captives released.

The most difficult challenge Carter faced in his presidency was the Iranian hostage crisis. Fifty-two Americans were held prisoner by Iranian militants for 444 days (below). They were finally set free just after Carter left office in January 1981.

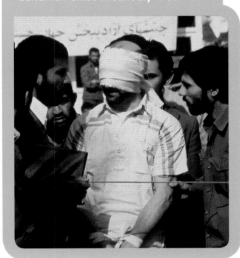

Jimmy Carter helped negotiate important treaties between Egyptian President Anwar Sadat (above, left) and Israel's Prime Minister Menachem Begin (above, right) in 1978. Their Camp David Accords were reached with Carter's help at the presidential retreat in Maryland. These agreements renewed hopes for peace in the Middle East, a region plagued by wars and terrorism.

Jimmy Carter, who was only 56 years old at the end of his presidency, went on to distinguish himself in the decades that followed as a peace-maker and moderator of democratic elections. His public service after leaving office earned him the Nobel Peace Prize (right) in 2002 at age 78.

As President, Carter's popularity ranged from very high to very low. It shifted depending on the state of the economy, the status of the hostage crisis, and his success at restoring confidence in government. He lost his reelection bid by a wide margin.

Just 56 years old, Carter began what is now the longest presidential retirement in U.S. history. He has written more than 20 books, for example, many of them best sellers. His greatest focus, however, has been devoted to the Carter Center, which he founded in Atlanta, Georgia, with his wife, Rosalynn, soon after his presidency ended.

Working through the center, Carter has helped negotiate peace agreements between nations, worked with others to verify that countries have fair elections, and directed efforts to improve health in developing lands. These and his other efforts to increase world peace earned him the Nobel Peace Prize in 2002. Only three other Presidents—Theodore Roosevelt, Woodrow Wilson, and Barack Obama—have been so honored. Carter is the only one to be recognized for postpresidential achievements.

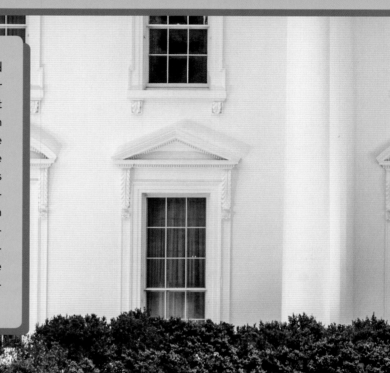

FOOTPRINTS ON THE GLOBAL FRONTIER

1981–PRESENT

The Cold War gave way near the end of the 20th century to a new frontier of shifting global alliances. The Soviet Union dissolved. The European Union expanded. Trade, population, even disease became more mobile. Although some nations moved closer to peace, old hatreds erupted elsewhere—often fueled by religious differences. Threats of terrorism began to rise among angry groups of outsiders. Nations sought to collaborate, compromise, and compete on a planet whose population is more connected and interdependent than ever.

1981
A new technology company named Microsoft helped launch the personal computer industry with its MS-DOS operating system. The software reached its sixth generation (above) within a dozen years.

1989
Berlin citizens marked the end of the Cold War by tearing down the wall that had divided their city into separate zones. East reunited with West to embrace democracy.

1992
Congress approved the North American Free Trade Agreement (NAFTA), allowing products to be sold easily between the U.S., Canada, and Mexico. Controversy followed when jobs left the U.S.

2001
On September 11 members of the al Qaeda terror network crashed hijacked jets into the World Trade Center in New York City and other targets. The towers were destroyed and more than 2,700 people died.

For all the changes in the world, some things stay constant: The White House remains home base for the nation's Presidents.

2008
Irresponsible investment strategies triggered a collapse of the U.S. housing market, resulting in global financial panic and the worst economic hardship since the Great Depression.

2011
Street protests sparked hopes for democracy in much of the Middle East during the so-called Arab Spring. Although many transitions started out peacefully (above, Egypt), conflict in the region grew.

2012
After the federal government started using drones to patrol U.S. borders (above) and conduct military missions, local governments and businesses began imagining peaceful uses for the unmanned aircraft.

2015
Representatives from 195 nations signed a deal to reduce human impact on Earth's climate while meeting in Paris on December 12. Rising global temperatures threaten species worldwide.

Everett Raymond Kins

RONALD REAGAN
40TH PRESIDENT OF THE UNITED STATES 1981–1989

No one older had ever become President when the 69-year-old Ronald Wilson Reagan took office. Yet this former Hollywood actor and governor of California brought a youthful optimism to his work. The "Great Communicator" strengthened support for the Republican Party and filled federal courts with conservative judges. He helped force the end of the Cold War through record spending on national defense, but his policies created financial challenges for future Presidents.

Reagan ended his presidential career near the end of the 20th century, having been born during a simpler era when the century was just beginning. He grew up in small towns in northern Illinois, particularly Dixon. His family called him "Dutch," short for "fat little Dutchman." He enjoyed playing sports and was a popular actor at the public schools he attended and at Eureka College in Eureka, Illinois.

After graduation he worked as a radio sports announcer in the Midwest. In 1937 Reagan moved to Hollywood. He made 53 movies and hosted two television shows during the next three decades. Even his World War II service involved making training films for the armed forces. Reagan "lived" so many lives through

Nancy Davis met her future husband, Ronald Reagan, when both of them were acting in Hollywood. They married three years later (above). Nancy Reagan appeared in a total of 11 films. As First Lady she encouraged children to "Just Say No" to illegal drugs.

Nancy Davis and Ronald Reagan starred together in *Hellcats of the Navy*, the last movie either of them made.

the parts he played in movies that sometimes he recalled combat scenes from his films with the conviction of someone who had actually lived through the experiences. Reagan married twice; both of his wives had been Hollywood actresses. He was the first President who had a marriage end in divorce.

Reagan's experiences as a union labor leader in Hollywood, public speaker, and political volunteer helped interest him in running for office. Although he had grown up loyal to the Democratic Party, he began supporting

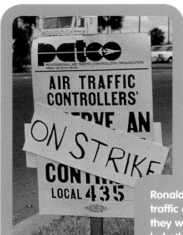

Ronald Reagan fired 13,000 air traffic controllers in 1981 when they went out on strike. His action led others to challenge the power of unionized workers, too.

American embassy workers held hostage after Iranians stormed their compound in 1979 gained their freedom on the first day of Reagan's presidency. Jimmy Carter's team had negotiated the release, but credit often falls to Reagan because of the timing.

A lone gunman attempted to assassinate Reagan in Washington, D.C., a few months after he took office. Prompt emergency care saved his life. During his recovery he joked to hospital staffers, "If I had had this much attention in Hollywood, I'd have stayed there."

Republicans during the Eisenhower era. He officially joined the Republican Party in 1962. In 1966 Californians elected him to the first of two terms as governor. Reagan sought his party's presidential nomination twice (in 1968 and 1976) before earning it in 1980. Citizens voted "yes" to elect Reagan as President because they generally answered "no" to his query about their lives during the Carter presidency: "Are you better off than you were four years ago?" He was reelected four years later.

In an effort to improve the economy, Reagan cut taxes, reduced federal spending in some areas, and increased government spending on defense by $1.5 trillion over seven years. He proposed the first trillion-dollar federal budget. His economic program came to be known as "Reaganomics." It suggested that if economic benefits such as tax cuts were made to the wealthy, these savings would "trickle down" and help less affluent citizens. This vision of "supply-side economics" became a cornerstone of the modern Republican Party. Although inflation and unemployment

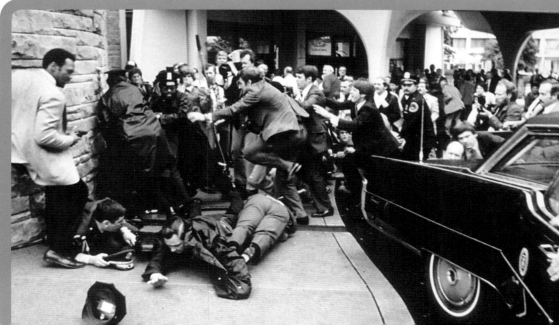

During his presidency, Ronald Reagan had the opportunity to place three justices on the U.S. Supreme Court, including Sandra Day O'Connor, its first female member (below, being sworn in on September 25, 1981). Reagan appointed new judges to half of the nation's federal court seats, too, allowing him to embed elements of his own judicial philosophy in the courts throughout the land.

Reagan's plan of increased spending on national defense put a strain on the U.S. economy and added to the national debt. His program was even tougher on the Soviet Union. America's old Cold War foe simply could not afford to keep up in the military arms race anymore. Mikhail Gorbachev (above, right), a more moderate Soviet leader, sought to reduce Cold War tensions through his glasnost initiative. In 1987 Reagan and Gorbachev signed an agreement to reduce stockpiles of nuclear missiles for the first time.

eventually improved during his administration, new problems developed. The collapse of the savings and loan industry, sizable annual budget deficits, and a growing national debt, for example, became costly concerns that would take years for future Presidents to solve.

A series of scandals unfolded during the Reagan Administration. The greatest one, the Iran-contra scandal, involved illegal sales of arms to the Middle Eastern nation of Iran. Profits from the sales were secretly diverted to support rebel forces in Nicaragua, a country in Central America. Upper-level administrators encouraged the activity. Other charges of illegal behavior forced the resignations of Reagan's secretary of labor, his attorney general, and senior staff members at the Environmental Protection Agency, the Central Intelligence Agency, the Defense Department, and the Department of Housing and Urban Development.

Reagan remained popular despite the scandals and criticisms of his presidency. Some credited this success to his Hollywood looks and his skill as the

Reagan's death in 2004 brought the nation its first presidential state funeral in more than 20 years. At one point during the weeklong series of events, his casket was moved by horse-drawn caisson to the U.S. Capitol for public viewing. When Nancy Reagan died in 2016, she was laid to rest beside her husband on the grounds of his presidential library in California.

Great Communicator. Others called him the "Teflon President" because, just like the nonstick pan surface, nothing bad ever "stuck" to his image.

Reagan was 77 years old when he retired with his wife, Nancy, to Los Angeles. In 1994 he was diagnosed with Alzheimer's disease, an illness that affects memory, and he led an increasingly secluded life. His death 10 years later prompted tributes on both coasts. After lying in state at the U.S. Capitol and receiving the honor of a state funeral, his body was flown home to California for a sunset burial.

"What I'd really like to do is go down in history as the President who made Americans believe in themselves again."

Ronald Reagan, 1981

GEORGE BUSH
41ST PRESIDENT OF THE UNITED STATES 1989–1993

George Herbert Walker Bush presided over a continued shift in Republican Party thinking toward conservative viewpoints. U.S. armed forces took part in two military actions, including the Persian Gulf War, during a presidency that witnessed the collapse of the Soviet Union. A sagging economy undercut Bush's wartime popularity and spoiled his reelection bid. Later, his eldest son became President.

Bush brought years of varied government experience and a distinguished personal background with him to the White House. The son of a wealthy U.S. senator, Bush attended elite private schools. He enlisted in the military after high school, became the Navy's youngest pilot, and earned a Distinguished Flying Cross. He was the last veteran of World War II to become President.

George Bush played baseball for Yale University. He was named after a grandfather, George Herbert Walker, who was known as "Pop." Bush was called "Little Pop" or "Poppy" into adulthood.

After the war, Bush graduated with honors from Yale University. He worked in the oil business in Texas for 18 years before seeking his first public office. He lost a 1964 U.S. Senate bid, but he gained a seat in the U.S. House of Representatives two years later. After two terms he made a second unsuccessful run for the Senate. Over the next 10 years, he was appointed by Republican Presidents Richard Nixon and Gerald R. Ford to a series of prominent posts: U.S. ambassador to the United Nations, chairman of the Republican National Committee, top U.S. diplomat in China, and director of the Central Intelligence Agency.

NICKNAME
Poppy

BORN
June 12, 1924, in Milton, MA

POLITICAL PARTY
Republican

CHIEF OPPONENT
Michael Stanley Dukakis, Democrat (1933–present)

TERM OF OFFICE
Jan. 20, 1989–Jan. 20, 1993

AGE AT INAUGURATION
64 years old

NUMBER OF TERMS
one

VICE PRESIDENT
James Danforth (Dan) Quayle III (1947–present)

FIRST LADY
Barbara Pierce Bush (1925–present), wife (married Jan. 6, 1945)

CHILDREN
George, Robin (died young), John (Jeb), Neil, Marvin, Dorothy

GEOGRAPHIC SCENE
50 states

SELECTED LANDMARKS
George Bush Presidential Library, Texas A&M University, College Station, TX

Bush married Barbara Pierce while on leave from World War II service. The couple had met two years before during an earlier shore leave. Both claim to have fallen in love at first sight.

As First Lady, Barbara Bush promoted literacy and other education programs. Entertainers were among those attending the third national literacy awards she hosted at the White House (above). The color of Barbara Bush's hair turned to a distinctive silver at an unexpectedly early age following the death of their three-year-old daughter to leukemia.

American soldiers wore gas masks and special clothing when they invaded Iraq in early 1991. Their protective gear was designed as defense against poisonous chemical weapons.

In 1989 the *Exxon Valdez* oil tanker ran aground off Alaska. The accident resulted in one of the largest oil spills in the nation's history. Almost 11 million gallons of oil polluted more than 1,000 miles of shoreline and killed hundreds of thousands of birds and other animals. The disaster destroyed the local fishing industry despite an extensive and costly cleanup effort.

Bush eyed the vice presidency in 1968 and 1974, and he sought the Republican presidential nomination in 1980. Instead, he earned eight years of experience as Ronald Reagan's Vice President before gaining the presidency himself in the election of 1988.

Bush inherited from Reagan a national and world scene that was in transition. Most notable was the rapid transformation of the Soviet Union from a Cold War superpower into a splintered collection of former communist states. First Poland, then East Germany, Czechoslovakia, Hungary, Yugoslavia, Bulgaria, Albania, and, finally, the Soviet Union itself, rejected the communist form of government. The Soviet Union dissolved, and Russia emerged as its most powerful descendant. Most of the momentum for these changes came from within the region itself, but the Bush Administration supported these moves toward democracy. The only remaining strongholds of communism by the end of the Bush presidency were China, Cuba, Laos, North Korea, and Vietnam.

In 1989 Bush ordered U.S. troops to invade Panama. Their mission was to seize Manuel Noriega, the country's military leader, and bring him to the United States so he could stand trial on charges of drug trafficking. He was captured four days later. (Eventually he was tried, convicted, and imprisoned for his illegal activity.) The invasion caused significant property damage, left 500 Panamanians dead, and cost the lives of 23 Americans.

Thirteen months later American soldiers were fighting again. Iraq's 1990 invasion of neighboring Kuwait, a tiny oil-rich nation on the Persian Gulf, provoked

George Bush poses with his four sons (left, from left to right: Neil, John (Jeb), George W., and Marvin). Two sons tried to follow their father to the White House. George W., the eldest, succeeded in 2000 while serving as governor of Texas. His younger brother Jeb, a former Florida governor, failed to win the 2016 Republican Party presidential nomination.

Commander in Chief George Bush reviews a ceremonial guard in 1989.

Four years after his presidency, George Bush made his first parachute jump since World War II (right). He repeated the feat in 2014 at age 90.

worldwide outrage. The United States led an international fight in the region several months later that liberated Kuwait and severely damaged Iraq's military defenses. Iraq's leader, Saddam Hussein, remained in command of his nation, but other governments agreed to enforce sanctions, or restrictions, on Iraq until the nation could prove it no longer possessed weapons of mass destruction. The war, which lasted only a few months, cost more than $60 billion, a sum that many nations helped pay. The United States lost 148 lives during the war. As many as 100,000 Iraqis died, most of them civilians.

These international events often overshadowed domestic policy during the Bush Administration. Nonetheless, the President worked to rescue the bankrupt savings and loan industry, fought rising

unemployment, signed a new Clean Air Act, and agreed to legislation that promoted equal rights of access for the disabled. Enormous budget deficits continued to swell the national debt. They forced Bush to break his 1988 campaign promise—"Read my lips: No new taxes." This change and a worsening economy cost Bush his reelection bid in the three-way race of 1992. Not since the multiparty race of 1912 had a sitting President fared so poorly at the polls. George and Barbara Bush retired to homes in Texas and Maine. They have been married longer than any other presidential couple, with the Carters coming in a close second.

> **"Out of these troubled times ... a new world order can emerge: a new era, freer from the threat of terror, stronger in the pursuit of justice, and more secure in the quest for peace."**
>
> George Bush, September 12, 1990

IN THE PRESIDENT'S SHADOW
SECURITY, THE MEDIA, AND PRESIDENTIAL PERKS

Today's Presidents may share the same residence as their predecessors, but their work and lifestyles are vastly different. The first Presidents handled much of their own paperwork, for example. They met freely with citizens who dropped by the White House, too. As the nation and its government grew in size, so did the complexity of the job for its Presidents.

Now Presidents travel by jet and limousine, not horse and buggy. The size of their staffs has grown from a handful to hundreds. The cost of running the White House has kept a parallel pace. The risks and realities of presidential assassinations have tightened the Presidents' freedom of movement. Gone are the days when John Quincy Adams could walk alone from the White House to the Potomac River and swim there in the nude.

Presidential planes date to the era of Franklin D. Roosevelt. Travel by jet began with Dwight D. Eisenhower.

Now more than two dozen Secret Service agents take turns guarding the President and family members around the clock. Other staff members help manage the President's busy calendar, assist with speechwriting, and advise the President on everything from foreign policy to party politics.

As a result, today's Presidents are more isolated than ever before from ordinary life. William Henry Harrison once strolled beyond the White House gates to do a little grocery shopping. Ulysses S. Grant took off by himself on speeding buggy rides. But no President sets foot beyond the grounds of the White House today just on a whim or all alone.

However, even as the lives of Presidents have

Secret Service agents began guarding the life of the U.S. President following the assassination of William McKinley in 1901.

Secret Service agents do everything from protecting the presidential limousine (right, in 1982) to supervising ordinary movements of the President and family members. Whether the Chief Executive wants to buy flowers for the First Lady, browse through a bookstore, or go for a jog, Secret Service agents ensure that the outing is safe and sound.

Presidential motorcades include many protective vehicles, even an ambulance.

Members of the news media stay near the President, whether on the road or back at the White House (below, with Barack Obama in the press briefing room).

Technically the term Air Force One refers to the aircraft currently in use by the President, but it's commonly considered the name for the President's jet. The presidential helicopter (right) is called Marine One.

become more controlled, their activities have grown in national visibility. Expanding media coverage by newspapers, radio, television, and the Internet ensures that the public knows more than ever about what a President says and does. All major news outlets assign one or more people to cover the President's activities. There are some 2,000 members of this presidential press corps.

This many reporters could not possibly follow every single move of the President. Instead, small groups of them—a few dozen or so at a time—take turns with the work. They are called the press pool because they pool, or collect, their reports, then share them with everyone in the press corps.

One representative of each day's press pool writes an eyewitness summary of the day's events. These reports are filled with colorful details so that other reporters will be able to visualize and write vivid news accounts. Additional members of the pool make still photos, video footage, and audio recordings to share with the press corps. The reports

of the press pool form the basis for the hundreds of news stories seen by the public.

Today's Presidents balance the demands and scrutiny of their jobs with many impressive perks, or benefits. For starters, they receive an annual salary of $400,000. (George Washington earned $25,000 a year.) They have free housing at the White House as well as at the presidential retreat of Camp David, in nearby Maryland.

These homes offer many luxuries that cushion the impact of their isolation. Presidents may enjoy swimming, bowling, horseback riding, skeet shooting, and woodland walks without ever leaving home. They can screen movies in a private theater and read the latest books in a private library, too.

When it's time to travel, Presidents may choose between a fleet of limousines, a jet known as Air Force One, a helicopter, a yacht, even a bulletproof train car. Yet at the end of the day, they tread the same stairs to bed as have all the Presidents since John Adams.

BILL CLINTON
42ND PRESIDENT OF THE UNITED STATES 1993–2001

William Jefferson Clinton brought the Democratic Party its first two-term presidency since the era of Franklin D. Roosevelt. Clinton earned respect internationally for his leadership and work for world peace. At home he balanced the federal budget for the first time in decades and reduced the national debt. These professional successes were undercut by bitter partisan political fighting over real and alleged scandals. Impeached by the House of Representatives on charges of misconduct, Clinton was tried and acquitted by the U.S. Senate.

Clinton was the first U.S. President born after World War II. He grew up in Hot Springs, Arkansas, where he did well in school. As a youth, Clinton joined the Boy Scouts, sang in the church choir, and raced to complete crossword puzzles. Later he graduated from Georgetown University in Washington, D.C., and

Bill Clinton's 1963 handshake with President John F. Kennedy helped cement his childhood ambition to be President. Clinton was known until age 16 by the birth name he shared with his natural father, William Jefferson Blythe, who died before Bill was born. Later, he adopted his stepfather's last name.

studied as a prestigious Rhodes Scholar at England's Oxford University before turning his attention to law. He met his future wife, Hillary Rodham, while the two of them were law students at Yale University.

William Clinton

NICKNAME
Comeback Kid

BORN
Aug. 19, 1946, in Hope, AR

POLITICAL PARTY
Democrat

CHIEF OPPONENTS
1st term: President George Bush, Republican (1924–present), and Henry Ross Perot, Independent (1930–present); 2nd term: Robert Joseph Dole, Republican (1923–present), and Henry Ross Perot, Reform (1930–present)

TERM OF OFFICE
Jan. 20, 1993–Jan. 20, 2001

AGE AT INAUGURATION
46 years old

NUMBER OF TERMS
two

VICE PRESIDENT
Albert Arnold Gore, Jr. (1948–present)

FIRST LADY
Hillary Diane Rodham Clinton (1947–present), wife (married Oct. 11, 1975)

CHILDREN
Chelsea

GEOGRAPHIC SCENE
50 states

SELECTED LANDMARKS
William J. Clinton Presidential Library and Museum, Little Rock, AR; home, Fayetteville, AR

During his youth, Bill Clinton played the saxophone in a jazz trio called the Three Blind Mice; sunglasses completed the musicians' attire. During presidential campaigns he performed twice on nationally televised talk shows. Clinton jammed with other musicians at a White House jazz festival (left).

Throughout his presidency, Bill Clinton tried to foster peaceful relations. In meetings with Israeli and Palestinian leaders (above), Clinton sought to improve understanding between people of different religions.

During the last six years of Bill Clinton's administration, Kenneth Starr (above, center) led a series of investigations into possible illegal behavior by the President and his associates. These proceedings became ensnared in bitter partisan, or political party, disputes. Republicans accused Democrats of hiding the truth, while Democrats accused Republicans of trying to undermine the Clinton presidency with false charges.

After graduating, Clinton taught law at the University of Arkansas and took up politics. By 1978, at age 32, he had become the nation's youngest governor. Although unseated in the next election, Clinton became known as the "Comeback Kid" after he regained his post in 1982. He went on to serve four consecutive terms as governor of Arkansas. As a presidential candidate in 1992, Clinton portrayed himself as a moderate Democrat, one who understood the perspective of a majority of Americans. Clinton and his vice presidential nominee, Tennessee senator Al Gore, became the youngest national ticket ever elected; they were the first all-Southern ticket since the Jackson Administration of 1828. The two men were reelected four years later. Clinton went on to become one of only five Presidents in the century to complete two terms of office.

As President, Clinton (helped by a booming economy) began balancing the federal budget for the first time in four decades. He created free trade between the United States, Canada, and Mexico with the North American Free Trade Agreement (NAFTA), and he normalized U.S. trade relations with China. As his presidency progressed, Clinton worked to improve relations with Russia and promoted peace and human rights in such places as Northern Ireland, the Middle East, Haiti, Bosnia, and Kosovo.

Clinton lived up to his image as the "Comeback Kid" during a presidency that was challenged by party politics, international instability, and personal scandal. In 1994 Republicans captured control of Congress for the first time in 40 years. Clinton struggled to focus attention on the nation's business as partisan lawmakers scrutinized his administrative and personal choices. He battled with members of Congress over how to manage the budget, taxes, health care, and trade while he labored to define the role of the United States as a peacemaker in a post–Cold War world.

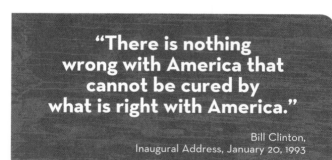

> **"There is nothing wrong with America that cannot be cured by what is right with America."**
>
> Bill Clinton,
> Inaugural Address, January 20, 1993

In retirement, Clinton teamed up with former rival George Bush to raise funds for disaster relief. Their efforts were recognized with Liberty Medals in 2006 (Bush, left, with Clinton).

The former President campaigned on behalf of his wife's two presidential bids (above, in 2008).

In 1998 Kenneth Starr, an independent prosecutor, accused Clinton of breaking laws to conceal an affair with a White House intern. The House of Representatives considered Starr's charges and voted to impeach the President, or recommend that he be tried by the Senate and removed from office. Members accused Clinton of lying under oath and using illegal means to keep the relationship a secret. Senate Democrats and some Republicans rejected the House charges during his 1999 trial. Clinton was acquitted. Andrew Johnson is the only other President impeached and tried by Congress.

Clinton succeeded at broadening the Democratic Party base of support during his presidency. Many past supporters of the Republican Party, particularly a wide variety of voters from middle-income levels, sided with the Democrats instead. However, the taint of personal scandal surrounding Clinton by the end of his administration limited how effectively he could support the presidential bid of his own Vice President in 2000.

Hillary Clinton assumed a broader range of responsibilities as First Lady than any other President's wife since Eleanor Roosevelt. She headed an effort to reform the nation's health care system, traveled extensively on behalf of her husband, promoted the rights of women and children, and wrote a weekly newspaper column. She protected the privacy of her teenage daughter and supported her husband during the scandals that plagued his presidency. While still serving as First Lady, she won election to the U.S. Senate, the first presidential spouse to seek and win elected office. Her subsequent service as secretary of state for Barack Obama was bookended by two unsuccessful attempts to become the nation's first female President.

Bill Clinton shared the spotlight during the celebration of his Inauguration in 1997 with his wife, Hillary, and the couple's teenage daughter, Chelsea. During his second term, opinion polls showed that most citizens supported Clinton's performance as President even though the House of Representatives was recommending that he be removed from office.

GEORGE W. BUSH
43RD PRESIDENT OF THE UNITED STATES **2001–2009**

George Walker Bush became the first President in more than a century to reach the White House without carrying the nation's popular vote. Only John Quincy Adams, Rutherford B. Hayes, and Benjamin Harrison did likewise. Unlike these predecessors, Bush was reelected four years later. Not since the Adamses had a father and his son each become President of the United States.

A family tradition of elected public service began while George W. Bush was growing up in Texas. He was six years old when his grandfather became a U.S. senator. Twelve years later his father made his first bid for elected office. As a child Bush played baseball and dreamed of becoming a star athlete. However, he shadowed his father's rise to political life by attending the same private high school as his father and the same college, Yale University. He graduated in 1968 with a major in history. Bush served in the Air Force National Guard during the Vietnam

Two future Presidents were captured in this family snapshot from 1955. George Bush, the nation's 41st Chief Executive, holds his young son, George W. Bush, who became the nation's 43rd President in 2001. Wife, mother, and future First Lady Barbara Bush looks on. During the son's presidency, the similar names of the men were distinguished by the use of the son's middle initial, W., a letter that had become his nickname as well. Some people referred to them by the number of their administrations: #41 and #43, or Bush 41 and Bush 43.

War and learned how to fly an F-102 fighter jet. Later he earned a degree from Harvard Business School.

In 1975 Bush returned to Texas and, like his father, found work in the oil industry. He married Laura Welch in 1977, just three months after they had met. The next year Bush made an unsuccessful bid for election to the U.S. House of Representatives. Later he became an owner and manager of the Texas Rangers baseball team. He was elected governor of Texas in 1994 and was reelected four years later.

During the Vietnam War, George W. Bush joined the Air Force National Guard (left). Questions over unfinished service requirements became a campaign issue during his presidential bids.

NICKNAME
Dubya (W.)

BORN
July 6, 1946, in New Haven, CT

POLITICAL PARTY
Republican

CHIEF OPPONENTS
1st term: Albert Arnold Gore, Jr., Democrat (1948–present), and Ralph Nader, Green (1934–present);
2nd term: John Kerry, Democrat (1943–present), and Ralph Nader, Independent (1934–present)

TERM OF OFFICE
Jan. 20, 2001–Jan. 20, 2009

AGE AT INAUGURATION
54 years old

NUMBER OF TERMS
two

VICE PRESIDENT
Richard Bruce Cheney (1941–present)

FIRST LADY
Laura Welch Bush (1946–present), wife (married November 5, 1977)

CHILDREN
Jenna, Barbara (twins)

GEOGRAPHIC SCENE
50 states

SELECTED LANDMARKS
George W. Bush Presidential Center (includes presidential library and museum), Dallas, TX

George W. Bush is the only President to be the father of twins (above, with his newborn daughters in 1981).

First Lady Laura Bush and her husband (above, visiting with children in Romania) emphasized their commitment to faith and family during his presidency.

The First Lady (above, walking in a wintry White House Rose Garden) promoted literacy during her husband's administration.

Bush campaigned for the presidency in 2000 against the sitting Vice President, Al Gore. Their contest ended with a hotly disputed debate over how to count election returns in Florida, a state governed by Bush's brother. Intervention by the U.S. Supreme Court some five weeks after Election Day secured the presidency for Bush even though he trailed Gore nationally by more than 500,000 popular votes. Bush took office with only a narrow margin of Republican control in the House of Representatives and the first ever equally divided U.S. Senate.

The Bush presidency featured many advisers who had served during his father's administration, including Vice President Dick Cheney, who was secretary of defense for the elder Bush and a staff member during the Nixon and Ford presidencies. Within months of taking office, Bush was forced to shift his focus from domestic concerns to international affairs. The catastrophic series of terrorist attacks on September 11, 2001, prompted the President and his advisers to renew security concerns about the Middle East from the administration of Bush's father.

The President's popularity soared as the United States invaded Afghanistan in an effort to capture those responsible for the attacks, including al Qaeda terrorist leader Osama bin Laden. The decision to attack Iraq in 2003 as a protective necessity met with general support at first, but public opinion splintered after reasons justifying the action proved unfounded. Critics also charged that missteps during the invasion helped to prolong the conflict and destabilize other countries in the Middle East. The administration's wartime use of torture further undermined support.

Bush sought to strengthen national defense through the creation of a Department of Homeland Security. The lack of further attacks on the U.S. and a willingness among many Americans to "stay the course" helped Bush secure reelection in 2004 against his Democratic Party challenger, Senator John Kerry.

During his second term the death of the Supreme

George W. Bush faced challenges both foreign and domestic during his two-term presidency, most notably with international conflicts (right, meeting with advisers in advance of the Iraq war).

The Bush Administration was criticized for its halting response to the impact of Hurricane Katrina on the Gulf Coast in 2005 (left, Bush visits the region).

During his retirement years, the President is collaborating with First Lady Laura Bush on outreach through the Bush Institute, a component of the presidential center in Dallas that includes his presidential library. Areas of focus include public education, democracy, global health, and economic prosperity.

Court's Chief Justice and the resignation of another justice enabled Bush to place two judicial conservatives on the nation's highest court. These appointments allowed him to preserve the conservative tilt of the Court.

As President, Bush succeeded at implementing some domestic policy initiatives, such as his No Child Left Behind program for education reform, but he failed to win congressional support for others, including Social Security modification and the reform of immigration laws. Charges of improper influence over the government by political appointees, especially those in the White House and Justice Department, led to a series of high-profile investigations.

Growing public dissatisfaction with the Bush Administration helped fuel midterm election victories in 2006 that put Democrats in control of the House and Senate for the first time in 14 years. Bush, determined to succeed in his so-called War on Terror,

> **"America was targeted for attack because we're the brightest beacon for freedom and opportunity in the world. And no one will keep that light from shining."**
>
> George W. Bush,
> September 11, 2001

sent additional U.S. troops to Iraq in 2007, a move that drew much criticism but did help stabilize the region for a while. A legacy of war continued there and in the region well beyond his presidency.

The administration's consistent support for tax cuts earned praise among conservatives, but was later seen as contributing to a dramatic rise in budget shortfalls. U.S. involvement in wars in Iraq and Afghanistan became costly, too. The growing unbalance in the federal budget, sluggish economic growth, soaring oil prices, and reduced government control of the housing and banking systems contributed to a worldwide economic crisis near the end of Bush's presidency.

In 2009 the President and First Lady retired to Texas to collaborate on planning for his presidential library. Bush took up portrait painting, too. His library opened in Dallas in 2013.

BARACK OBAMA
44TH PRESIDENT OF THE UNITED STATES 2009–2017

Barack Hussein Obama became the nation's first African-American President in the historic election of 2008. Worldwide economic uncertainties, continuing wars, and random acts of terrorism presented him with dizzying challenges in a nation increasingly polarized by political disagreements. His eight-year administration included the implementation of landmark legislation on health care.

The son of a white mother born in Kansas and a black father from Africa, Obama spent most of his childhood in Hawaii, where he was raised by his mother and her parents. He was the first President born there and the first born to a nation of 50 states. He attended Occidental College in Los Angeles, completed his undergraduate degree at New York's Columbia University, and, after working with disadvantaged residents of Chicago, earned a law degree from Harvard. After winning election to the Illinois State Senate in 1996, Obama advanced to the U.S. Senate and the White House. He was the first senator since John F. Kennedy to become President and, in 2012, became the first Chief Executive since Ronald Reagan to win back-to-back elections with majority support.

Obama assumed office during an economic crisis more severe than any since the Great Depression; many called it the Great Recession. Concerted action by the President, Congress, and the Federal Reserve

During his studies at Harvard Law School (above), Barack Obama became the first African American to head the prestigious *Harvard Law Review*. His father's enrollment at Harvard years earlier had separated him from his family when his son was only two. With the exception of a month-long visit when Obama was 10, the father and son never saw each other again. The future President spent four years of his childhood living in Asia when his mother, then divorced, married an Indonesian. Obama has a half-sister from that union.

halted the nation's economic nosedive and ultimately fueled the longest streak of job creation in American history. Some regions and segments of the population rebounded better than others, though, and unease spread as an elite class of ultra-wealthy citizens prospered while others did not. A divide widened in the political landscape, too, as the growth of the 24-hour news cycle, partisan cable channels, and social media fed more conflict than compromise. Although Democrats held nominal control of the House and Senate, Republicans

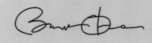

NICKNAME
Barry

BORN
August 4, 1961, in Honolulu, HI

POLITICAL PARTY
Democrat

CHIEF OPPONENT
1st term: John McCain, Republican (1936–present);
2nd term: Mitt Romney, Republican (1947–present)

TERM OF OFFICE
Jan. 20, 2009–Jan. 20, 2017

AGE AT INAUGURATION
47 years old

NUMBER OF TERMS
two

VICE PRESIDENT
Joseph R. Biden, Jr. (1942–present)

FIRST LADY
Michelle Robinson Obama (1964–present), wife (married October 3, 1992)

CHILDREN
Malia, Sasha

GEOGRAPHIC SCENE
50 states

The Haynes brothers (Jacob, with arm extended, and James) posed for a selfie with Barack Obama during their 2015 visit with the President in the Oval Office.

To monitor the military mission that killed Osama bin Laden in 2011, Obama gathered in the White House Situation Room with his advisers, including Vice President Joe Biden (on sofa), and Hillary Clinton, his secretary of state (opposite Obama).

flexed their minority party muscle in ways that slowed, diminished, or defeated many of the President's efforts.

Nonetheless, there were legislative successes, including the repeal of the ban against gays serving in the military, greater regulation of the financial industry, increased fuel efficiency standards for vehicles, and enhanced support for the rights of women to equal pay for their work. Obama's signature achievement, the Affordable Care Act of 2010, passed without a single Republican vote. The program, which took effect in 2014, achieved a long-sought Democratic goal: guaranteed access to health care for all Americans. The law withstood multiple legal challenges as well as dozens of attempted repeals; it expanded health insurance coverage to more than 10 million citizens.

In 2010 a so-called Tea Party movement developed within the Republican Party to oppose Obama and his party. Its supporters helped Republicans gain control of the Senate that year and the House in 2015. Legislation ground to a virtual standstill, so political power shifted to the remaining branches of government. Obama used his executive authority to advance key elements of his policy agenda, from regulations for cleaner air, to a strengthening of worker rights, to a ban against torture during military interrogations, to the expansion of protected wilderness. In the judicial branch, liberals

First Lady Michelle Obama displayed a style, grace, and example of good works that influenced everything from fashion to health. Her "Let's Move" initiative emphasized the importance of childhood nutrition and fitness. She promoted the value of fresh foods by starting the White House Kitchen Garden (right) as a living laboratory and source of produce for family members, area residents, and state guests.

benefited from some Supreme Court decisions, but conservatives made gains, too, with rulings that created new avenues for funding political campaigns and made it easier to restrict voting rights.

Growing instability in the Middle East kept U.S. forces engaged in that region throughout Obama's presidency. Almost 7,000 American soldiers died in Iraq and Afghanistan during his tenure and his predecessor's, and more than 50,000 were wounded. Gains made fighting the al Qaeda terrorist network—most notably the death at American hands of its leader Osama bin Laden—were undercut by the development of a new terrorist threat, the so-called Islamic State, sometimes referred to as ISIS or ISIL. Obama, who in 2009 became the fourth U.S. President to earn a Nobel Peace Prize, overcame long-standing international animosities to end an embargo against Cuba that had stood since before his birth. His administration helped broker the first U.S. treaty with Iran since the presidency of Jimmy Carter,

Global instability sparked the largest international refugee crisis since World War II (above, refugees reach Greece after fleeing war-torn regions of the Middle East).

Critics condemned health care reform as Obamacare, creating a term the President and supporters soon embraced (advocates outside the Supreme Court in 2012).

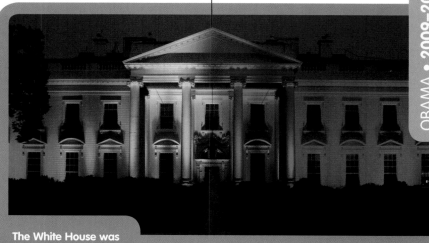

The White House was lit with a symbolic rainbow when the Supreme Court issued its marriage equality ruling on June 26, 2015. The 5–4 decision eliminated all barriers to same-sex marriage nationwide in a hard-fought victory for members and allies of the LGBT community that dismayed many conservatives.

When two vacancies opened on the Supreme Court during his first two years of office, Obama replaced retiring male justices with women. His action placed the first person of Latino heritage on the high court and raised the number of female justices on the court to three, a record. The death of Justice Antonin Scalia, a conservative icon, early in the President's final year of office gave him an unexpected opportunity to reshape the court's judicial direction. Alarmed Republicans refused to consider Obama's moderate nominee, justifying their inaction by the fact that it was an election year. Although high court nominations had become complicated during previous election years, none had ever before failed to receive at least a hearing. The resulting vacancy became the longest in Supreme Court history. The remaining eight justices continued to work, but some legal matters were left unresolved when they deadlocked with 4–4 votes.

By delaying, Republicans hoped to win back the White House and restore the court's conservative majority, a strategy that seemed to work with the victory of Donald Trump. Trump's defeat of Obama's preferred successor, his former secretary of state Hillary Clinton, followed a long-standing pattern. Only once since World War II has a two-term President—Ronald Reagan—been succeeded by a member of the same party.

one that limited Iran's ability to develop nuclear weapons. It advanced global efforts to reduce climate change, too, culminating in 2015 with an unprecedented international agreement for action.

Issues of racial equality, which had inspired so many with Obama's election, became more divisive during his presidency. Some tensions arose among those not prepared to support an African American as President, but technology made a difference, too. Social media and the development of cell phone cameras allowed citizens to share visual evidence of the use of excessive force by police officers against people of color. Unsettling videos forced the nation to face matters of racial injustice to a degree not seen since the 1960s, and a Black Lives Matter movement emerged to promote change.

> "For as long as I live, I will never forget that in no other country on Earth is my story even possible."
>
> Barack Obama,
> March 18, 2008

ELECTION 2016
A DRAMATIC FINISH TO AN UNPRECEDENTED RACE

Donald Trump's come-from-behind Electoral College victory in the 2016 presidential race capped a campaign of long-shot odds that repeatedly defied historical precedent and confounded political analysts. Few expected the outspoken real estate developer and reality TV star to succeed given his lack of experience in public service, fondness for making judgmental statements, and disregard for standard campaign practices. Even on Election Day, most forecasts predicted his defeat. His triumph over Democratic nominee Hillary Clinton prevented her from becoming the nation's first female President despite her breadth of accomplishments as a First Lady, U.S. senator, and secretary of state.

The candidates' divergent backgrounds, policy positions, personalities, and temperaments fueled a battle for victory that broke long-standing patterns for presidential contests. On the Republican Party side, Trump emerged as the unexpected victor in a crowded field of 17 contenders that included five former or current U.S. senators and nine former or current governors, including Jeb Bush, who is the son and brother of former Presidents. Yet Trump thrived even as others left the race, despite, or perhaps because of, his disregard for accepted campaign strategy and traditional rules of conduct. Initially six candidates vied for the Democratic Party nomination, but the race soon resolved into a robust matchup between Clinton and U.S. Senator Bernie Sanders.

Candidates faced an electorate still recovering from the economic woes of the Great Recession, and the victorious party nominees offered opposing visions for how to remedy a broad range of voter concerns. Donald Trump promised in his campaign slogan to "Make America Great Again" while Hillary Clinton argued that the country was already great and, as her slogan put it, could be made even "Stronger Together." Trump's approach appealed

After earning his party's nomination, Republican candidate Donald Trump (above, left, with running mate Mike Pence) enjoyed the same traditional balloon drop that Democrats would shower on rival Hillary Clinton a week later. Trump ignored other standard political practices, such as staffing hundreds of field offices with campaign workers.

The large field of Republican candidates had to be divided into two groups during the fall 2015 party debates. Political polls determined participation (right, the nine leading candidates in the Las Vegas debate in December). Donald Trump (fifth from left), a wealthy political outsider, argued that his business experience and financial independence made him the superior choice. His steady stream of homespun, provocative Tweets kept him in the public eye without the need for advertising.

particularly to working-class white males who felt threatened by the forces of global trade, mechanization, and population diversity. For them, Trump's promise recalled a mid-20th-century era that had seemed greater. Yet that same era represented a period of oppression and lack of opportunity for many of Clinton's strongest supporters: women, African Americans, Latinos, and other minority groups. Her calls for greater equality, financial fairness, and affordable college education appealed widely to these constituencies as well as to many younger voters.

The two candidates suffered from self-inflicted wounds as much as from those caused by their opponents, and victory seemed to rest with whoever best succeeded at pointing out the other person's faults. Decisions Clinton made while serving as secretary of state—especially storing official emails on a private server—created the opportunity for her rival to accuse her of taking risks with national security. Meanwhile the disparaging statements Trump frequently made about women, Muslims, immigrants, minorities, veterans, and others allowed Clinton to brand him as hotheaded and unqualified to be President.

Political polls showed Clinton leading Trump among potential voters throughout the general election. Her chance of victory increased after performing well in the fall presidential debates, and she gained further ground when the release of a 2005 videotape revealed Trump judging women as physical objects. Key Republican leaders, even the party's two former Presidents, refused to embrace his campaign. Tallies on Election Day revealed a nation almost equally divided, with Clinton earning a slim majority of popular votes. Trump gained the White House by emerging victorious in the Electoral College.

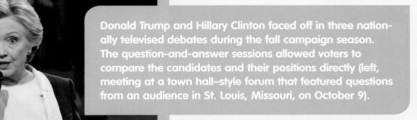

Donald Trump and Hillary Clinton faced off in three nationally televised debates during the fall campaign season. The question-and-answer sessions allowed voters to compare the candidates and their positions directly (left, meeting at a town hall–style forum that featured questions from an audience in St. Louis, Missouri, on October 9).

Neither major nominee entered the fall campaign season with positive approval ratings, a historical first that reflected misgivings both within and beyond each party base (above, opponents of Donald Trump's candidacy; below, opposing opinions about Hillary Clinton).

When Vermont senator Bernie Sanders called for a political revolution as a presidential candidate, he sparked widespread support among younger voters and progressives. Even though he considers himself a political independent and a democratic socialist, Sanders sought the Democratic Party's presidential nomination because he works closely with that party in the Senate.

DONALD TRUMP
45TH PRESIDENT OF THE UNITED STATES **2017–PRESENT**

Donald John Trump assumed the presidency confident in his ability to convert a lifetime of experience in business into the management of the federal government. He is the first person ever to become President without having performed some sort of public service either through the military or by holding an elected or appointed office. Not since 1940, when the respected business leader Wendell Willkie failed to derail the third-term bid of Franklin D. Roosevelt, has a major party nominee pursued such an untraditional pathway to the presidency.

The real estate developments of Trump's father in the outlying areas of New York City supported a privileged family life that included servants, limousines, and private schools. Donald, the fourth of five children and the second son, earned his high school diploma at the New York Military Academy and spent two years at Fordham University before completing his education at the University of Pennsylvania's Wharton School of Finance and Commerce (known now as the Wharton School). When he returned to New York and began pursuing real estate developments in the heart of Manhattan, he surpassed his father's successes. The son's ever ambitious investments grew into a global empire that made the Trump name synonymous with wealth and power. Trump boosted his public profile further by hosting the popular *Apprentice* reality TV shows. This fame and name recognition helped pave his way to the presidency.

Donald Trump hosted a reality TV show (above, season 6 of *The Apprentice*) from 2004 to 2015.

Prior to 2017, Ronald Reagan had been the nation's oldest President, assuming office at age 69. Trump eclipsed that record by about eight months. The two are the only Presidents to have been divorced. Trump's third wife, Melania (a native of Slovenia), is the first foreign-born First Lady since Louisa Adams in 1825 (who came from Great Britain). Barron, the couple's son, is the latest youth to call the Executive Mansion home.

NICKNAME
The Donald

BORN
June 14, 1946, in Queens, NY

POLITICAL PARTY
Republican

CHIEF OPPONENT
Hillary Clinton, Democrat (1947–present)

TERM OF OFFICE
Jan. 20, 2017–present

AGE AT INAUGURATION
70 years old

VICE PRESIDENT
Mike Pence (1959–present)

FIRST LADY
Melania Knauss Trump (1970–present), wife (married Jan. 22, 2005)

PREVIOUS WIVES
Ivana Zelníčková Winklmayr Trump (1949–present), married 1977, divorced 1992; Marla Maples (1963–present), married 1993, divorced 1999

CHILDREN
Born to Ivana Trump (first wife): Donald, Ivanka, Eric; born to Marla Maples (second wife): Tiffany; born to Melania Trump (third wife): Barron

GEOGRAPHIC SCENE
50 states

The family interest in real estate development began with Donald Trump's grandfather, a German immigrant who eventually settled in New York City and began acquiring properties (left, Donald Trump with his father, Fred, in Manhattan, 1987).

FORMER PRESIDENTS
EXPERIENCED ELDERS WITH A LASTING INFLUENCE

For U.S. Presidents, it's only a matter of time before their jobs come to an end. No matter how popular they may be or how much they relish their work, four to eight years after taking office, they're out of work.

Presidents have completed their administrations when they were as young as 50 (Theodore Roosevelt) and as old as 77 (Ronald Reagan). Some have enjoyed lengthy retirements. Jimmy Carter broke Herbert Hoover's record of 31 years in 2012. Other retirements are very brief, such as James K. Polk's (three months).

Usually the nation has at least one living former President at any given time, but on five occasions there have been none. Richard Nixon was President during the last such period. There have never been more than five former Presidents alive at once.

Some former Presidents have continued in public service after leaving the White House. John Quincy Adams and Andrew Johnson joined the U.S. Congress. William Howard Taft was appointed Chief Justice of the United States. Others, like Herbert Hoover and Jimmy Carter, have played less formal

roles but have assisted in government studies, peacemaking, or international humanitarian efforts. Carter earned a Nobel Peace Prize for his postpresidential work.

Other former Presidents have kept busy by writing and speaking about their lives, by teaching, with travel, or by just having fun. In recent decades former Presidents have spent considerable time helping to establish their presidential libraries, too.

In a show of respect, Chief Executives continue to be addressed as President even after they leave office. The earliest ones departed the White House with little more than this title. Not until 1958 did Congress begin appropriating money for presidential retirement funds. Harry S.

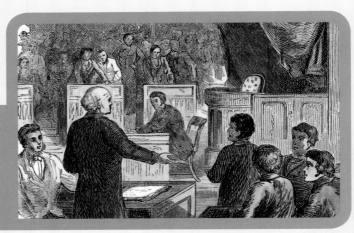

Two years after his presidential retirement, John Quincy Adams won election to the U.S. House of Representatives. He served there for 17 years (right) until his death near the chamber at age 80.

Bill Clinton, like many former Presidents, wrote his autobiography after leaving office.

William Howard Taft, who had always wanted to serve on the Supreme Court, earned that distinction (first row, center), eight years after his presidency by becoming Chief Justice.

Truman received the first such pension; it totaled $25,000 a year. Presidential widows were granted pensions of $10,000; later this sum was increased to $20,000.

Today Presidents earn an annual retirement salary of about $200,000. In addition they receive office support, health care benefits, some paid travel expenses, free U.S. postage, and assistance with their presidential libraries. All former Presidents are entitled to receive lifetime protection for themselves and their spouses by members of the Secret Service. Their children are similarly protected through age 15.

Although Presidents have no formal role in the government after leaving the White House, they often remain influential at home and abroad. Sitting Presidents may seek their advice. Former Presidents and their spouses gather for important events, such as state funerals. Occasionally they may publicly voice their opinions about government, especially in a show of support for the current President. Only rarely do they openly criticize a sitting President, and in such cases their views are treated seriously and with respect. They may offer their endorsement of new candidates for President, too.

Former Presidents often find

that their popularity fluctuates with time. Even those who may not have been well regarded on leaving office can gain public support later on, as did Jimmy Carter, for example. Reputations continue to evolve and shift, even after the Presidents' deaths.

The death of a former President starts off a period of national mourning and recognition. U.S. flags fly at half-staff for 30 days. Some Presidents may request simple burial services. Others prefer more elaborate events, such as state funerals in the nation's capital. Whether simple or complex, funeral plans are prepared after each President leaves office, then saved until the former leader's death.

"Now is the best time of all," President Jimmy Carter has said about his retirement. He has combined recreational pursuits—from fly-fishing to time with grandchildren—with decades of writing, teaching, and community service (at right, volunteering with his wife, Rosalynn, on a Habitat for Humanity construction site).

The death of a President brings together surviving peers. Four former Presidents joined President George W. Bush (front row, far left) to mourn the passing of Ronald Reagan in 2004. Those in attendance with their wives were (second row, from left) George Bush, Jimmy Carter, Gerald R. Ford, and (front row, second from right), Bill Clinton.

CHART OF PRESIDENTIAL ELECTION RESULTS
1789–PRESENT

Election Year	Number of Presidency	Name of President, Years of Office, and Chief Opponents	Name of Political Party	Name of Vice President	Percentage of Popular Vote	Electoral Vote
1789	1	George Washington, 1789–1797	Federalist	John Adams		69
		John Adams	Federalist			34
		Others				35
1792		George Washington, 1789–1797	Federalist	John Adams	.	132
		John Adams	Federalist			77
		George Clinton	Federalist			50
		Others				5
1796	2	John Adams, 1797–1801	Federalist	Thomas Jefferson		71
		Thomas Jefferson	Democratic-Republican			68
		Thomas Pinckney	Federalist			59
		Aaron Burr	Democratic-Republican			30
		Others				48
1800	3	Thomas Jefferson, 1801–1809	Democratic-Republican	Aaron Burr		73
		Aaron Burr	Democratic-Republican			73
		John Adams	Federalist			65
		Charles C. Pinckney	Federalist			64
		John Jay	Federalist			1
1804		Thomas Jefferson, 1801–1809	Democratic-Republican	George Clinton		162
		Charles C. Pinckney	Federalist			14
1808	4	James Madison, 1809–1817	Democratic-Republican	George Clinton		122
		Charles C. Pinckney	Federalist			47
		George Clinton	Democratic-Republican			6
1812		James Madison, 1809–1817	Democratic-Republican	Elbridge Gerry		128
		DeWitt Clinton	Federalist			89
1816	5	James Monroe, 1817–1825	Democratic-Republican	Daniel D. Tompkins		183
		Rufus King	Federalist			34
1820		James Monroe, 1817–1825	Democratic-Republican	Daniel D. Tompkins		231
		John Quincy Adams	Democratic-Republican			1
1824	6	John Quincy Adams, 1825–1829	Democratic-Republican	John C. Calhoun	30.5%	84
		Andrew Jackson	Democratic-Republican		43.1%	99
		William Crawford	Democratic-Republican		13.1%	41
		Henry Clay	Democratic-Republican		13.2%	37
1828	7	Andrew Jackson, 1829–1837	Democratic	John C. Calhoun	56.0%	178
		John Quincy Adams	National Republican		44.0%	83
1832		Andrew Jackson, 1829–1837	Democratic	Martin Van Buren	54.9%	219
		Henry Clay	National Republican		42.4%	49
		Others			2.6%	18
1836	8	Martin Van Buren, 1837–1841	Democratic	Richard M. Johnson	50.9%	170
		William Henry Harrison	Whig		36.6%	73
		Others			12.4%	51

Election Year	Number of Presidency	Name of President, Years of Office, and Chief Opponents	Name of Political Party	Name of Vice President	Percentage of Popular Vote	Electoral Vote
1840	9	William Henry Harrison, 1841	Whig	John Tyler	52.8%	234
		Martin Van Buren	Democratic		46.8%	60
		James G. Birney	Liberty		0.3%	0
	10	John Tyler, 1841–1845	Whig	None		
1844	11	James K. Polk, 1845–1849	Democratic	George M. Dallas	49.6%	170
		Henry Clay	Whig		48.1%	105
		James G. Birney	Liberty		2.3%	0
1848	12	Zachary Taylor, 1849–1850	Whig	Millard Fillmore	47.4%	163
		Lewis Cass	Democratic		42.5%	127
		Martin Van Buren	Free-Soil		10.1%	0
	13	Millard Fillmore, 1850–1853	Whig	None		
1852	14	Franklin Pierce, 1853–1857	Democratic	William R. D. King	50.9%	254
		Winfield Scott	Whig		44.1%	42
		John P. Hale	Free-Soil		5.0%	0
1856	15	James Buchanan, 1857–1861	Democratic	John C. Breckinridge	45.3%	174
		John C. Frémont	Republican		33.1%	114
		Millard Fillmore	Know-Nothing		21.6%	8
1860	16	Abraham Lincoln, 1861–1865	Republican	Hannibal Hamlin	39.8%	180
		Stephen A. Douglas	Democratic		29.5%	12
		John C. Breckinridge	Democratic		18.1%	72
		John Bell	Constitutional Union		12.6%	39
1864		Abraham Lincoln, 1861–1865	Republican	Andrew Johnson	55.0%	212
		George B. McClellan	Democratic		45.0%	21
	17	Andrew Johnson, 1865–1869	Democratic	None		
1868	18	Ulysses S. Grant, 1869–1877	Republican	Schuyler Colfax	52.7%	214
		Horatio Seymour	Democratic		47.3%	80
1872		Ulysses S. Grant, 1869–1877	Republican	Henry Wilson	55.6%	286
		Horace Greeley	Democratic		43.9%	0
1876	19	Rutherford B. Hayes, 1877–1881	Republican	William A. Wheeler	48.0%	185
		Samuel J. Tilden	Democratic		51.0%	184
1880	20	James A. Garfield, 1881	Republican	Chester A. Arthur	48.5%	214
		Winfield S. Hancock	Democratic		48.1%	155
		James B. Weaver	Greenback-Labor		3.4%	0
	21	Chester A. Arthur, 1881–1885	Republican	None		
1884	22	Grover Cleveland, 1885–1889	Democratic	Thomas A. Hendricks	48.5%	219
		James G. Blaine	Republican		48.2%	182
		Others			3.3%	0
1888	23	Benjamin Harrison, 1889–1893	Republican	Levi P. Morton	47.9%	233
		Grover Cleveland	Democratic		48.6%	168
		Others			3.5%	0
1892	24	Grover Cleveland, 1893–1897	Democratic	Adlai E. Stevenson	46.1%	277
		Benjamin Harrison	Republican		43.0%	145
		James Weaver	Populist		8.5%	22
		John Bidwell	Prohibition		2.2%	0
1896	25	William McKinley, 1897–1901	Republican	Garret A. Hobart	51.1%	271
		William J. Bryan	Democratic		47.7%	176

Election Year	Number of Presidency	Name of President, Years of Office, and Chief Opponents	Name of Political Party	Name of Vice President	Percentage of Popular Vote	Electoral Vote
1900		William McKinley, 1897–1901	Republican	Theodore Roosevelt	51.7%	292
		William J. Bryan	Democratic/Populist		45.5%	155
		John C. Woolley	Prohibition		1.5%	0
	26	Theodore Roosevelt, 1901–1909	Republican	None		
1904		Theodore Roosevelt, 1901–1909	Republican	Charles W. Fairbanks	56.4%	336
		Alton B. Parker	Democratic		37.6%	140
		Eugene V. Debs	Socialist		3.0%	0
		Silas C. Swallow	Prohibition		1.9%	0
1908	27	William Howard Taft, 1909–1913	Republican	James S. Sherman	51.6%	321
		William J. Bryan	Democratic		43.1%	162
		Eugene V. Debs	Socialist		2.8%	0
		Eugene W. Chafin	Prohibition		1.7%	0
1912	28	Woodrow Wilson, 1913–1921	Democratic	Thomas R. Marshall	41.9%	435
		Theodore Roosevelt	Progressive		27.4%	88
		William H. Taft	Republican		23.2%	8
		Eugene V. Debs	Socialist		6.0%	0
		Eugene W. Chafin	Prohibition		1.5%	0
1916		Woodrow Wilson, 1913–1921	Democratic	Thomas R. Marshall	49.4%	277
		Charles E. Hughes	Republican		46.2%	254
		Others			4.4%	0
1920	29	Warren G. Harding, 1921–1923	Republican	Calvin Coolidge	60.4%	
		James M. Cox	Democratic		34.2%	127
		Eugene V. Debs	Socialist		3.4%	0
		P. P. Christensen	Farmer-Labor		1.0%	0
	30	Calvin Coolidge, 1923–1929	Republican	None		
1924		Calvin Coolidge, 1923–1929	Republican	Charles G. Dawes	54.0%	382
		John W. Davis	Democratic		28.8%	136
		Robert M. La Follette	Progressive		16.6%	13
1928	31	Herbert Hoover, 1929–1933	Republican	Charles Curtis	58.2%	444
		Alfred E. Smith	Democratic		40.9%	87
1932	32	Franklin D. Roosevelt, 1933–1945	Democratic	John N. Garner	57.4%	472
		Herbert Hoover	Republican		39.7%	59
		Norman Thomas	Socialist		2.2%	0
1936		Franklin D. Roosevelt, 1933–1945	Democratic	John N. Garner	60.8%	523
		Alfred M. Landon	Republican		36.5%	8
		William Lemke	Union		1.9%	0
1940		Franklin D. Roosevelt, 1933–1945	Democratic	Henry A. Wallace	54.8%	449
		Wendell Willkie	Republican		44.8%	82
1944		Franklin D. Roosevelt, 1933–1945	Democratic	Harry S. Truman	53.5%	432
		Thomas E. Dewey	Republican		46.0%	99
	33	Harry S. Truman, 1945–1953	Democratic	None		
1948		Harry S. Truman, 1945–1953	Democratic	Alben W. Barkley	50%	303
		Thomas E. Dewey	Republican		49.9%	189
		J. Strom Thurmond	States' Rights		2.4%	39
		Henry A. Wallace	Progressive		2.4%	0
1952	34	Dwight D. Eisenhower, 1953–1961	Republican	Richard Nixon	55.1%	442
		Adlai E. Stevenson	Democratic		44.4%	89

Election Year	Number of Presidency	Name of President, Years of Office, and Chief Opponents	Name of Political Party	Name of Vice President	Percentage of Popular Vote	Electoral Vote
1956		Dwight D. Eisenhower, 1953–1961	Republican	Richard Nixon	57.6%	457
		Adlai E. Stevenson	Democratic		42.1%	73
1960	35	John F. Kennedy, 1961–1963	Democratic	Lyndon B. Johnson	49.9%	303
		Richard Nixon	Republican		49.6%	219
	36	Lyndon B. Johnson, 1963–1969	Democratic	None		
1964		Lyndon B. Johnson, 1963–1969	Democratic	Hubert H. Humphrey	61.1%	486
		Barry M. Goldwater	Republican		38.5%	52
1968	37	Richard Nixon, 1969–1974	Republican	Spiro T. Agnew	43.4%	301
		Hubert H. Humphrey	Democratic		42.7%	191
		George C. Wallace	American Independent		13.5%	46
1972		Richard Nixon, 1969–1974	Republican	Spiro T. Agnew	60.6%	520
				Gerald R. Ford		
		George S. McGovern	Democratic		37.5%	17
	38	Gerald R. Ford, 1974–1977	Republican	Nelson A. Rockefeller		
1976	39	Jimmy Carter, 1977–1981	Democratic	Walter F. Mondale	50.1%	297
		Gerald R. Ford	Republican		47.9%	240
1980	40	Ronald Reagan, 1981–1989	Republican	George Bush	50.9%	489
		Jimmy Carter	Democratic		41.2%	49
		John B. Anderson	Independent		7.9%	0
1984		Ronald Reagan, 1981–1989	Republican	George Bush	59.0%	525
		Walter F. Mondale	Democratic		41.0%	13
1988	41	George Bush, 1989–1993	Republican	Dan Quayle	53.4%	426
		Michael S. Dukakis	Democratic		45.6%	111
1992	42	Bill Clinton, 1993–2001	Democratic	Al Gore	43.0%	370
		George Bush	Republican		37.0%	168
		H. Ross Perot	Independent		19.0%	0
1996		Bill Clinton, 1993–2001	Democratic	Al Gore	49.0%	379
		Robert J. Dole	Republican		41.0%	159
		H. Ross Perot	Reform		8.0%	0
2000	43	George W. Bush, 2001–2009	Republican	Dick Cheney	48.0%	271
		Al Gore	Democratic		48.5%	266
		Ralph Nader	Green		2.7%	0
		Others			0.8%	0
		Abstained				1
2004		George W. Bush, 2001–2009	Republican	Dick Cheney	51.0%	274
		John Kerry	Democratic		48.0%	252
		Ralph Nader	Independent		1.0%	0
2008	44	Barack Obama, 2009–2017	Democratic	Joe Biden	52.5%	365
		John McCain	Republican		46.3%	173
2012		Barack Obama, 2009–2017	Democratic	Joe Biden	51.0%	332
		Mitt Romney	Republican		48.0%	206
2016*	45	Donald Trump, 2017–present	Republican	Mike Pence	47.5%	290
		Hillary Clinton	Democratic		47.7%	228
		Gary Johnson	Libertarian		3%	0
		Jill Stein	Green		1%	0
		Others			0.8%	0

* Tallies reflect popular vote percentages as determined at press time; 20 Electoral College votes were not yet allocated.
  Electoral College vote allocations remain provisional until confirmed by electors in December.

FIND OUT MORE

BOOKS

Allen, Thomas B. *George Washington, Spymaster: How the Americans Outspied the British and Won the Revolutionary War*. Washington, D.C.: National Geographic, 2004.

Bausum, Ann. *Our Country's First Ladies*. Washington, D.C.: National Geographic, 2007.

___. *With Courage and Cloth: Winning the Fight for a Woman's Right to Vote*. Washington, D.C.: National Geographic, 2004.

Bunch, Lonnie G. et al. *The American Presidency: A Glorious Burden*. Washington, D.C.: Smithsonian Institution Press, 2000.

Ethier, Eric. *Wit and Wisdom of the Presidents*. Lincolnwood, Ill.: Publications International, 1998.

Freidel, Frank. *The Presidents of the United States of America*. Washington, D.C.: White House Historical Association and National Geographic Society, 1995 (14th edition).

Harness, Cheryl. *Abe Lincoln Goes to Washington, 1837–1865*. Washington, D.C.: National Geographic, 1997.

___. *George Washington*. Washington, D.C.: National Geographic, 2000.

___. *The Revolutionary John Adams*. Washington, D.C.: National Geographic, 2003.

___. *Thomas Jefferson*. Washington, D.C.: National Geographic, 2004.

___. *Young Abe Lincoln: The Frontier Days, 1809–1837*. Washington, D.C.: National Geographic, 1996.

___. *Young Teddy Roosevelt*. Washington, D.C.: National Geographic, 1998.

Johnston, Robert D. *The Making of America: The History of the United States from 1492 to the Present*. Washington, D.C.: National Geographic, 2002.

Klapthor, Margaret Brown. *The First Ladies*. Washington, D.C.: White House Historical Association and National Geographic Society, 1995.

Kunhardt, Jr., Philip B., Philip B. Kunhardt III, and Peter W. Kunhardt. *The American President*. New York: Riverhead Books, Penguin Putnam Inc., 1999.

McPherson, James M., general editor. *"To the Best of My Ability": The American Presidents*. New York: Dorling Kindersley, 2001 (revised edition).

Provensen, Alice. *The Buck Stops Here*. New York: Browndeer Press, Harcourt Brace, 1997.

Sandler, Martin W. *Presidents: A Library of Congress Book*. New York: HarperCollins, 1995.

Schanzer, Rosalyn. *George vs. George: The American Revolution as Seen From Both Sides*. Washington, D.C.: National Geographic, 2004.

St. George, Judith. *In the Line of Fire: Presidents' Lives at Stake*. New York: Holiday House, 1999.

___. *So You Want to Be President?* New York: Philomel, 2004 (revised edition).

Walker, Diana. *Public & Private: Twenty Years Photographing the Presidency*. Washington, D.C.: National Geographic, 2002.

VIDEOS AND TELEVISION PROGRAMS

1600 Pennsylvania Avenue: The White House. National Geographic Educational Film and Video, 1997.

Air Force One. National Geographic Television Special and Video, 1996.

The American President (listed as a book) is also a film series distributed by PBS.

Inside the U.S. Secret Service. National Geographic Channel, 2004.

Inside the White House. National Geographic Television Video, 2001.

The Presidents. The American Experience, Public Broadcasting Service. pbs.org/wgbh/amex/presidents/intro.html

WEBSITES

American President: A Reference Resource, Miller Center, University of Virginia
millercenter.org/president

About the White House, First Ladies
whitehouse.gov/1600/first-ladies

About the White House, Presidents
whitehouse.gov/1600/presidents

Museum of the Moving Image, Campaign Commercials, 1952–present
livingroomcandidate.org

National Archives and Records Administration, Electoral College
archives.gov/federal_register/electoral_college

National Popular Vote
nationalpopularvote.com

Smithsonian National Museum of American History
americanhistory.si.edu

White House Historical Association
whitehousehistory.org

Presidential Libraries
archives.gov/presidential-libraries

Presidential Speeches
millercenter.org/president#speeches-nav

PLACES TO VISIT

"The American Presidency," permanent exhibit, National Museum of American History, Smithsonian Institution, Washington, D.C.

The White House, Washington D.C.

See also pages 96–97 and each President's fact box.

BIBLIOGRAPHY

Aikman, Lonnelle. *The Living White House*. Washington, D.C.: White House Historical Association and National Geographic Society, 1996 (10th edition).

___. *We, the People: The Story of the United States Capitol— Its Past and Its Promise*. Washington, D.C.: The United States Capitol Historical Society and National Geographic Society, 1991 (14th edition).

Boller, Paul F., Jr. *Presidential Anecdotes*. New York: Oxford University Press, 1981.

___. *Presidential Wives*. New York: Oxford University Press, 1988.

Brinkley, Alan and Davis Dyer, editors. *The Reader's Companion to the American Presidency*. Boston: Houghton Mifflin, 2004.

Caroli, Betty Boyd. *First Ladies*. New York: Oxford University Press, 1995 (expanded edition).

DeGregorio, William A. *The Complete Book of U.S. Presidents*. New York: Wings Books, Random House, 2005 (sixth edition, revised).

Freidel, Frank. *The Presidents of the United States of America*. Washington, D.C.: White House Historical Association and National Geographic Society, 1995 (14th edition).

Gibbs, Nancy and Michael Duffy. *The Presidents' Club: Inside the World's Most Exclusive Fraternity*. New York: Simon & Schuster, 2012.

Graff, Henry F., editor. *The Presidents: A Reference History*. New York: Charles Scribner's Sons, 1996 (second edition).

Hamilton, Alexander, James Madison, and John Jay. *The Federalist Papers*. New York: New American Library, 1961.

Kane, Joseph Nathan. *Facts About the Presidents: A Compilation of Biographical and Historical Information*. New York: H. W. Wilson Company, 2001 (seventh edition), with new co-authors: Janet Podell and Steven Anzovin.

Keyssar, Alexander. *The Right to Vote: The Contested History of Democracy in the United States*. New York: Basic Books, 2000.

Klapthor, Margaret Brown. *The First Ladies*. Washington, D.C.: White House Historical Association and National Geographic Society, 1999 (ninth edition).

Kruh, David and Louis Kruh. *Presidential Landmarks*. New York: Hippocrene Books, Inc., 1992.

Pearce, Lorraine. *The White House: An Historic Guide*. Washington, D.C.: White House Historical Association and National Geographic Society, 1999 (20th edition).

Purcell, L. Edward, editor. *Vice Presidents: A Biographical Dictionary*. New York: Checkmark Books, Facts On File, 2001.

Schaefer, Peggy. *The Ideals Guide to Presidential Homes and Libraries*. Nashville: Ideals Press, 2002.

The World Almanac and Book of Facts. New York: World Almanac Books, 2004.

Additional resources were consulted for individual essays, including presidential biographies, newspaper articles, and Internet sites.

ANN BAUSUM is the author of 13 works of nonfiction history, including the recent title *The March Against Fear* (2017). Her books have received numerous awards, including a Sibert Honor, the Jane Addams Children's Book Award, the SCBWI Golden Kite Award, and the Carter G. Woodson Award (twice). The Children's Book Guild of Washington, D.C., recognized the body of her work by naming her the 2017 recipient of its nonfiction award, a coveted distinction for children's authors. Notable titles from her writing career include *Stonewall; Stubby the War Dog; Marching to the Mountaintop; Denied, Detained, Departed; Freedom Riders; With Courage and Cloth;* and, of course, *Our Country's First Ladies*. The daughter of a history professor, Bausum grew up with a love of research and American history. She tackled each presidency as its own assignment, immersing herself in reference volumes, historical documents, and period anecdotes. Finding the facts she knows kids will love is her favorite part of research. A graduate of Beloit College, she makes her home in Wisconsin. Bausum's website is annbausum.com.

Consultant **ROBERT D. JOHNSTON** is associate professor and director of the Teaching of History Program at the University of Illinois at Chicago. He is also the author of National Geographic's *The Making of America: The History of the United States From 1492 to the Present*, which was named a *School Library Journal* Best Book of the Year. Johnston lives in Chicago with his wife, Anne, and two sons, Sandy and Isaac.

ILLUSTRATIONS CREDITS

Abbreviations:
LC = Library of Congress; WHHA = White House Historical Association
t = top; b = bottom; l = left; r = right; cen = center

Cover (flag), Triff/Shutterstock; (George Washington), White House Historical Association; (Thomas Jefferson), White House Historical Association; (Abraham Lincoln), White House Historical Association; (Ronald Reagan), White House Historical Association; (Barack Obama), Pete Souza/The White House; (Donald Trump), Dan Hallman/Invision/AP; back cover (presidential seal), Larry Downing/Sygma/Getty Images; (U.S. Capitol building), Orhan Cam/Shutterstock; spine (The White House), Orhan Cam/Shutterstock; (bald eagle), FloridaStock/Shutterstock; (Grand Canyon), Francesco R. Iacomino/Shutterstock; (Mount Rushmore), Ashley Werter/Dreamstime

1, Larry Downing/Sygma/Getty Images; 2-3, ESB Professional/Shutterstock; 5, Ashley Werter/Dreamstime; 6, Brooks Kraft LLC/Corbis Premium Historical/Getty Images; 7, The White House; 8 (t), Larry Downing/Getty Images; (b), Stock Montage/Getty Images; 9 (b), Photoquest/Getty Images; 9 (tl), Universal History Archive/Getty Images; 9 (tr), Bettmann/Getty Images; 10 (t), Jupiterimages/Getty Images

THE PRESIDENCY AND HOW IT GREW
12-13, WHHA; 12 (l-r), National Archives; Chase Manhattan Bank, Money Museum; Chicago Historical Society; Doris S. Clymer; 13 (l-r), U.S. Supreme Court; New York Public Library, Stokes Collection; The Granger Collection, NY; Courtesy Alamo Museum; 14, WHHA; 15 (both), LC; 16 (tr), LC; 16 (tl), Frances Tavern Museum; 16 (b), The White House; 17 (l), LC; 17 (r), VA. Museum of Fine Arts, Richmond. Gift of Edgar & Bernice Chrysler Garbisch. Photo: Ron Jennings; 18 (b), Courtesy Acacia Mutual Life Ins. Co.; 18 (t), Continental Insurance Companies; 19 (b), Metropolitan Museum of Art, bequest of William Nelson, 1903; 19 (t), LC; 20, WHHA; 21 (t), Adams National Historic Site/Bob Allnut; 21 (b), Newsweek; 22 (t), Joe Bailey/Larry Kinney, NGS; 22 (b), Lisa Biganzoli, NGS; 23 (l), New York Public Library; 23 (r), Collection of New York Historical Society; 24 (b), The White House; 24 (t), Smithsonian Institution; 25 (b), WHHA; 25 (t), From the collection of Mac G. and Janelle Morris; 26, WHHA; 27 (r), WHHA; 27 (l), Vlad Kharitnov; 28 (t), Courtesy Rhode Island Historical Society; 28 (b), Painting by Thure DeThulestrup/Louisiana Historical Society; 29 (t), Marie-Louise Brimberg; 29 (b), Painting by W. Goodacre, Betts Collection, Special Collections Dept., Univ. of Virginia Library; 30 (t), Arthur Liddov; 30 (b), NGS Image Collection; 31 (t, both), Linda Bartlett; 31(b), Louis Glanzman; 32, WHHA; 33 (t), WHHA; 33(b), Eastern National Park & Monument; 34 (t), New York Historical Society; 34 (cen), Culver Pictures; 34 (b), New Haven Colony Historical Society; 35 (tl), Painting by Thomas Brick/Jack Fletcher; 35 (tr), James A. Sugar; 35 (b), Newman Galleries Inc; 36 (t), The White House, Michael Evans; 36 (bl), The Granger Collection, NY; 36 (br), The White House; 37 (background), Vlad Kharitnov; 37 (bl), Collection of New York Historical Society; 37 (bc), Culver Pictures; 37 (br), Bettmann/Corbis; 38, WHHA; 39 (b), WHHA; 40, WHHA; 41(t), LC; 41 (ctr), WHHA; 41 (b), LC; 42, WHHA; 43, Chicago Historical Society; 44, Chip Somodevilla/Getty Images; 45 (t, both), Brendan Smialowski/AFP/Getty Images; 45 (b), AP Photo; 45 (b), Mandel Ngan/AFP/Getty Images; 46, WHHA (WHC); 47 (t), Joseph H. Bailey, NG Image Collection; 47 (b), Chicago Historical Society; 48 (tl), Collection New York Historical Society; 48 (tr), LC; 48 (b), Chicago Historical Society; 49 (t), Yale University Art Gallery/Ken Heinen; 49 (bl), David S. Boyer; 49 (br), Culver Pictures

FROM SEA TO SHINING SEA
50-51, Universal History Archive/Getty Images; 50 (l-r), Bettmann/Corbis; Werner Wolff/Black Star; LC; Bettmann/Corbis; 51 (l-r), Association of American Railroads, DC; Painting by William Heine from Mrs. Mary C. Owens/George Mobley, NG Historical Picture Services; Culver Pictures; Thomas Gilcrease Institute; 52, WHHA; 53 (t), LC; 53 (b), Stock Montage Inc; 54 (t), Bettmann/Corbis; 54 (b), Museum of the City of New York/Bridgeman Images; 55 (t), Woolaroc Museum; 55 (b), Colombia County Historical Society; 56, WHHA; 57 (t), Culver Pictures; 57 (b), LC; 58, WHHA; 59 (b), Pierre Mion, NGS; 59 (t), Benjamin Perley Poore; 60 (b), The White House; 60 (t), North Wind Picture Archives; 61 (tl), Bettmann/Corbis; 61 (br), Getty Images News Service; 61 (tr), The White House; 61 (bl), Bettmann/Corbis; 62, WHHA (WHC); 63 (t), Bettmann/Corbis; 63(b), Bettmann/Corbis; 64 (t), Bettmann/Corbis; 65 (t), Culver Pictures; 64 (b), LC; 65 (b both), Culver Pictures; 66 (t), Bettman/Corbis; 66 (b), Steve Schapiro/Corbis; 67 (tr), AP Images/North Wind Picture Archives; 67(b), Francis Dean/Rex/Rex USA; 67 (tl), Bettman/Corbis; 67 (cen), AP Images/Denis Cook; 68, WHHA; 69 (b), LC; 69 (t), Culver Pictures; 70, WHHA; 71 (both), Culver Pictures; 72 (l), Corbis; 73 (cen), Flip Schulke/Corbis; 73 (b), Corbis; 72(r), Reuters/Corbis; 73 (t), Matthew Cavanaugh/epa/Corbis; 74, WHHA; 75 (t), LC; 75 (b), Culver Pictures; 76, WHHA; 77 (b), Bettmann/Corbis; 77 (t), Missouri Historical Society, St. Louis

A NEW BIRTH OF FREEDOM
78-79, Peter Newark Military Pictures/Bridgeman Images; 78 (l-r), Lowdermilk Print Shop; Joe Bailey, NGS; Leslie Carlson; Bettmann/Corbis; 79 (l-r), LC; Western Historical Collection/University of Oklahoma Library; Corcoran Gallery of Art; The American Automobile Manufacturers Association; 80, WHHA; 81 (b), Lloyd Ostendorf; 81 (t), LC; 82 (l), Chicago Historical Society; 82 (r), LC; 83 (t), Bettmann/Corbis; 83 (b), LC; 84 (t, both), LC; 84 (b), Collection of New York Historical Society; 85 (tl), LC; 85 (tr), Victor Boswell, NGS; 85 (bl), Drawing by Beighaus, courtesy National Park Service; 85 (br), Museum of the City of New York; 86, WHHA; 87 (both), LC; 88 (b), FDR Library; 88 (t, both), Vlad Kharitnov; 89 (tl), Ripon Commonwealth Press; 89 (tr), Bettmann/Corbis; 89 (bl), UPI; 89 (bc & br), Brown Brothers; 90, WHHA; 91 (t), Chicago Historical Society; 91 (b, both), LC; 92 (tl), Stock Montage/Stock Montage/Getty Images; 92 (tr), LC; 92 (b), Bettmann/Corbis; 93 (tl), Bettmann/Corbis; 93 (tr), Getty Images; 93 (bl), LC; 94, WHHA; 95 (t), Rutherford B. Hayes Presidential Center; 96 (t), Johnny Thompson; 97 (r), LC; 96 (b), Corbis; 97 (l), Abraham Lincoln Presidential Library & Museum; 98, WHHA; 99, Kiplinger Washington Collection; 100, WHHA; 101 (t), LC; 101 (b), U.S. National Park Service; 102, WHHA; 103, Bettmann/Corbis; 105 (tl), LC; 104 (t), Niday Picture Library/Alamy Stock Photo; 104 (b), LC; 105 (tr), Culver Pictures; 105 (b), Bettmann/Corbis; 106 (t), Buyenlarge/Getty Images; 106 (bl), Gerald R. Ford Library; 107 (br), Bettmann/Corbis; 106 (br), Gerald R. Ford Library; 108, WHHA; 109 (t), LC; 109 (b), Bettmann/Corbis

AMERICA TAKES CENTER STAGE
110-111, Apic/Getty Images; 110 (l-r), LC; LC; The LeBaron Collection; Ken Marschall; 111 (l-r), LC; LC; Archive Photos; NG Image Collection; 112, WHHA; 113 (t), LC; 113 (b), Culver Pictures; 114 (b), Chicago Historical Society; 114 (t), LC; 115 (t), LC; 115 (b), Bettmann/Corbis; 116, WHHA; 117 (t), Bob Oakes, NGS; 117 (b), LC; 118 (t), Culver Pictures; 118 (br), Culver Pictures; 118 (bl), FPG Int'l; 119 (tl), Brown Brothers; 119 (tr), LC; 119 (b), Theodore Roosevelt Collection, Harvard College Library; 120, LC; 121 (tc), Buyenlarge/Getty Images; 121 (tr), LC; 121 (cen r), Popperfoto/Getty Images; 121 (cen), Alex Ross; 121 (bl), LC; 121 (b), AP Images/Rex Features; 121 (tl), Corbis; 122, WHHA; 123 (t), LC; 123 (b), Emory Kristof, NGS; 124 (tl), LC; 124 (tr), Culver Pictures; 124 (b), Culver Pictures; 125 (tl, tr, b), LC; 125 (cen), George Mobley, NGS; 126 (t), John Kuo/iStockPhoto.com; 126 (b), Corbis; 127 (t, l-r), Bettmann/Corbis; Jim Watson/AFP/Getty Images; 127 (b), The Collection of the Supreme Court of the United States/MCT via Getty Images; 128, WHHA; 129 (t), Punch; 129 (b), LC; 130 (tr), UPI; 130 (tl), Culver Pictures; 130 (b), UPI; 130 (cen), Hulton Archive/Getty Images; 131 (t), Brown Brothers; 131 (b), LC; 132 (tl), Mort Kuntsler; 132 (tr, b), Getty Images News Service; 133 (t), Corbis; 133 (cen), Gustav LeGray, The J. Paul Getty Museum; 133 (bl), AP Images/Rex Features; 133 (br), Rex Features via AP Images; 134, WHHA; 135, LC; 136, WHHA; 137 (t), Bettmann/Corbis; 137 (b), Stock Montage Inc.; 138 (t), Andrey_Popov/Shutterstock; 138 (cen), Wikimedia Commons; 138 (br), The Historical Collection/Detroit Public Library/Library of Congress; 138 (bl), Alexander Helser/FPG/Archive Photos/Getty Images; 138 (b cen), Stock Montage/Getty Images; 139 (t), Pete Souza/WH/Handout/Corbis; 139 (b), Everett Historical/Shutterstock; 140, WHHA; 141 (t), National Archives; 141(b), LC

SEEKING STABILITY IN THE ATOMIC AGE
142-143, Universal History Archive/Getty Images; 142 (b,l-r), Roger Viollet/Getty Images; Keystone/Getty Images; IBM; UPI; 143 (l-r), Bernie Boston; NASA; Scott Shapiro/Index Stock; Black Star; 144, WHHA; 146 (tr), Hartford University; 146 (both), FDR Library; 146 (tl), Bettmann/Corbis; 146 (bl), Social Security Administration; 146 (br), AP/Wide World Photos; 147 (tr), FPG Int'l; 147 (b), Hartford University; 147 (tl), AP/Wide World Photos; 148 (l), Bettmann/Corbis; 148 (r), FPG Int'l; 149 (t), Bettmann/Corbis; 149 (bl), Sandra Baker/Index Stock; 149 (bl), Time-Life Pictures; 150 (t), WHHA; 150 (bl), Bettmann/Corbis; 150 (br), Louis S. Glanzman, NGS; 151 (tl), Joe Bailey, NGS; 151 (cen r), Patrick T. Fallon/Bloomberg/Getty Images; 151 (tr), Steve Adams; 151 (br), UPI; 151 (cen), LC; 151 (cen r), Olivier Douliery/Abaca Press/MCT/Newscom; 151 (bl), Olivier Douliery/Abaca Press/MCT)/Newscom; 152, WHHA; 153 (t), UPI; 153(b), Harry S. Truman Library; 154 (bl), U.S. Army; 154 (br), FPG Int'l; 154 (t), UPI; 155 (t), Time-Life Pictures; 155 (bl), Arthur Shilstone; 155 (br), AP/Wide World Photos; 157, Keystone/Getty Images; 156-157, Amy Sancetta/Associated Press; 158, WHHA; 159 (both), Courtesy Dwight D. Eisenhower Library; 160 (t, both), Courtesy Dwight D. Eisenhower Library; 160 (b), Transcendental Graphic/Getty Images; 161 (tl), AP/Wide World Photos; 161 (tr), UPI; 161 (b), AP/Wide World Photos; 161 (cen),Courtesy Dwight D. Eisenhower Library; 162, WHHA; 163 (t), Courtesy JFK Library; 163 (cen), Fred Ward/Black Star; 163 (b), Courtesy JFK Library; 164 (tl), Corbis; 164 (tr), LC; 164 (b, l-r), Hulton/Getty; Cecil W. Stoughton; 165 (tl), Hank Wolfe, Time-Life Pictures; 165 (tr), Archive Photos; 165 (b), Bettmann/Getty Images; 166 (t & bl), James P. Blair, NGS; 166 (br), LC; 167 (tl), LC; 167 (tc), Bettmann/Corbis; 167 (tr), FDR Library; 167 (bl), Archive Photos; 167 (br), Arlon Wiker; 168, WHHA; 169 (t), LBJ Library; 169 (b), AP/Wide World Photos; 170 (t), George Mobley, NGS; 170 (b), LBJ Library; 171 (tl), LC; 171(tc), LBJ Library; 171 (tr), Dennis Brack/Black Star; 171 (bl), Al Chang; 171 (br), LBJ Library; 172, WHHA; 173 (both), National Archives/Nixon Archives; 174 (t), Ken Garrett; 174 (cen), James L. Stanfield, NGS; 174 (b), The White House; 175 (tl), National Archives/Nixon Archives; 175 (br), Joe Bailey, NGS; 175 (bc), Black Star; 175 (bl), Stephen St. John; 176, WHHA; 177 (both), Gerald R. Ford Library; 179, Corbis; 180, WHHA; 181 (t), Jimmy Carter Library; 181 (b), Grace-Sygma/Corbis; 182 (l), Wilbur E. Garrett, NGS; 182 (r), Liaison; 183 (tl), D. B. Owen/Black Star; 183 (tr), Alain Mingam/Liaison; 183 (b), Getty Images

FOOTPRINTS ON THE GLOBAL FRONTIER
184-185, Sean Pavone/Getty Images; 184 (l-r), Shahn Kermani; Mike Persson/Liaison; Josh Roberts/AFP/Getty Images; Reuters/Rich Wilking/Archive Photo; 185 (l-r), Spencer Platt/Getty Images; Chris Hondros/Getty Images; AP Images/John Miller; Sonia Moskowitz/Archive Photo; 186, WHHA; 187 (both), The White House; 188 (cen), David Alan Harvey, NGS; 188 (tr), Consolidated News Pictures/Getty Images; 188 (tl), Shahn Kermani/Getty Images; 188 (b), Archive Photo/Getty Images; 189 (tl), White House /AP Photo; 189 (tr), Liaison/Getty Images; 189 (b), Getty Images News Service; 190, WHHA (WHC); 191 (both), Courtesy George Bush Presidential Library; 192 (cen), Archive/Getty Images; 192 (br), Natalie Fobes; 192 (t), Mike Theiler/Archive Photos/Getty Images; 193 (t), Newmakers/Liaison/Getty Images; 193 (bl), BradMarkel/Liason/Getty Images; 193 (br), Adees A. Latiff/ArchivePhotos/Corbis; 194 (t), Clinton Presidential Library; 194 (b), Bettmann/Corbis; 194 (cen), Getty Images News Services; 195 (t), Ilker Akgungor/Getty Images; 195 (br), AP Images/Pablo Martinez Monsivais; 195 (bl), The White House; 196, WHHA; 197 (t), Archive Photos/Getty Images; 197 (both), Sygma/Corbis; 198 (tl), Sygma/Corbis; 198 (tr), Mark Reinstein/Index Stock; 198 (b), Arnie Sachs/Archive Photo; 199 (tl), Jeff Swensen/Getty Images; 199 (tr), George Widmanpool/Getty Images; 199 (b), Sygma/Corbis; 200, WHHA; 201 (t), Newsmakers/Liaison/Getty Images; 201 (b), Texas National Guard/Corbis; 202 (t), The White House; 202 (l), Getty Images; 202 (b both),The White House; 203 (tl), The White House; 203 (bl), Larry Downing/Reuters/Corbis; 203 (br), Reuters/Corbis; 204, Ron Sachs/CNP/Corbis; 205 (t), Harvard University/Corbis; 205 (b), White House Photo/Alamy Stock Photo; 206 (tl), Win McNamee/Getty Images; 206 (tr), Pete Souza/The White House/Getty Images; 206 (b) Mark Wilson/Getty Images; 207 (b), Mark Wilson/Getty Images; 207 (tl), Ayhan Mehmet/Anadolu Agency/Getty Images; 207 (tr), Drew Angerer/Bloomberg/Getty Images; 208 (tl), Jabin Botsford/The Washington Post via Getty Images; 208 (cen), Paul Morigi/WireImage/Getty Images; 208-209 (b), Ethan Miller/Getty Images; 209 (tl), Rick T. Wilking/Pool/AP; 209 (tr), Victor J. Blue/Bloomberg/Getty Images; 209 (bl), Tom Williams/CQ Roll Call/Getty Images; 209 (br), Patrick T. Fallon/Bloomberg/Getty Images; 210, Dan Hallman/Invision/AP Photo; 211 (t), Mathew Imaging/FilmMagic/Getty Images; 211 (b), Dennis Caruso/NY Daily News Archive/Getty Images; 212 (t), North Wind Picture Archives; 212 (bl), Bettmann/Corbis; 212 (br), Chip East/Corbis; 213 (t), Black Star; 213 (b), David Hume Kennerly/Getty Images; 224, Jerry Driendl/Getty Images

INDEX

For my sons, Jake and Sam, with love
—AB

Since 1888, the National Geographic Society has funded more than 12,000 research, exploration, and preservation projects around the world. The Society receives funds from National Geographic Partners, LLC, funded in part by your purchase. A portion of the proceeds from this book supports this vital work. To learn more, visit natgeo.com/info.

For more information, visit nationalgeographic.com, call 1-800-647-5463, or write to the following address:

National Geographic Partners
1145 17th Street N.W.
Washington, D.C. 20036-4688 U.S.A.

Visit us online at nationalgeographic.com/books

For librarians and teachers: ngchildrensbooks.org

More for kids from National Geographic:
kids.nationalgeographic.com

For information about special discounts for bulk purchases, please contact National Geographic Books Special Sales: specialsales@natgeo.com

For rights or permissions inquiries, please contact National Geographic Books Subsidiary Rights: bookrights@natgeo.com

Art directed by Callie Broaddus
Designed by Carol Norton

Hardcover edition ISBN: 978-1-4263-2685-1
Reinforced library edition ISBN: 978-1-4263-2686-8
Scholastic edition ISBN: 978-1-4263-2944-9

Printed in the United States of America
16/QGT-QGL/1

The publisher gratefully acknowledges the kind assistance of presidential historian Michael Beschloss for his review of the first edition of this title in page proof form and Robert D. Johnston, associate professor and director of the Teaching of History Program at the University of Illinois at Chicago, for reviewing and commenting on all subsequent editions of the book, including this one. The publisher would also like to recognize the generous support of the late William B. Bushong, longtime staff historian for the White House Historical Association, who reviewed the first four editions of this title. The author is grateful to the staffs of the Beloit College Library and the Beloit Public Library for the assistance provided during her research and extends special appreciation to the production team for this book, including Suzanne Fonda (project editor), Priyanka Lamichhane (project manager), Alix Inchausti and Joan Gossett (production editors), Anne LeongSon (design production assistant), Michael McNey (maps), Lori Epstein and Jeff Heimsath (photo editors), and, of course, art director Callie Broaddus and designer Carol Norton, who have enlivened the book with its new design. Thank you, one and all.

PAGE 1: The presidential seal was altered by President Harry S. Truman so that the eagle faced toward the olive branch, a symbol of peace, rather than toward the arrows of war.

PAGE 2: The arching columns of the South Portico were added to the White House in 1824. In 1948, at the suggestion of President Truman, workers added a second-floor balcony to the structure. The addition is called the Truman Balcony in his honor.

PAGE 6: The Oval Office serves as the command center for a presidency. Each President redecorates the room after taking office.

Presidential monuments to Abraham Lincoln (foreground) and George Washington punctuate the evening skyline in the nation's capital (with the U.S. Capitol Building shown behind). The Washington Monument was the tallest structure in the world when it was completed in 1884, measuring 555 feet 5⅛ inches high.